Francis Eales
Steve Oakes

speakout

Elementary
Flexi Course Book 2

BBC

Pearson Education Limited
Edinburgh Gate
Harlow
Essex CM20 2JE
England

and Associated Companies throughout the world.

www.pearsonELT.com

© Pearson Education Limited 2011

The right of Frances Eales and Steve Oakes to be identified as authors of this Work has been asserted by them in accordance with the Copyright, Designs and Patents Act 1988.

All rights reserved; no part of this publication may be reproduced, stored in a retrieval system, or transmitted in any form or by any means, electronic, mechanical, photocopying, recording, or otherwise without the prior written permission of the Publishers.

First published 2011

Third impression 2014

ISBN: 978-1-4082-9198-6

Set in Gill Sans Book 9.75/11.5

Printed in Slovakia by Neografia

La presente publicación se ajusta a la cartografía oficial establecida por el Poder Ejecutivo Nacional de la República Argentina a través del IGN-Ley 22.923 y fue aprobada por Expte. No GG11 1595/5 de Mayo de 2011.

Acknowledgements

The publishers and authors would like to thank the following people and their institutions for their feedback and comments during the development of the material:

Reporters: Australia: Jane Comyns-Carr; **Germany:** Irene Ofteringer; **Ireland:** Fiona Gallagher; **Italy:** David Barnes, Elizabeth Gregson, Elizabeth Kalton, Thomas Malvica, Claire Maxwell; **Poland:** Dorota Adaszewska, Sylwia Sroda; **Spain:** Robert Armitage, Anabel Fernandez, Will Moreton; **United Kingdom:** Filiz Aydinlioglu, Andrew Briston, Olivia Date, Gareth Eldridge, Helen Elmerstig, Eileen Flannigan, Paula Kler, Alastair Lane, Andrea Merckel, Sheila Parrott, David Penny, Rich Quarterman, Emma Stobart, Alison Tomura

We are grateful to the following for permission to reproduce copyright material:

Text: Interview 3.2 adapted from Interview with Vladimir Chernenko "Family of 19 is never bored", *The Sacramento Bee*, 5 January 2006 (Erika Chavez), copyright © The Sacramento Bee 2006; Extract 3.2 from "Birds of a feather meet the southside's broodiest mom" published on www.bbc.co.uk 15 January 2003 copyright © The BBC; Extract 7.2 adapted from www.oz-bus.com copyright © OzBus; Extract 11.3 from "Good Samaritan?" by Michael Coombes published on www.bbc.co.uk 26 July 2006 copyright © The BBC.

Fawlty Towers written by John Cleese and Connie Booth

Illustration acknowledgements: Lyndon Hayes pgs9, 163t, 166; **Mister Paul** pgs10, 11, 48, 137; **Harry Malt** pgs28, 81, 92, 101, 106, 109, 129, 132, 134, 135, 141, 142, 143, 147, 150, 164, 166; **Jurgen Ziewe** p38; **Infomen** pgs40, 41, 72, 73, 163b; **Peter Grundy** pgs53, 121; **Joel Holland** p54; **Vince McIndoe** pgs88, 89; **Otto Steininger** p109; **Dermot Flynn** p111; **Matt Herring** p112.

Photo acknowledgements: The publisher would like to thank the following for their kind permission to reproduce their photographs:

(Key: b-bottom; c-centre; l-left; r-right; t-top)
7 Andrew Hackett, www.viewphotographic.co.uk: Andrew Hackett / photographersdirect.com (p12). **BBC Photo Library:** (p14). **Corbis:** Heide Benser (p8). **Photolibrary.com:** Lester Lefkowitz (p10). **8 BBC Photo Library:** (A). **Getty Images:** Andersen Ross (D); David Lees (C). **Photolibrary.com:** Photo Alto (B). **Rex Features:** Image Source (E). **12 Alamy Images:** Ken Welsh (B). **Axiom Photographic Agency Ltd:** Andrew Watson (A). **13 Alamy Images:** Vanda Woolsey (D). **Art Directors and TRIP photo Library:** (C). **Getty Images:** Andrew Hetherington (b). **14 BBC Photo Library:** (tl) (tr). **14-15 BBC Photo Library:** (b). **15 BBC Photo Library:** (br). **17 Alamy Images:** Chris Howes/Wild Places Photography (p22); funkytravel London - Paul Williams (p24). **Buzz Pictures:** Dean O'Flaherty (p20). **Corbis:** Roy Morsch (p18). **18 Photolibrary.com:** Corbis (t); Digital Vision (tc); Moodboard (bc). **PunchStock:** moodboard (b). **19 Alamy Images:** David Stares. **20 www.dreamstime.com:** (E) (F). **iStockphoto:** (D) (I). **Jupiter Unlimited:** (A) (H) (B) (C). **Photolibrary.com:** Fancy (G). **21 BBC Photo Library:** Jeff Overs (cl). **Corbis:** Barry Lewis (t). **Rex Features:** Nils Jorgensen (bl). **22 www.dreamstime.com:** (A). **Adrian Japp :** Adrian Japp / Photographersdirect.com (D). **alveyandtowers.com:** (E). **PunchStock:** Digital Vision (tourists). **Rosina Redwood :** Rosina Redwood / Photographersdirect.com (F). **Ureche Marius Liviu Photography:** Ureche Marius Liviu Photography / Photographersdirect.com (B); Ureche Marius Liviu / Photographersdirect.com (C). **22-23 Photoshot Holdings Limited:** World Pictures (t/background). **23 DK Images:** Nigel Hicks (r). **iStockphoto:** (l) (c). **24 Photolibrary.com:** Comstock (bl). **Rex Features:** Nils Jorgensen (tl). **24-25 Alamy Images:** funkytravel London - Paul Williams (main). **27 Alamy Images:** Ian Walter (p30). **Getty Images:** Louis Laurent Grandadam (p28); Neo Vision (p32). **Spectrum Photofile:** Spectrum Photofile / Photographersdirect.com (p34). **29 Getty Images:** Eileen Bach. **30 Getty Images:** Monica Davey / AFP. **31 Photolibrary.com:** Purestock. **32 Alamy Images:** Directphoto.org (l). **Corbis:** Jon Hicks (r). **33 Alamy Images:** John Elk III (bc/montage); Sergio Pitamitz (br/montage). **Gareth Boden:** (br). **Rex Features:** Ilpo Musto (t/montage). **34 Rex Features:** Geoffrey Swaine (bl). **34-35 Photolibrary.com:** Walter Bibikow (main). **35 Alamy Images:** Mary Evans Picture Library (sheet music). **iStockphoto:** (biscuits) (coal) (cleaning items). **37 Photolibrary.com:** Blend Images (p42); Shubroto Chattopadhyay (p44). **Rex Features:** Ken Straiton (p40). **View Pictures Ltd:** Edmund Sumner (p38). **38 Smoothe / Piercy Conner Architects :** (tl). **40 Alamy Images:** amama images inc. (b). **42 Alamy Images:** Rubberball (b). **Photolibrary.com:** Image Source (t). **42-43 Photolibrary.com:** Digital Vision (background). **43 Getty Images:** Andersen Ross (b). **Photolibrary.com:** Digital Vision (t). **44 Alamy Images:** Images of Africa Photobank (B). **Corbis:** Arnaud Chicurel (C). **FLPA Images of Nature:** Suzi Eszterhas/Minden Pictures (D). **International Photobank Ltd:** (A). **Photolibrary.com:** Image Source (E). **44-45 Corbis:** Ron Watts (background). **47 Alamy Images:** Agripicture Images (p50); foodfolio (p48). **BBC Photo Library:** (p54). **iStockphoto:** (p52). **49 iStockphoto:** (c) (r). **Photolibrary.com:** Creatas (l). **50 www.dreamstime.com:** (K). **Alamy Images:** Alistair Heap (beans can). **Alamy Images:** Alistair Heap (beans can); The Daniel Heighton Food Collection (B). **DK Images:** Susanna Price (J). **iStockphoto:** (H) (I). **Jupiter Unlimited:** (A) (D) (E) (F) (G) (C) (tr). **POD - Pearson Online Database:** (br). **51 Alamy Images:** David Muscroft (t). **Getty Images:** Bay Hippisley (b). **52 Photolibrary.com:** Digital Vision (b); John Howard (t). **52-53 Getty Images:** Mike Blank (t). **54-55 Corbis:** Jon Hicks (background). **55 BBC Photo Library:** (bl). **56 Copyright (c) Brand X Pictures. 57 Corbis:** John Turner (p58). **Getty Images:** Rick Gershon (p60). **Rex Features:** Steve Bell (p64). **SuperStock:** Corbis (p62). **58 Alamy Images:** United Archives GmbH (A). **Getty Images:** Vladimir Rys/Bongarts (B). **Press Association Images:** (E). **Rex Features:** Lehtikuva OY (C); © Universal/Everett (F) (D). **60 Steven Oakes:** (l) (c) (r). **61 Steven Oakes:** (l) (c) (r). **62 Photolibrary.com:** Goodshoot (b). **SuperStock:** Comstock (t). **63 Alamy Images:** Colin Underhill (tl). **Press Association Images:** Paul Faith (tr). **64 FAMOUS:** (tl). **iStockphoto:** (football). **Lebrecht Music and Arts Photo Library:** Laurie Lewis (br). **Photolibrary.com:** Chad Ehlers (bl); Roy Rainford (building). **Pictures Colour Library Ltd:** (cars). **65 Lebrecht Music and Arts Photo Library. 67 Photolibrary.com:** Chad Ehlers (p74); Digital Vision (p72); Image Source (p68). **Rex Features:** The Travel Library (p70). **68 Alamy Images:** Caro (D). **Photolibrary.com:** Digital Vision (B). **Rex Features:** The Travel Library (C). **TopFoto:** Spectrum Colour Library / HIP (A). **69 Hesvan Huizen Fotografie B.V. :** Hesvan Huizen Fotografie B.V. / Photographersdirect.com (tent). **Photolibrary.com:** Cultura (beach); Image Source (boat); Noel Hendrickson (horse riding). **Rex Features:** Stuart Black/The Travel Library (sign post). **70 Axiom Photographic Agency Ltd:** J. Sparshatt (A). **Rex Features:** David Pearson (D); Image Source (E). **STILL Pictures The Whole Earth Photo Library:** Biosphoto / Klein J.-L. & Hubert M.-L (C). **Travel Library Ltd, The:** John Carr (B). **71 Alamy Images:** D A Barnes (tl). **Corbis:** David Samuel Robbins (r). **Rex Features:** Image Source (bl). **Spectrum Photofile:** (bus). **72 Alamy Images:** M J Perris (C). **Rex Features:** KPA/Zuma (B); The Travel Library (A). **73 Photolibrary.com:** Corbis. **74 Alamy Images:** Aflo Co. Ltd. (bl). **Getty Images:** altrendo images (cr); Nicolas Russell (tl). **Photolibrary.com:** Brand X Pictures (br); Oswald Jan (cl). **TopFoto:** (tr). **74-75 Getty Images:** Chad Ehlers (main). **75 Getty Images:** altrendo images (br). **76 iStockphoto. 77 Alamy Images:** Jack Hobhouse (p84). **Getty Images:** John D McHugh/AFP (p80). **Press Association Images:** Fiona Hanson (p78). **Vickie Burt:** Vickie Burt / Photographersdirect.com (p82). **78 Corbis:** Daniel Attia (t); Moons (l). **Photolibrary.com:** Jochen Tack (br). **79 Getty Images:** Zac Macaulay (b). **Photolibrary.com:** Corbis (t). **80 Corbis:** Kurt Krieger (tr); Peter Andrews (br); Rafael Roa (bl). **Getty Images:** Frederick M. Brown (tl). **81 Corbis:** Kurt Krieger (t). **Getty Images:** Avik Gilboa (b). **82 Ronald Grant Archive:** 20th Century Fox (E); 20th Century Fox (B); New Line Cinema (A); Paramount Pictures (H). **Rex Features:** Magnolia/Everett (F). **83 Getty Images:** Workbook Stock/ Kristin Burns (b). **Ronald Grant Archive:** Columbia Pictures (D); © Walt Disney (G). **Kobal Collection Ltd:** Universal / Playtone (C). **84 Alamy Images:** David Pearson (tl); Mai Chen (br). **84-85 Alamy Images:** Edward Westmacott (background). **85 Press Association Images:** Jon Crwys-Williams (br). **87 Getty Images:** Elis Years (p92). **Photolibrary.com:** Xavier Subias (p90). **Science Faction:** Peter Ginter (p94). **SuperStock:** Etienne (p88). **90 Alamy Images:** Pablo Valentini. **91 POD - Pearson Online Database:** Image Source (bl); Photodisc (t). **93 Alamy Images:** Jack Sullivan (br). **Getty Images:** Christopher Furlong (tr); Tim Graham (bl). **Press Association Images:** Matt Dunham (tl). **94-95 Corbis:** Ashley Cooper (aeroplane); Ralf-Finn Hestoft (background). **95 Alamy Images:** CoverSpot (tr/montage); vario images GmbH & Co.KG (cl/montage). **Corbis:** Marc Asnin (bl/montage). **Getty Images:** Photo and Co (tl/montage). **Photolibrary.com:** Image Source (br/montage); Will Datene (cr/ montage). **97 Alamy Images:** E.J. Baumeister Jr. (p104). **Corbis:** Simon Marcus (p102). **Getty Images:** Gregor Schuster (p98). **Photolibrary.com:** Geoff Renner (p100). **98 Photolibrary.com:** Blend Images (couple). **TopFoto:** (shop). **99 Alamy Images:** Ace Stock Ltd (jogger); Bubbles Photolibrary (bags); Ian Thraves (barbecue); igroover (at desk). **Getty Images:** Paul Viant (wedding couple); Stuart O'Sullivan (shaking hands). **Photolibrary.com:** Corbis (with plant). **100 Alamy Images:** Chris Cooper-Smith (tl); Daniel H. Bailey (tr); Travelscape Images (br). **Corbis:** Alfred Saerchinger (bl). **102 Alamy Images:** Lars Johansson (c); PYMCA (tr). **Corbis:** Anthony West (cl). **Getty Images:** Jim Cummins (tl). **Photolibrary.com:** Brand X Pictures (bl); Creatas (br). **SuperStock:** Corbis/Tim Pannell (cr). **104 Alamy Images:** Ian Dobbs (A); Steve Bloom Images (D). **Corbis:** Onne van der Wal (B). **iStockphoto:** (E) (C). **Photolibrary.com:** (F). **104-105 iStockphoto:** (background). **105 Alamy Images:** Alex Segre (tl); David Noble Photography (tr) (bl). **Photolibrary.com:** (br). **107 Alamy Images:** D. Hurst (p108). **Aurora Photos Inc:** Daniel Lai (p114). **Getty Images:** Felbert + Eickenberg (p112); Tao Associates (p110). **108 Alamy Images:** Charles Mistral (B); Chris Rout (C). **Corbis:** Steve Prezant (D); Turbo (A). **Getty Images:** Oliver Lang (E). **110 PhotoDisc. 112 Alamy Images:** Alvey and Towers (r). **Photofusion Picture Library:** Bob Watkins (l). **113 Alamy Images:** Sally and Richard Greenhill (b). **alveyandtowers.com:** Peter Alvey (t). **114 iStockphoto:** (A) (D). **Jupiter Unlimited:** (F) (C). **Photolibrary.com:** Corbis (E); Corbis (B). **Rex Features:** Richard Young (b). **117 Ronald Grant Archive:** New Line Cinema (p120). **Image Quest Marine:** (p124). **Masterfile UK Ltd:** (p122). **Rex Features:** The Travel Library (p118). **118 Alamy Images:** David Noble Photography (E). **Ardea:** Chuck McDougal (A). **Corbis:** Jose Fuste Raga (B); Peter Adams (D). **Eye Ubiquitous / Hutchison:** Elliot Walker (C). **120 Ronald Grant Archive:** (tl); LucasFilm/Paramount Pictures (br). **Kobal Collection Ltd:** LucasFilm Ltd/ Paramount (bl); MGM / EON / Jay Maidment (tr). **121 Alamy Images:** Martin Florin Emmanuel. **122-123 Getty Images:** Don Spiro. **123 Alamy Images:** Chris Howes/Wild Places Photography (inset). **124 Alamy Images:** Buzz Pictures (r). **iStockphoto:** (shark) (rat) (tiger) (spider) (bear) (snake). **124-125 Image Quest Marine:** (main). **152 iStockphoto:** (D) (E) (H) (I) (M) (N) (t) (B) (C) (L). **Jupiter Unlimited:** (J) (G) (O). **Pearson Education Ltd:** (A). **Rex Features:** 24/7 Media (F). **shutterstock:** (K). **153 Alamy Images:** Danny Clifford (J). **Blend:** (G). **iStockphoto:** (D) (A) (F) (M) (O) (Q) (L) (B). **Jupiter Unlimited:** (H) (I) (K) (N). **Photolibrary.com:** Corbis (P); White (E). **Rex Features:** Ron Sachs (C). **154 Bananastock:** (E) (F) (H) (I) (J) (C). **iStockphoto:** (A) (D) (B). **Jupiter Unlimited:** (G). **155 www.dreamstime.com:** (D) (E) (G). **iStockphoto:** (A). **Jupiter Unlimited:** (F) (H) (inset H) (B) (C). **156 www.dreamstime.com:** (A) (N) (B) (L). **Alamy Images:** Adrian Sherratt (J); Gary Roebuck (G); LondonPhotos - Homer Sykes (M); Peter Titmuss (K); uk retail Alan King (C). **iStockphoto:** (E) (H). **Jupiter Unlimited:** (D) (F). **Photolibrary.com:** Polka Dot (I). **157 www.dreamstime.com:** (P) (S) (Q). **Trevor Clifford:** (I) (J) (G) (K) (C) (L). **Copyright (c) Brand X Pictures:** (A) (V) (X). **iStockphoto:** (E) (D) (H) (M) (U) (Z) (R) (T). **Jupiter Unlimited:** (F) (N) (O) (W) (Y) (B). **158 Alamy Images:** Johnny Greig people (cr/top row). **Corbis:** Kate Mitchell (r/top row). **Getty Images:** Jose Luis Pelaez (cl/top row). **iStockphoto:** (r/centre row). **Pearson Education Ltd:** (bl) (bc) (br). **Photolibrary.com:** Corbis (cl/centre row); Creatas (l/centre row); Digital Vision (cr/centre row); Tim Garcha (l/top row). **159 www.dreamstime.com:** (N) (O). **iStockphoto:** (D) (E) (G) (H) (I) (J) (K) (M) (P) (B) (L). **Jupiter Unlimited:** (A) (C). **Photolibrary.com:** Image Source (F). **160 Corbis:** VALLON FABRICE (br). **Getty Images:** PNC (bl). **iStockphoto:** (tc). **Newspix:** Cifra Manuela (tr). **Photolibrary.com:** Digital Vision (bc). **162 Alamy Images:** Ian Dagnall (b). **Jupiter Unlimited:** Stockexpert (t). **164 Corbis:** VALLON FABRICE (br). **iStockphoto:** (tr). **Newspix:** Cifra Manuela. **Photolibrary.com:** Digital Vision (bl). **165 Alamy Images:** Jon Arnold Images Ltd

All other images © Pearson Education

Every effort has been made to trace the copyright holders and we apologise in advance for any unintentional omissions. We would be pleased to insert the appropriate acknowledgement in any subsequent edition of this publication.

Frances Eales
Steve Oakes

speakout

Elementary
Students' Book

with ActiveBook

BBC

CONTENTS

LESSON	GRAMMAR/FUNCTION	VOCABULARY	PRONUNCIATION	READING
UNIT 7 HOLIDAYS page 67 — Video podcast | How was your last holiday?				
7.1 Travel partners page 68	comparatives	travel	stressed syllables	
7.2 The longest bus ride page 70	superlatives	places (1)	strong and weak forms of *the*	read an article about a long journey
7.3 Can you tell me the way? page 72	giving directions	places (2)	sentence stress for correcting	
7.4 Buenos Aires page 74		phrases to describe a town/city		read a travel article
UNIT 8 NOW page 77 — Video podcast | What was the last film you				
8.1 In the picture page 78	present continuous	verbs + prepositions	weak forms of prepositions and articles	read blogs about what people are doing now
8.2 Looking good page 80	present simple and present continuous	appearance		
8.3 What do you recommend? page 82	recommending	types of film	word linking	
8.4 Festival Highlights page 84		festival activities; phrases to describe an event		read a festival review
UNIT 9 TRANSPORT page 87 — Video podcast | How do you get to work?				
9.1 Travel in style page 88	articles: *a/an*, *the*, no article	transport collocations	strong and weak forms of *a* and *the*	
9.2 Citybikes page 90	*can/can't*, *have to/don't have to*	adjectives (1)	strong and weak forms of *can*, *can't*, *have to* and *don't have to*	read an article about Paris Citybikes
9.3 Sorry I'm late page 92	apologising	excuses	intonation to show being happy or unhappy	
9.4 Airport page 94		phrases to describe and complain about problems		read an email
UNIT 10 THE FUTURE page 97 — Video podcast | What are your plans for the future?				
10.1 Life's a lottery page 98	*be going to*; *would like to*	plans	*going to* and *would*	read a news story about a lottery win
10.2 Survive! page 100	*will*, *might*, *won't*	phrases with *get*	contracted form of *will*	read an extract from a survival instruction book
10.3 Let's do something page 102	making suggestions	adjectives (2)	stressed syllables	read an article about things to do with friends
10.4 Wild Weather page 104		phrases to describe weather		
UNIT 11 HEALTH page 107 — Video podcast | Do you have a healthy lifestyle?				
11.1 My head hurts page 108	*should/shouldn't*	the body; health	consonant clusters	read an article about cold cures around the world
11.2 Never felt better page 110	adverbs of manner	common verbs (2)		read a quiz about how fit you are
11.3 Help! page 112	offering to help	problems		read an article about a social experiment
11.4 The Optician page 114		phrases to describe a problem and to give advice		
UNIT 12 EXPERIENCES page 117 — Video podcast | What's the most exciting thing you've				
12.1 Unforgettable page 118	present perfect	outdoor activities		
12.2 Afraid of nothing page 120	present perfect and past simple	prepositions (3)		read an article about a dangerous job
12.3 I've got a problem page 122	telephoning	telephoning expressions	sentence stress	
12.4 Shark Therapy page 124		phrases to describe an experience		

IRREGULAR VERBS page 127   LANGUAGE BANK page 128   PHOTO BANK page 140

CONTENTS

LISTENING/DVD	SPEAKING	WRITING
listen to people discuss how they like to travel	talk about how you like to travel; compare places and holidays	
	plan and talk about a long journey	learn to check and correct information; write about a holiday
understand directions; learn to check and correct directions	give directions in the street	
BBC Holiday 10 Best: watch an extract from a travel show about Buenos Aires	describe a town/city you know	write a short article about a town/city
	talk about taking photos; talk about what people are doing	write a blog entry about what you are doing
listen to a radio programme about ideas of beauty	discuss what you know about various film stars; describe people's appearance	
learn to link words to speak faster	ask and answer a questionnaire about films; ask for and give recommendations	
BBC Inside Out: watch an extract from a documentary about an English music festival	describe an event	write a review of an event
listen to a guide giving a tour around a transport museum	talk about types of transport	
	talk about ways to travel around towns/cities	
listen to a man talk about his problems getting to work	apologise for being late; tell a long story	learn to use linkers and write a story
BBC Airport: watch an extract from a documentary about a day at Heathrow airport	deal with problems when flying	write an email about an experience at an airport/on a plane
listen to a radio interview with lottery winners	talk about your future plans/wishes	
	make predictions about situations	improve your use of linkers: *too, also* and *as well* and write a short story
learn to respond to suggestions; listen to people discussing which activities they want to do	make some suggestions and invite your friends to join you	
BBC Wild Weather: watch an extract from a documentary about the wettest place in Europe	talk about weather and how it makes you feel	write a message board notice about your country
listen to a radio programme about colds and flu	talk about what to do when you don't feel well and give advice; discuss cures for the common cold	
	do a quiz about your fitness; talk about healthy weekends	learn to use adverbs in stories and how to make stories more interesting
listen to different scenarios of people needing help and thanking someone	give advice and offer help; thank someone	
BBC The Two Ronnies: watch an extract from a sitcom about an unusual shopping experience	ask for help in a pharmacy	write some advice for a health message board
listen to people talking about their experiences	talk about unusual experiences	learn to use postcard phrases and write a postcard
	describe movement from one place to another; talk about past experiences	
listen to different scenarios on the phone	describe difficult situations/problems; say telephone numbers; phone someone about a problem	
BBC Shark Therapy: watch an extract from a documentary about sharks	describe an exciting/frightening experience	write a story about an exciting/frightening experience

COMMUNICATION BANK page 148   AUDIO SCRIPTS page 152

UNIT 7

SPEAKING
- Talk about how you like to travel
- Compare places, transport, hotels and holidays
- Plan and talk about a long journey
- Give directions in the street
- Describe a town/city you know

LISTENING
- Understand directions
- Watch an extract from a travel show about Buenos Aires

READING
- Read an article about a bus ride from London to Sydney

WRITING
- Check and correct information about a holiday
- Write a short article about a town/city

BBC CONTENT
- Video podcast: How was your last holiday?
- DVD: Holiday 10 Best

UNIT 7

holidays

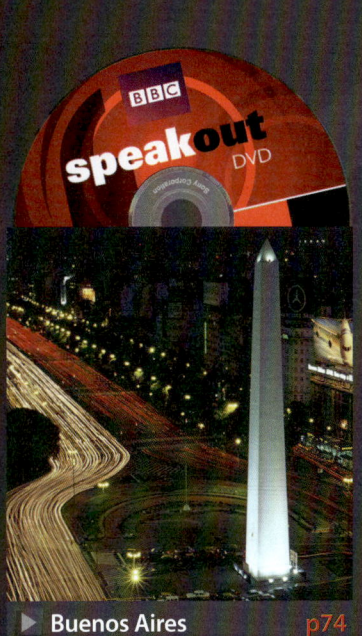

▶ Travel partners   p68
▶ The longest bus ride   p70 
▶ Can you tell me the way?   p72 
▶ Buenos Aires   p74

7.1 TRAVEL PARTNERS

▶ GRAMMAR | comparatives   ▶ VOCABULARY | travel   ▶ HOW TO | compare places and holidays

A

B

C

D

VOCABULARY travel

1A Work in pairs. What places/things can you see in the photos? Make a list of adjectives to describe them.
Train: fast, comfortable …

B Match the adjectives in column A with the opposites in column B.

A	B
good	noisy
fast	empty
crowded	bad
expensive	boring
hot	cheap
comfortable	cold
interesting	uncomfortable
quiet	slow

C ▶ 7.1 Listen and underline the stressed syllable in each adjective. Then listen again and repeat.
<u>crow</u>ded

D Work in pairs and take turns. Student A: choose one of the photos A–D. Describe it using four adjectives from Exercise 1B. Student B: guess the photo.
A: *It's really comfortable and I think it's expensive. It's quite big and it isn't noisy.*
B: *Photo D?*

SPEAKING

2A Do the travel quiz below. Circle your answers.

B Work in pairs and compare your answers. Are you good travel partners? Why/Why not?

TRAVEL QUIZ

Going on holiday this year? Do the quiz and find your perfect travel partner …

1 **How do you like to travel?**
   a) By plane   b) By train

2 **Where do you like to stay?**
   a) In a hotel   b) In a self-catering apartment

3 **What do you prefer to do?**
   a) Go sightseeing   b) Relax on a beach

4 **When do you like to go?**
   a) In spring   b) In summer

5 **What do you like to eat?**
   a) Local dishes   b) The food I usually eat

6 **What do you like to do in the evening?**
   a) Go to a club   b) Go to a restaurant

7 **How long is your perfect holiday?**
   a) A week   b) A month

LISTENING

3A ▶ 7.2 Listen to two people doing the quiz. Answer the questions.
1 How many of their answers are the same?
2 Are they good travel partners?

B Listen again. Write man (M) and woman (W) next to the answers in the quiz in Exercise 2A.

C Work in pairs and discuss. Is the man or the woman a good travel partner for you? Why/Why not?

GRAMMAR comparatives

4A Look at audio script 7.2 on page 152 and complete the sentences.
1 Flying is fast____ _____ going by train.
2 Summer is hot____ _____ spring.
3 A hotel is _____ expensive _____ an apartment.

B ▶ 7.3 Underline the stressed words in the sentences above. Listen and check. Then listen again and repeat.

C Complete the table.

short adjectives	fast	fast*er*	adjective + -_____
long adjectives	comfortable	_____ comfortable	_____ + adjective
irregular adjectives	good/bad	better/worse	

➡ page 128 **LANGUAGEBANK**

PRACTICE

5A Write comparative sentences. Use the adjectives in brackets.
1 cafés, restaurants (expensive)
   Restaurants are more expensive than cafés.
2 autumn, spring (romantic)
3 travelling by car, travelling by train (fast)
4 English, my language (easy)
5 shoes, trainers (comfortable)
6 water, coffee (good for you)
7 book, magazine (interesting)
8 city, beach (relaxing)

B Work in pairs and compare your answers.

6A Choose two places you know, e.g. cities, cafés, nightclubs. Which one do you like more? Write two sentences about each place using comparatives.
I like Edinburgh more than London because it's friendlier and cheaper.

B Work in pairs and take turns. Tell each other about your places.
A: *I like Edinburgh more than London.*
B: *Why?*
A: *It's friendlier and cheaper.*

SPEAKING

7A Write notes about a good/bad holiday you went on. Think about the questions below and use the photos to help.
* Where/When did you go?
* Who did you go with?
* Where did you stay? Was it good?
* What did you do? Did you enjoy it?
* Where did you eat? Did you like the food?
* Was it hot?
* Did you like it more than your town/city? Why/Why not?

B Work in pairs. Ask and answer the questions above.
A: *Where did you go?*
B: *I went to France …*

7.2 THE LONGEST BUS RIDE

▶ GRAMMAR | superlatives   ▶ VOCABULARY | places   ▶ HOW TO | talk about a journey

VOCABULARY places

1A Work in pairs. Look at photos A–E. Which of the things in the box can you see?

> a mountain   a bridge   a village   a lake   a river   a jungle   a city   a market
> a famous building   a desert

OZBUS an exciting way to travel from London to Sydney

The OZBUS is the longest bus ride in the world and the ultimate journey for backpackers. In twelve weeks it travels 16,000 kilometres through twenty different countries.

'Most people fly from London to Sydney at 40,000 feet and never see anything,' says Mark Creasey from Ozbus. 'On the Ozbus people can see the most beautiful places in the world. We go across Europe, through Turkey, India, China, Malaysia and Australia. We travel through deserts, mountains and jungles – it's amazing.'

Jeff Lane travelled on the Ozbus last summer. 'The best thing was the Taj Mahal,' he said. 'The most exciting place was the tiger reserve in the Himalayas, and I really enjoyed visiting the base camp of Mount Everest.' And what were the worst things? 'Well, in Tehran the bus broke down and we waited a whole day for a new one. That wasn't so good. And I didn't always enjoy camping at night. Sometimes I wanted to stay somewhere more comfortable!'

The Ozbus takes up to forty people of all ages. At night, the passengers usually stay in camps or sometimes in small hotels. Everyone takes turns to buy food in local markets and cook for the group.

The greatest journey in the world? Creasey thinks so: 'If you want a truly awesome experience, then the Ozbus is for you.'

READING

2A Read the introduction to the article about the Ozbus and answer the questions.
1 What is the Ozbus?
2 How many countries does it travel through?

B Work in pairs. What else would you like to know about the Ozbus? Write three questions using the words in the box to help.

> countries   price   sleep   people   food   sights

How many countries does it visit?

3A Read the article. Did you find the answers to your questions?

B Read the article again. Are sentences 1–6 true (T) or false (F)?
1 The Ozbus travels through twelve countries in twenty weeks.
2 Ozbus passengers fly from London to Sydney.
3 Jeff Lane took the Ozbus in the summer.
4 He liked the Taj Mahal, the tiger reserve and camping.
5 Most Ozbus passengers are forty years old.
6 They stay in hotels and camps.

B Work in pairs. Look at the words in the box above and write an example for each word. Use your country if possible.
A mountain: Mount Velino (Italy)

C Would you like to go on the Ozbus? Why/Why not?

7.2

PRACTICE

5A Make questions about the Ozbus trip. Use the prompts below to help.
1 What / cold / place you visited?
   What was the coldest place you visited?
2 What / hot / place?
3 What / friendly / place?
4 What / long / you travelled in one day?
5 What / beautiful / building you saw?
6 What / amazing / experience of the journey?

B Match answers a)–f) with questions 1–6.
a) The Red Desert in Australia.
b) The Taj Mahal
c) Seeing a tiger
d) 400 kilometres
e) Mount Everest
f) I can't say. We met so many fantastic people.

C ▶ 7.5 Listen to a conversation with an Ozbus passenger and check your answers.

SPEAKING

6A Work in groups. Plan a long journey to another country. Make a list of five places to visit: the most exciting, the most beautiful, the highest, etc.

B Prepare to tell the class about your journey. Use these phrases:
First we go to … then we visit the oldest/most famous … in …

C Work in pairs and take turns. Tell the class about your journey. Ask and answer questions about each journey.
A: *Where do you sleep at night?*
B: *In small hotels.*

D Discuss. Which journey is the most interesting?

WRITING   checking and correcting

7A Read the student's homework below. Find and correct ten mistakes with:
• the spelling   • past tense forms   • singular and plural

>   desert
> On Saturday we went by bus across the dessert. We meet a lot of peoples. The peoples in the villages was friendlyer than in the city. At night we staid in a camp. It was not very comftable, but it was more cheaper than the hotels. We buyed all our food in the market.

B Write four sentences about your last holiday.

C Work in pairs. Check each other's sentences. Use the list in Exercise 7A to help.

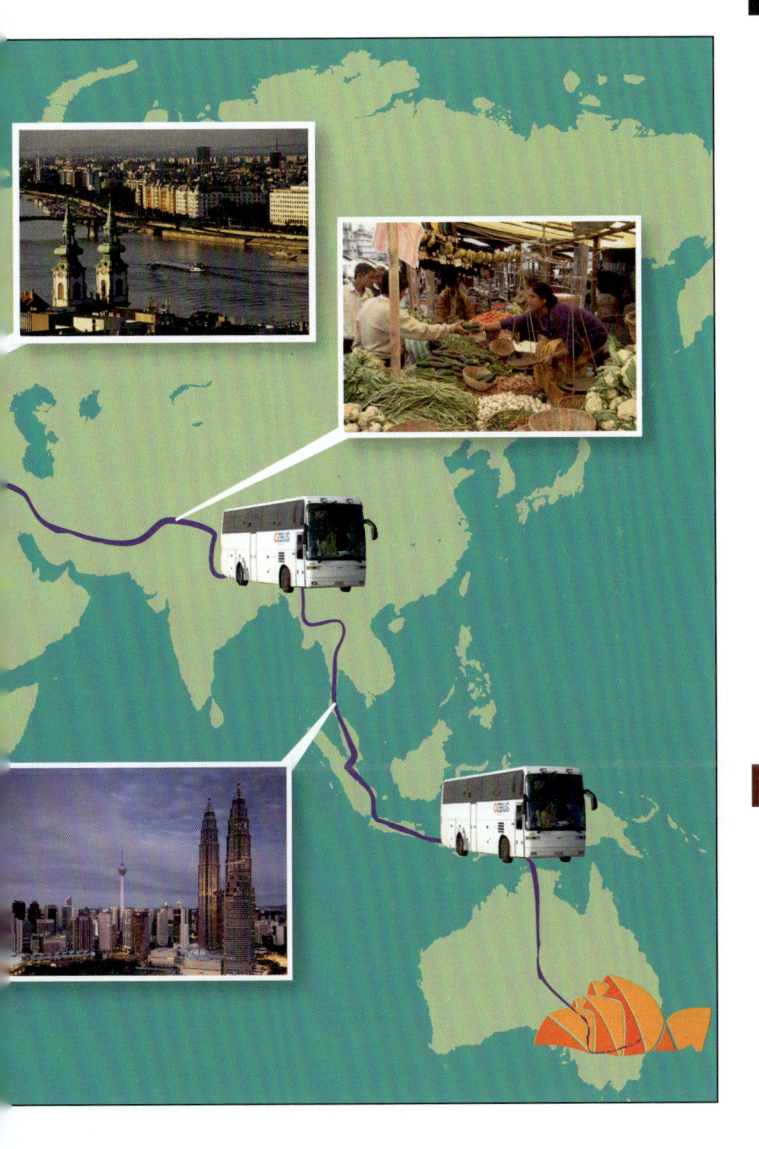

GRAMMAR   superlatives

4A Complete the sentences with words from the article above.
1 The Ozbus is the _____ bus ride in the world.
2 People can see the _____ beautiful places in the world.
3 The _____ thing was the Taj Mahal.

B Underline other examples of superlatives in the article. Then complete the table below.

			the + adjective +
short adjectives	great	*the greatest*	
longer adjectives	exciting		
irregular adjectives	good		
	bad		

C ▶ 7.4 Listen to the pronunciation of *the* in the sentences in Exercise 4A. Then listen and repeat.

➡ page 128 **LANGUAGE**BANK

7.3 CAN YOU TELL ME THE WAY?

▶ **FUNCTION** | giving directions   ▶ **VOCABULARY** | places   ▶ **LEARN TO** | check and correct directions

VOCABULARY   places

1A Read the leaflet below and look at the photos A–C. What can you see and do in Brighton? Would you like to go there? Why/Why not?

WELCOME TO BRIGHTON AND HOVE

Just 80km south of London on England's south coast, it is a great place to visit. Brighton is one of the most exciting cities in Britain – with its fantastic shopping, good-value restaurants, great arts and music and famous beach and pier – it's a popular place to visit or stay. It has even got its very own royal palace, the exotic Royal Pavilion.

B Look at the map of Brighton and find the places in the box below.

> a bus station   a theatre   a car park
> a Tourist Information centre   a pier
> a museum   a clock tower
> an art gallery   a park   a square
> a library   a swimming pool

FUNCTION   giving directions

2A Work in pairs and look at the map. Find three different routes from the Clock Tower to Brighton Pier.

B ▶ 7.6 Listen to the directions. Draw the route on the map.

C Listen again and complete the dialogue. Then listen and repeat.

A: Excuse me. Can you ¹_____ me the way to the ²_____, please?
B: Yeah … you ³_____ down West Street until the ⁴_____.
A: Straight ⁵_____?
B: Yeah. And then turn ⁶_____ and you'll see the Pier.
A: Thanks very much.

3A Match directions 1–8 to diagrams A–H.

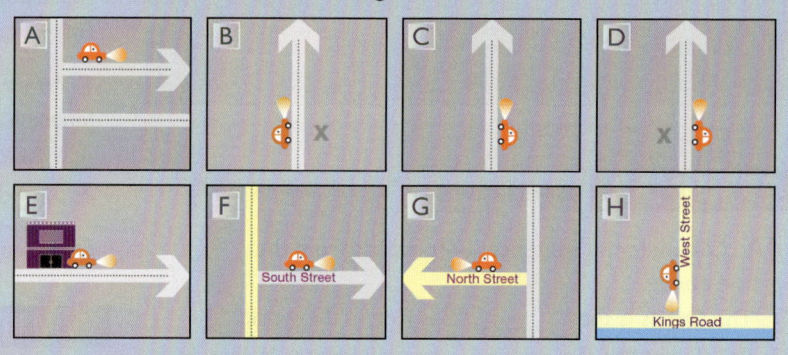

1 go straight on   C
2 turn left into North Street
3 turn right into South Street
4 go down West Street until the end
5 take the second right
6 go past the cinema
7 it's on the right
8 it's on the left

B ▶ 7.7 Listen and check. Then listen and repeat.

▶ page 128 **LANGUAGEBANK**

4A Choose two places in the box below. Write directions to them from the Clock Tower.

> the Royal Pavilion   the Museum and Art Gallery   the swimming pool
> Church Street car park   the Town Hall   the Theatre Royal

B Work in pairs and take turns. Student A: Read your directions. Student B: follow the directions. Where are you?

C Give directions for two more places.

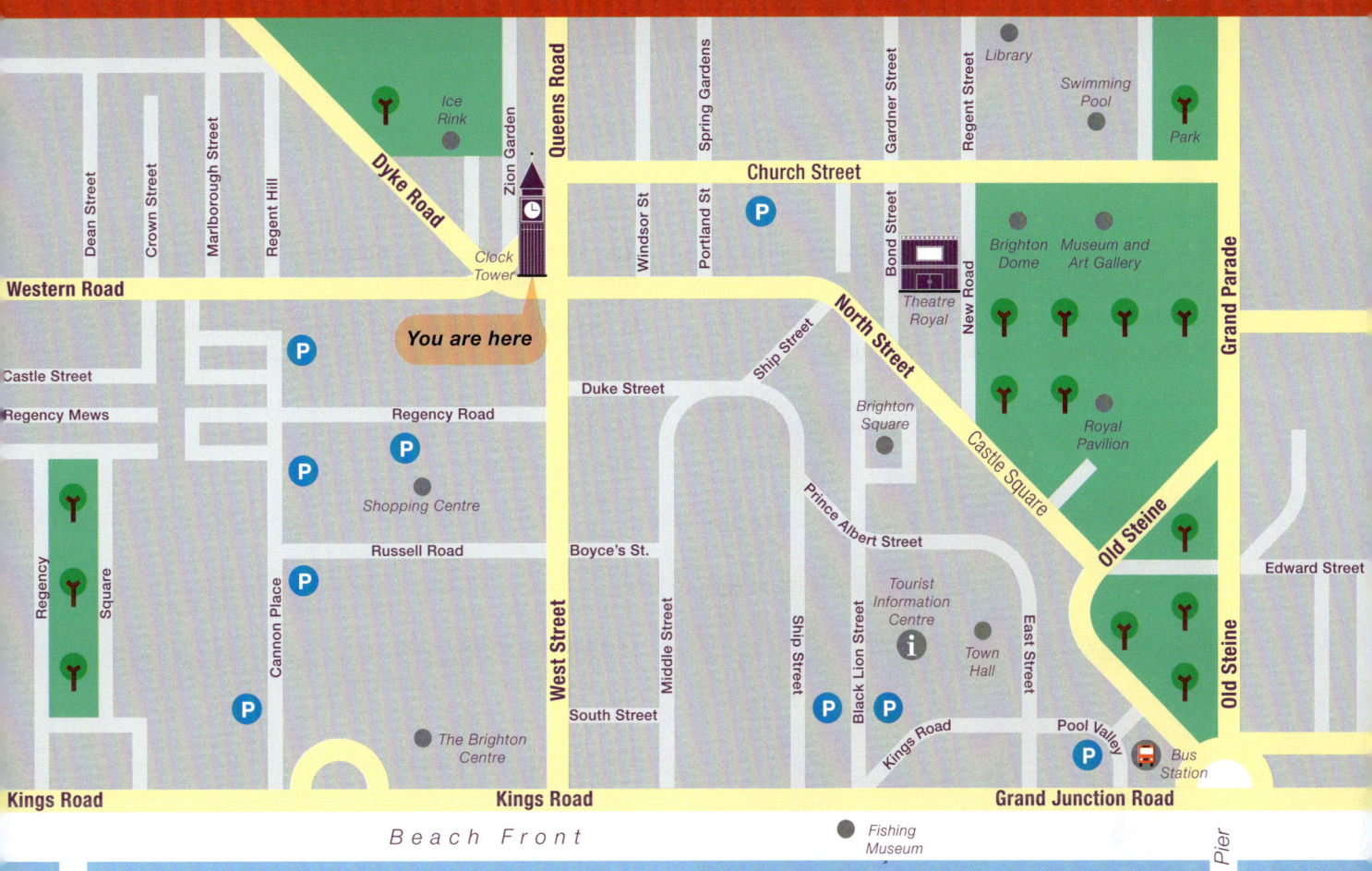

LEARN TO check and correct directions

5A ▶ 7.8 Find Church Street car park. Listen to the conversation and follow the directions. Where are you?

B Read the extract and listen again. How does the woman check the directions? Underline the phrases she uses.

A: You go out of this car park and turn right. So that's right into Church Street. Then take the third right, I think it's called New Road.
B: The first right?
A: No, the third right. And you go straight on until the end of the road and then turn left. After about one minute you'll see it on the left. You can't miss it!
B: So third right, erm, left at the end of the road and then … ?
A: It's on the left.
B: On the left.

C Work in pairs. Student A: read the part of A above, sentence by sentence. Student B: cover the extract. Listen to Student A and repeat to check you understand.
A: You go out of this car park and turn right.
B: Turn right?

6A ▶ 7.9 Look at the conversation extracts below. Listen and underline the stressed words in B's answers.
1 A: The first right?
   B: No, the third right.
2 A: So I turn left and then …
   B: No, you turn right.
3 A: So I go past the Pavilion and …
   B: No, past the Pier.
4 A: It's in Church Street.
   B: No, it's in Church Road.

B Listen again and repeat the man's answers.

speakout TIP

When you want to correct a mistake, you can use stress. Remember to say the correct word **higher**, **louder** and **longer**.
Is it fifty-two High Street?   No, it's **thirty**-two.

C Work in pairs and take turns. Student A: look at page 149. Student B: look at page 150.

SPEAKING

7 Work in pairs and take turns. Choose a starting point in your town/city that you both know. Student A: you are a tourist. Ask for directions to three places. Check you understand the directions. Student B: give directions and correct the directions if necessary.

7.4 CITY OF BUENOS AIRES

DVD PREVIEW

1A Work in pairs. Look at the photos and answer the questions below.
1 What can you see/do in Buenos Aires City?
2 What sports are popular in Argentina?

B Read the text and check your answers.

BBC Holiday 10 Best

In the last of ten programmes looking at exciting holidays, Nicki Chapman takes us on a quick tour of Argentina's capital. She starts her tour at the amazing Avenue 9th July, and then visits La Boca, where football legend Diego Maradona started his career. She also watches people dance the tango, tries the popular sport of polo and eats some famous Argentinian beef.

DVD VIEW

2A Watch the DVD. Number the photos in the order Nicki talks about them.

B Match the words/names below with descriptions a)–f).
1 the Avenue 9th July
2 La Boca
3 Diego Maradona
4 the tango
5 polo
6 Argentinian beef

a) is one of the poorest parts of Buenos Aires City
b) is the best in the world
c) is the widest street in the city
d) is a famous dance
e) is a sport you do on a horse
f) is one of the most famous football players in the world

C Work in pairs and compare your answers.

D Watch the DVD again. Complete the extracts below with the words in the box.

| famous | vegetables | south | football |
| widest | meat | emotion | career |

The twenty-lane Avenue 9th July is the ^{1}_____ street on the planet and it cuts through the city from north to ^{2}_____.

The people of La Boca share one of Argentina's greatest passions: ^{3}_____. La Boca is where Diego Maradona, one of football's leading legends, began his ^{4}_____.

We are also ^{5}_____ for the tango. People started dancing the tango in the 1800s. It's a dance full of passion and ^{6}_____.

You can't be a vegetarian, can you, with all this fantastic ^{7}_____? If you want, we have very good ^{8}_____ here! Very social, isn't it?

3 Work in pairs. Answer the questions.
1 What do you think are the two most interesting things to do or to see in Buenos Aires City?
2 Do you think Buenos Aires City is a good place for a holiday? Why/Why not?

speakout describe a town/city

4A Work in pairs. Choose a town/city you both know. Make a list of interesting facts and information about it. Think about:
- general information, e.g. where it is, how big it is
- important places
- famous people
- special food/local dishes

B Prepare to tell other students about the town/city. Use the key phrases to help.

> **keyphrases**
> We want to talk about …
> It's [the capital city/an old town] …
> It's got [a/some] …
> One of the most important places in … is …
> Here you can see …
> A famous person from … is …
> He/She's famous because …
> A typical food from [town/city] is …
> It's a (very) … place. You can … there.

C ▶ 7.10 Listen to two students talk about Rimini in Italy. Which things from Exercise 4A don't they talk about?

D Listen again and tick the key phrases you hear.

E Work in groups. Tell other students about the town/city. Which places would you like to visit?

writeback a travel article

5A Read the description of Rimini below. Divide the article into four paragraphs:
- a description of the place
- a famous person
- a typical food
- your opinion

> Rimini is an old city on the Adriatic Sea in Italy. It's famous for its beautiful beach and also for the cathedral and the Arch of Augustus. The Rimini nightlife is amazing. There are lots of places to dance and have fun. One of the most famous people from Rimini is the film director Federico Fellini. He made many films, for example *Amarcord*, *La Dolce Vita* and *La Strada*. His ideas for his films sometimes came from his childhood in Rimini. A typical food in Rimini is 'puntarelle'. This is a pasta dish with fresh vegetables. It's very simple but delicious. Rimini is also a good place to eat fish. I like travelling, and I like going to new places, but I go to Rimini every year because I love the beaches and the nightlife.

B Now write an article of 80–100 words about your town/city for a travel website. Use the ideas and phrases from Exercise 4 and the article above to help.

75

7.5 ◀◀ LOOKBACK

COMPARATIVES

1A Look at the information below about two ways of travelling from Moscow to Beijing. Write eight sentences comparing them. Use the words in the box to help.

> cheap fast expensive slow
> crowded boring comfortable
> interesting uncomfortable
> exciting relaxing

The train is cheaper than the plane.

Trans-Siberian Railway:
580 euros 2nd class,
7 days, 35 stops,
4 beds per compartment,
restaurant on train

China Airlines flight:
1,100 euros 2nd class,
7 hours 20 minutes, 0 stops,
2 meals, 2 movies

B Work in pairs and discuss. Which way of travelling from Moscow to Beijing is better: the train or plane? Why?

VOCABULARY: PLACES

2 Work in pairs. Look at the words in the box below and find:

> a mountain   a village   a city
> a desert   a jungle   a lake
> a market   a river

1 two places where you can swim.
2 one place that has a lot of trees.
3 two places where people live.
4 one place where you can buy things.
5 one place that's hot in the day and cold at night.
6 one place that's very high.

SUPERLATIVES

3A Complete the quiz with superlatives of the adjectives in brackets.

City Quiz

1 *The friendliest* (friendly) city in the world is:
   a) Rio de Janeiro   b) Cairo
   c) Kuala Lumpur

2 The world's _____ (big) city is:
   a) Seoul   b) Mexico City
   c) Tokyo

3 _____ (good) place to live is:
   a) Zurich   b) Vancouver
   c) Melbourne

4 _____ (safe) city in the world is:
   a) Istanbul   b) Singapore
   c) Dublin

5 _____ (beautiful) city is:
   a) Cape Town   b) Sydney
   c) Prague

6 _____ (popular) tourist destination in the world is:
   a) Spain   b) The USA
   c) France

7 _____ (fast)-growing cities in the world are in:
   a) China   b) Africa   c) India

8 _____ (busy) shopping street is in the world is in:
   a) London   b) Hong Kong
   c) Shanghai

Key: 1a 2c 3b 4a 5a 6c 7b 8a

B Work in pairs and do the quiz. Then check your answers in the key.

CHECKING AND CORRECTING

4A Complete the sentences with false information about you.
1 I spell my name …
2 I'm from …
3 I live in …
4 My teacher is …
5 I like …

B Work in pairs and take turns. Look at your partner's information and check statements with him/her.
A: *So, you spell your name d-y-a-n-a.*
B: *No, my name's Diana! I spell my name d-i-a-n-a.*
A: *And, you're from Poland.*
B: *No, I'm from France.*

GIVING DIRECTIONS

5A Put the words in order. Start with the underlined words.
1 <u>Go</u> / take / left. / and / down / the / Grand / first / Avenue
2 on. / bank / <u>Turn</u> / and / right / go / at / straight / the
3 turn / into / Park / right / Lane. / <u>Take</u> / the / right / then / third
4 's / left. / on / <u>It</u> / the
5 straight / turn / road / end / on / right. / and / of / until / <u>Go</u> / then / the / the
6 way / you / to / tell / the / <u>Can</u> / me / supermarket? / the

B Work in pairs and take turns. Student A: think of a place near where you are now. Give directions. Student B: guess the place.
A: *Go out of the main entrance and turn left …*

BBC VIDEO PODCAST

Watch people talking about where they went on their last holidays on ActiveBook or on the website.

Authentic BBC interviews

www.pearsonELT.com/speakout

UNIT 8

SPEAKING
- Talk about what people are doing
- Describe people's appearance
- Ask for and give recommendations
- Talk about an event

LISTENING
- Listen to a radio programme about ideas of beauty
- Watch an extract from a documentary about an English music festival

READING
- Read blog entries about what people are doing now

WRITING
- Write a blog about what you are doing
- Write a review of an event

BBC CONTENT
- Video podcast: What was the last film you saw?
- DVD: Inside Out

UNIT 8

now

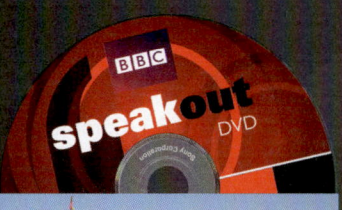

| In the picture p78 | Looking good p80 | What do you recommend? p82 | Festival Highlights p84 |

8.1 IN THE PICTURE

▶ **GRAMMAR** | present continuous   ▶ **VOCABULARY** | verbs + prepositions   ▶ **HOW TO** | talk about the present

SPEAKING

1A Read the sentences. Underline the alternative which is true for you.
1. I take photos *every day/on holiday/only on special occasions.*
2. I take photos with *my camera/my mobile/ my camera and my mobile.*
3. I share photos with *my family/my friends/ everyone.*
4. I put my photos *on a website/in a book/on my computer.*
5. My favourite subjects are *people/places/ nature.*

B Work in pairs and compare your answers.

GRAMMAR present continuous

2A Look at the website page. Match sentences 1–5 below to photos A–E.
1. We're listening to live jazz.
2. I'm cleaning up after the party.
3. I'm lying on the beach in Cannes.
4. Patrizia's looking at paintings at the Hermitage.
5. He's singing *My Way* at a karaoke bar.

Cannes, 1p.m.
Caracas, 7.30a.m.
Singapore, 1p.m.

B Underline the verbs in sentences 1–5 above. Then complete the table.

I	___ ly _ing_	on the beach.
We	___ listen ___	to live jazz.
He	___ sing ___	*My Way.*

C Look at the sentences again and underline the correct alternative to complete the rule.

> Rule: Use the present continuous to talk about your life *every day/at this moment.*

D ▶ 8.1 Complete the questions with *is* or *are*. Then listen and check.
1. What ___ you doing?
2. What ___ he singing?

E Listen again and underline the stressed words. Then listen and repeat.

▶ page 130 **LANGUAGEBANK**

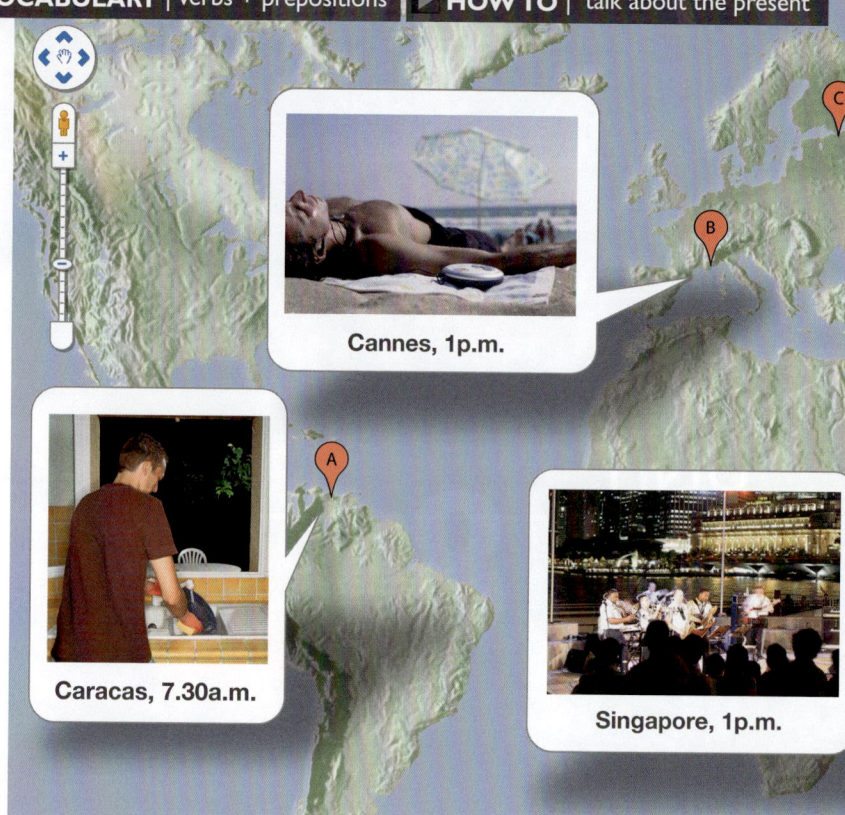

PRACTICE

3A Complete the sentences with verbs from the box.

~~dance~~ take read have swim chat feel make enjoy listen

1. Some people *are dancing* to the music. We _____ to each other and _____ the band.
2. People _____ photos of the paintings.
3. I _____ about the film festival here in Cannes. Cath and Jim aren't here – they _____ in the sea, I think.
4. Everyone _____ to him sing – he's fantastic! We _____ a really good time!
5. It's a beautiful day, but I _____ really tired. Karen _____ some coffee and I really need it!

B Match photos A–E on the website page with sentences 1–5 above.

C Work in pairs. Cover the sentences above. Ask and answer questions about the people from the website.
A: What's he doing? What are they doing?
B: He's …

D Work in pairs and take turns. Write the names of three people you know. What do you think they are doing at the moment? Tell your partner.
My friend Julia lives in Sydney. I think she's getting up now or maybe she's having breakfast.

speakout TIP

Practise English in your head. When you do something, think of the sentence, e.g. *I'm walking, I'm doing my homework, I'm washing my hands …*

St Petersburg, 3p.m.

Tokyo, 9p.m.

VOCABULARY verbs + prepositions

4A Underline the correct alternative.
1 listen *with/to* the radio
2 take photos *of/about* a friend
3 wait *to/for* a train
4 read *on/about* a film star
5 lie *on/at* a bed
6 chat *to/from* my partner
7 be *for/on* the phone
8 look *on/at* a photo
9 think *about/on* your friend
10 ask *about/to* pronunciation

B ▶ 8.2 Listen and check. Notice the weak sound of the prepositions and articles. Then listen and repeat.

1 *listen* /təðə/ *radio*

C Work in pairs and take turns. Student A: say a verb from Exercise 4A. Student B: say the whole verb phrase. Then think of other possible nouns.

A: listen
B: listen to the radio
A: listen to an MP3 player
B: listen to …

SPEAKING

5 Work in pairs. Student A: look at page 149. Student B: look at page 151.

READING

6 Read the two blogs from WhatRUdoing.com. Write the number of the missing sentences from Exercise 3A in the correct places.

Next Blog >>

Jules

I'm having a great time here. I'm staying with my two best friends from college. I last saw **them** five years ago. **They**'re still the same – just a bit older. At the moment I'm relaxing and _____. Their apartment is only ten minutes from the festival. Yesterday we went to see our first film. Angelina Jolie was in **it**. I didn't like **it** much – but I thought **she** was very good!

Next Blog >>

Rafael

Hi, everyone. So what am I doing today? Not much! _____. We didn't get to bed until four in the morning, but it was great! Non-stop music and dancing, good food and all our friends. I think **they** enjoyed themselves. I got some fantastic presents: especially a digital camera. I used **it** to put a photo on WhatRUdoing.com. Take a look. That's me, with the dirty dishes!

WRITING pronouns

7A Look at the sentences below from the first blog. What does *them* refer to?

I'm staying with (my two best friends). I last saw **them** five years ago.

B Look at the pronouns in bold in the blogs. What do they refer to? Circle the pronouns and draw an arrow to the correct word.

C Read the blog entry below. Use pronouns to make four more changes.

Next Blog >>

Last night I went to Jazz Stop with Dan and Lisa.
                              We
~~Dan, Lisa and I~~ saw Will Brown. Will Brown has got a new CD and Will Brown played songs from his new CD. Lisa and Dan danced a lot but I just chatted with Lisa and Dan between dances and took photos. I put one of the photos on WhatRUdoing.com. WhatRUdoing.com is my favourite website.

D Write your own blog entry. Write about a concert, a party, an art gallery or a karaoke bar. Use pronouns and include the names of two other students.

8.2 LOOKING GOOD

▶ GRAMMAR | present simple/continuous   ▶ VOCABULARY | appearance   ▶ HOW TO | describe people

SPEAKING

1A Work in pairs and discuss. Match the information with the film star.

She was in a lot of James Bond films.

He played Che Guevara in *The Motorcycle Diaries*.

She's American.

He also sings – he's a rapper.

He started acting in the 1950s.

She was born in Malaysia.

B What other information do you know about the film stars?

Sean Connery is Scottish.

C Do you think any of the film stars are good-looking? Why/Why not?

VOCABULARY | appearance

2A Work in pairs. Look at the photos and answer the questions.

1 Which of the film stars has got:
a) short grey hair?
b) long blonde hair?
c) dark curly hair?
d) a beard and a moustache?
e) brown eyes?

2 Which of the film stars is:
a) black?
b) in his/her seventies/eighties?
c) in his/her twenties/thirties?
d) wearing make-up?
e) wearing earrings?

B ▶ 8.3 Listen to a man describing two of the film stars. Which two is he talking about?

1 _____
2 _____

C Listen again and write the questions. Use the prompts to help.

1 Is / man / or / woman?
2 What / she / look like?

D Work in pairs and take turns. Student A: choose one of the film stars and describe him/her. Student B: ask the questions in Exercise 2 and guess the film star.

▶ page 146 **PHOTOBANK**

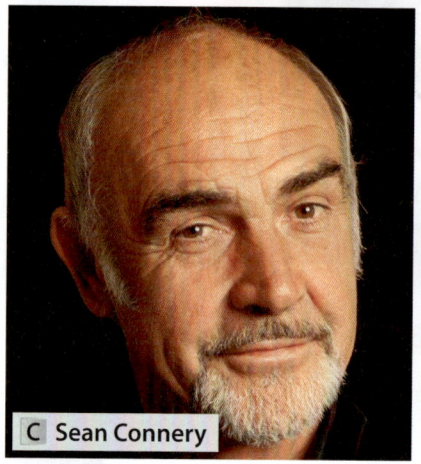

A Michelle Yeoh

B Scarlett Johansson

C Sean Connery

D Will Smith

LISTENING

3A ▶ 8.4 Listen to the first part of a radio programme. Is the programme about film stars, ideas of fashion or ideas of beauty?

B Read the information below. Then listen again and underline the words you hear.

Do men today *really* like women with [1]*blonde/black* hair and [2]*brown/blue* eyes? And do women like the James Bond look – tall, [3]*grey/dark* and very [4]*masculine/feminine*, or do they like something different now?

C ▶ 8.5 Listen to the second part of the radio programme. Which film stars do the people like?

D Listen again. What do the people talk about? Complete the table.

	height/build	hair/beard	eyes	other
Woman 1		beard		
Woman 2				nice smile
Woman 3				
Man 1				beautiful clothes
Man 2	slim			

E Work in groups and discuss. What's your idea of beauty?

8.2

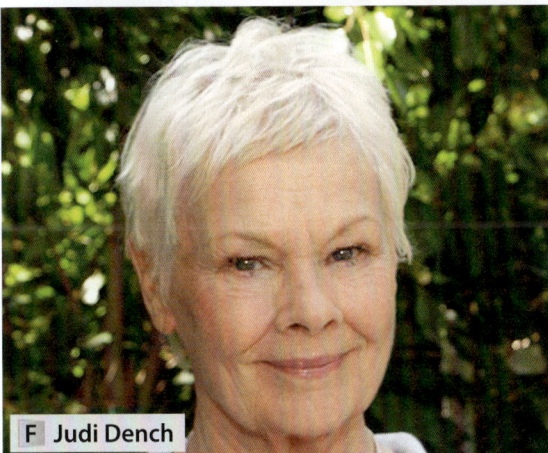

E Gael García Bernal

F Judi Dench

GRAMMAR present simple/continuous

4A Look at the sentences and underline the verbs. Which tenses are they?
1 She always wears beautiful clothes.
2 He's wearing a white T-shirt.

B Underline the correct alternative to complete the rules.

> Rules:
> 1 Use the *present simple/present continuous* for something we do every day or usually.
> 2 Use the *present simple/present continuous* for something we're doing now or at this moment.

C Complete the table with the verb *wear*.

| What | ____ | you | usually | ____ | to work/school? |
| What | ____ | you | | ____ | now? |

| I | usually ____ | | a suit. |
| Now, I | ____ | | jeans and a sweater. |

➡ page 130 LANGUAGEBANK

PRACTICE

5A Look at the cartoons and discuss. What are the problems?

B Underline the correct alternatives below.

> In an office, men usually ¹*wear/are wearing* dark suits, ties and shoes, but Sam ²*wears/'s wearing* jeans, a T-shirt and trainers. He ³*doesn't wear/isn't wearing* a tie. Another problem is that he ⁴*wears/'s wearing* sunglasses and most businessmen ⁵*don't wear/aren't wearing* sunglasses at work.

C Complete the information about the second cartoon.

> Walkers ¹_____ (not) usually ²_____ skirts; they ³_____ trousers and walking jackets. Jenny's boyfriend ⁴_____ boots but she ⁵_____ high-heeled shoes – dangerous on a country walk. Another problem is that she ⁶_____ (not) a backpack. She ⁷_____ a handbag!

6 Work in pairs. Sit back to back and take turns. Student A: say six things you're wearing – four true and two false. Student B: say which things are false.

A: *I'm wearing a grey shirt.*
B: *True!*

SPEAKING

7A Work in pairs and discuss. What clothes do you usually/never wear for:
- a walk in the country?
- dinner at a friend's house?
- a job interview?
- meeting friends in a bar or club?
- a party?
- an exercise class?

B Work with a new partner. Student A: say the clothes you usually/never wear for the situations above. Student B: guess the situation.

A: *I usually wear jeans and a top. I never wear shorts.*
B: *A walk in the country?*

8.3 WHAT DO YOU RECOMMEND?

▶ FUNCTION | recommending   ▶ VOCABULARY | types of film   ▶ LEARN TO | link words to speak faster

SPEAKING

1A Complete the questionnaire below.

MOVIEWATCH

1. What was the last film you saw?
2. What's your favourite film?
3. Who is your favourite film actor?
4. Who is your favourite film actress?
5. Do you like watching films:
   a) *at home/at the cinema*?
   b) *on TV/on your computer*?
   c) *on your own/with someone*?
   d) *only once/more than once*?

B Work in pairs and compare your answers.

VOCABULARY types of film

2A Match the posters in pictures A–H with the types of film in the box.

> ~~romantic film~~ A   horror film   drama
> animated film   musical   action film
> comedy   sci-fi film

B Complete the sentences with the types of film.
1. People fall in love in a <u>romantic film</u>.
2. There's a lot of singing and dancing in a _____.
3. I laugh a lot when I watch a _____.
4. There are often UFOs and aliens from space in a _____.
5. A _____ can be too scary for me.
6. There are usually a lot of guns and car chases in an _____.
7. I sometimes cry when I watch a _____.
8. Drawings seem to move and talk in an _____.

C Work in pairs and discuss. Do you like the same films? Why/Why not? Which types of films <u>don't</u> you like? Why?
A: *Which types of films do you like?*
B: *I like musicals.*
A: *Oh, really? Why? …*

82

8.3

FUNCTION recommending

3A ▶ 8.6 Listen to two conversations. Which types of film from Exercise 2A do the people talk about?

B Listen again. Do the people decide to watch the films? Why/Why not?

4A Put the words in the correct order.
1 you / do / recommend? / What
   What do you recommend?
2 *French Kiss*? / about / How
3 you / I'd / Do / it? / like / think
4 you'd / it / like / think / don't / I
5 I / French / like / that / film / you'd / think

B ▶ 8.7 Listen and check. Then listen and repeat.
➡ page 130 LANGUAGEBANK

5 Work in pairs and take turns. Look again at the film posters A–H. Student A: ask your partner to recommend a film. Student B: ask questions and recommend a film.

A: *I want to watch a DVD this weekend. What do you recommend?*
B: *Hmm. What kind of films do you like?*

LEARN TO link words to speak faster

6A Read the flowchart and complete questions 1–5.

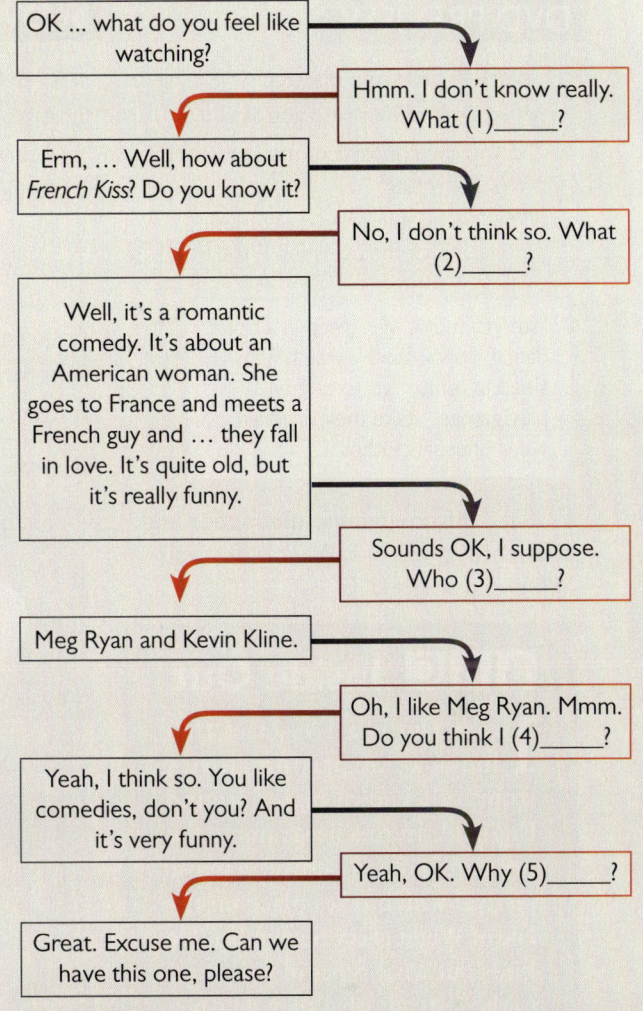

- OK ... what do you feel like watching?
- Hmm. I don't know really. What (1)_____?
- Erm, ... Well, how about *French Kiss*? Do you know it?
- No, I don't think so. What (2)_____?
- Well, it's a romantic comedy. It's about an American woman. She goes to France and meets a French guy and ... they fall in love. It's quite old, but it's really funny.
- Sounds OK, I suppose. Who (3)_____?
- Meg Ryan and Kevin Kline.
- Oh, I like Meg Ryan. Mmm. Do you think I (4)_____?
- Yeah, I think so. You like comedies, don't you? And it's very funny.
- Yeah, OK. Why (5)_____?
- Great. Excuse me. Can we have this one, please?

speakout TIP

Word linking can help your speaking sound more natural. Remember you can link the consonant at the end of one word and the vowel at the beginning of the next word, e.g. What's˯it˯about?

B ▶ 8.8 Listen and check your answers.

C Look at the questions in Exercise 6A and draw the links. Then practise saying them.

D Work in pairs and take turns. Cover the man's part and practise the conversation.

7A Work as a class and make a list of eight films. Write the titles in English or in your language.

B Work in pairs. Student A: choose one of the films and answer Student B's questions. Student B: ask questions 1–3 from Exercise 6A. Guess the film.

SPEAKING

8 Work with a new partner. Recommend one of your favourite films or a film you saw recently.

A: *One of my favourite films is ... / Last week I saw ...*
B: *What's it about? Do you think I'd like it?*

8.4 FESTIVAL HIGHLIGHTS

DVD PREVIEW

1 Work in pairs and discuss.
1 What type of music do you like?
2 Do you like concerts or music festivals? Why/Why not?
3 What do people often do at music festivals? Tick the activities in the box:

listen to music ✓   sleep in a hotel
dance   cook food   watch films
sleep in tents   go to bed early
play games   take their children
wear unusual clothes

2 Read the programme information and answer the questions. What is Bestival? When and where is it?

BBC Inside Out

Inside Out is a TV series that looks at surprising stories from well-known places around England. In this programme the presenter goes to Bestival, a music festival which takes place on the Isle of Wight every September. He finds out what types of people go to the festival, what they do when they are there and why they go.

▶ DVD VIEW

3A Before you watch, underline the alternative you think is correct.
1 A woman in a red dress is *singing/dancing*.
2 A man is carrying some *boots/socks*.
3 Some people are sitting outside on a *chair/sofa*.
4 A man is sitting and eating in front of a *beach hut/tent*.
5 A child is playing with a big *orange/white* ball.
6 Some people are putting up a *hut/tent*.
7 A band is playing *at night/in the afternoon*.
8 Families are *playing games/eating and drinking* in the tea tent.

B Watch the DVD and check your answers.

4 Why do people come to the festival? Watch the DVD again and listen to what the people say. Are the sentences true (T) or false (F)?
1 It's a holiday for the family.   T
2 People are away from their normal jobs.
3 People can buy music CDs.
4 Festivals are a playground for grownups (adults).
5 People can meet famous bands and singers.
6 Young people and old people can mix together.

5 Listen again and complete the sentences.

'It's like opening your back door, going down to the end of your ¹_____, getting in your shed with your baby and ²_____, and then calling it a ³_____.'

'Well, I suppose it gives everybody a chance just to be themselves, and just … be ⁴_____ … and be away from their normal ⁵_____.'

'The community getting together and the ⁶_____ mixing with the older ⁷_____. We make ⁸_____, we do pop festivals, we'll go anywhere, do anything.'

speakout describe an event

6A Think about a recent event you went to, e.g. a festival, a concert, a sports event, an exhibition, a play/dance or comedy show. Use the questions below to make notes about it.
- What was it?
- When and where was it?
- What did you do or see?
- What did you think of it?
- Do you recommend it?

B ▶ 8.9 Listen to someone talking about an event he/she went to recently. What was it? Did he/she enjoy it?

C Read the key phrases below. Then listen again and tick the ones you hear.

keyphrases
[Last week/month/year/Recently] I went to …
It was in (place).
I/We went because …
I think it was good for [children/families/teenagers/music lovers].
It cost … / It was free.
I thought it was [great/terrible].
I [really liked/really enjoyed/didn't really like/hated] it because …

D Work in groups and take turns. One student: talk about your event. Use the key phrases to help. Other students: listen and ask two questions about each event.

writeback a review

7A Read this web review from the Edinburgh Festival. What type of event is it?

26-09-11
listener

Posting 1

Last night we went to see Adam Hills at the Stand. We went because a good friend of mine recommended the show. Hills is a popular comedian from Australia and this is his first time in Europe. His show is called *Happy Feet* because he loves dance music from 1930s America. He's a very good story-teller – really funny. We never stopped laughing and one hour was too short. We wanted more! I really recommend the show – I thought Hills was great! Go and see him before he returns to Australia.

B Read the review again and put the topics in the correct order.
a) What was good/bad about it?
b) Why did you go?
c) What was it?
d) When and where was it? 1

C Write a review of 80–100 words about the event you talked about in Exercise 6D. Use phrases from the review above to help you.

8.5 ‹‹ LOOKBACK

ACTIVITIES

1A Complete the puzzle with the verb phrases and find the hidden message.

1. take photos
2. l_ _ _ the beach
3. l_ _ _ jazz
4. h_ _ _ _ _ reat time
5. l_ _ k _ art
6. h_ _ _ _ ffee
7. r_ _ _ book

(hidden word: **f_ _ _ _ _ _**)

B Work in groups and discuss. Which two activities above do you usually do with other people/alone/outside?

PRESENT CONTINUOUS

2A Complete the sentences. Use the present continuous of the verb in brackets.

1. It _____. (rain)
2. A plane _____ over the building. (fly)
3. Someone _____ and reading. (sit)
4. Students _____. (talk)
5. Someone _____ on his/her computer. (work)
6. People _____ past the building. (drive)
7. Children _____. (play)
8. Someone _____ a phone call. (make)

B Work in pairs. Which of the things above are happening outside your classroom at the moment?

DESCRIBING APPEARANCE

3A Use the prompts below to write complete questions.

1. man / woman? *Is it a man or a woman?*
2. he/she / dark hair? *Has he/she got dark hair?*
3. he/she / long hair?
4. he/she / tall?
5. he/she / black sweater?
6. he/she / in her/his twenties?
7. he/she / brown shoes?
8. he/she / blue eyes?

B Work in groups and take turns. One student: think of a student in the class. Answer questions with *yes* or *no*. The other students: ask the questions above and your own questions. Guess the name of the student.

CLOTHES

4A What are the clothes? Add the vowels.

1. tr_a_ _i_ ners
2. sh_ _ s
3. s_ cks
4. j_ _ ns
5. tr_ _ s_ rs
6. sk_ rt
7. T-sh_ rt
8. j_ ck_ t
9. t_ p

B Work in pairs and take turns. Student A: say an item of clothing. Student B: say the name of a person who is wearing it in the class.

PRESENT SIMPLE AND PRESENT CONTINUOUS

5A Write questions about students in your class. Use the present simple and present continuous.

1. wear glasses (*usually/today*)
   Does Mia usually wear glasses? Is she wearing them today?
2. use an electronic dictionary (*usually/now*)
3. chew gum (*often/at the moment*)
4. speak English (*always in class/now*)
5. wear black (*often/today*)

B Work in pairs and take turns. Ask and answer the questions.

RECOMMENDING

6A Write the conversation in full.

A: I want / read a good book. What / recommend?
B: What kind / books / you like?
A: Travel books and good stories.
B: I / got *Life of Pi* by Yann Martel. It / very good.
A: What / it about?
B: It / about a boy and a tiger on a boat.
A: you / think I / like it?
B: Yes, I do.
A: OK. Can / borrow it?
B: Sure.

B Ask three other students for book recommendations. Which of the books would you like to read?

BBC VIDEO PODCAST
Watch people talking about films on ActiveBook or on the website.

Authentic BBC interviews

www.pearsonELT.com/speakout

UNIT 9

SPEAKING
- Talk about types of transport
- Apologise for being late
- Tell a long story
- Deal with problems when flying

LISTENING
- Listen to a museum tour
- Listen to a man talk about his problems getting to work
- Watch an extract from a documentary about a day at Heathrow airport

READING
- Read an article about Paris Citybikes

WRITING
- Write a story using linkers
- Write an email about your experience at an airport

BBC CONTENT
- Video podcast: How do you get to work?
- DVD: Airport

transport

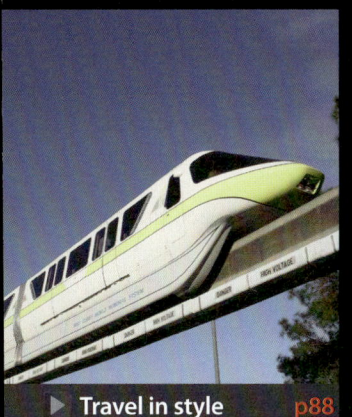

▶ Travel in style p88
▶ Citybikes p90 
▶ Sorry I'm late p92 
▶ Airport p94

9.1 TRAVEL IN STYLE

▶ GRAMMAR | articles   ▶ VOCABULARY | transport collocations   ▶ HOW TO | talk about ways to travel

VOCABULARY transport collocations

1A Work in pairs. Which types of transport can you see in the pictures? Tick the correct words in the box.

> bus plane train taxi car helicopter bike
> horse motorbike foot

B Look at the word webs below and cross out the type of transport which does <u>not</u> go with the verb. Then add a correct type of transport to each word web.

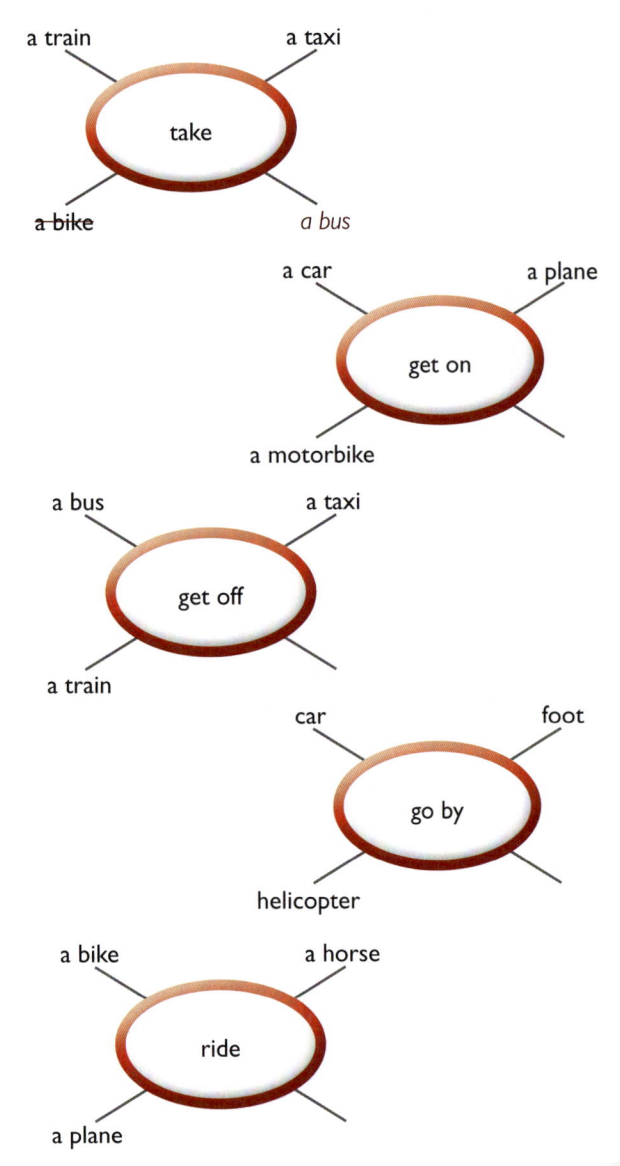

take: a train, a taxi, ~~a bike~~, a bus

get on: a car, a plane, a motorbike

get off: a bus, a taxi, a train

go by: car, foot, helicopter

ride: a bike, a horse, a plane

▶ page 147 PHOTOBANK

C Work in pairs and take turns. Student A: say a type of transport. Student B: say the verbs that can go with it.
A: *bike*
B: *go by bike, get on a bike, ride a bike …*

D Work in pairs and discuss.
1 How do you usually get to work/school?
2 What's your favourite type of transport? Why?
3 Which types of transport <u>don't</u> you like using? Why not?

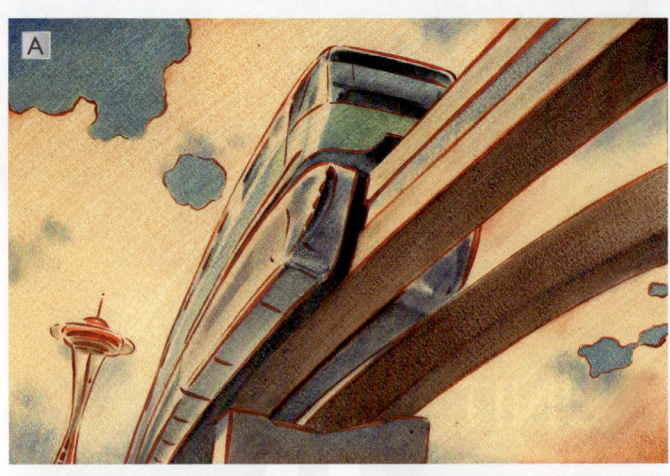

A

B

C

LISTENING

2A Match pictures A–C with the titles below.
1 A monorail train from the World Fair in Seattle, USA, 1962
2 The 'Hiller Hornet' – a home helicopter, 1951
3 A plane with a car that comes off, 1948

B ▶ 9.1 Listen to a museum guide and answer the questions.
1 Which transport ideas from above does he talk about?
2 What are his favourite ways of travelling?

C Listen again. What's the problem with each transport idea?

D Work in pairs and discuss. What do you like about each idea? Which one was successful? Why?

9.1

GRAMMAR articles: a/an, the, no article

3A ▶ 9.2 Listen to an extract from the museum tour and complete the text with *a/an*, *the*, – (no article).

Look at this photo on ¹_____ left. It's from ²_____ World Fair in ³_____ Seattle. That was in 1962. ⁴_____ monorails were ⁵_____ very popular idea in ⁶_____ America at that time. ⁷_____ people wanted to leave their cars at ⁸_____ home and go to ⁹_____ work by ¹⁰_____ public transport.

B Find examples for rules a)–f) from the text above.

Rules:
a) Usually use *a/an* before singular nouns:
   I've got a car. __5__
b) Usually use no article before plural nouns:
   I love cars. _____
c) Usually use no article before cities and countries:
   Madrid is in Spain. _____
d) Use no article in some phrases: *by car, on foot, go to school, at work*. _____
e) Usually use *the* before nouns when there's only one:
   the sun. _____
f) Use *the* in some phrases: *in the morning, on the right, in the city centre*. _____

▶ page 132 **LANGUAGEBANK**

C ▶ 9.3 We usually pronounce *a* /ə/ and *the* /ðə/ in phrases/sentences. Listen and write the four phrases you hear. Then listen again and repeat.
1 _____
2 _____
3 _____
4 _____

D Listen again and check your answers. Then listen and repeat.

PRACTICE

4A Work in pairs and complete the sentences. Use *a/an*, *the* or – (no article).
1 There was _a_ big problem with each one.
2 There are some monorails in ___ world … but not very many.
3 Look at this photo. Is that ___ car under ___ plane?
4 People wanted to fly from ___ Los Angeles to ___ New York.
5 There was ___ engineering problem.
6 We laugh at this now, but ___ people were very serious about it.
7 People wanted to leave ___ home in ___ morning and go to ___ work by ___ private helicopter.
8 ___ helicopters are very difficult to fly.

B Check your answers in audio script 9.1 on page 153.

5A Look at questions 1–5. Choose one of the endings and write a short answer.
1 How do you get *to school / to work / home*?
   By car.
2 What are three things *you like / you don't like / you liked when you were a child*?
3 What's a famous city in *India / China / Africa*?
4 When do you *check your emails / do your homework / relax*?
5 What's the name of *the President of the USA / the student next to you / the teacher*?

B Work in pairs and take turns. Student A: read your answers to the questions above. Student B: close your book and guess the question.
A: *By car.*
B: *How do you get to school?*
A: *No.*
B: *How do you get to work?*
A: *Yes!*

speakout TIP

When you write a noun in your notebook, put it in a short phrase. This shows how to use the word with the articles *a/an*, *the* or no article. For example: *in the city centre, he's a doctor, I like cats*.

SPEAKING

6A Work in pairs. Look at the pictures of transport inventions below. Think of two problems with each invention.
The Horseless Sulky – it's difficult to turn.

B Work in pairs. Student A: look at page 150. Student B: look at page 148.

The Horseless Sulky

The Lightning Bug

9.2 CITYBIKES

▶ **GRAMMAR** | can/can't, have to/don't have to   ▶ **VOCABULARY** | adjectives   ▶ **HOW TO** | talk about transport

SPEAKING

1 Work in pairs and discuss.
1 Is there a lot of traffic where you live?
2 When is the worst time to travel?
3 Do you prefer to travel around your town/city by car, by public transport, by bike or on foot? Why?

VOCABULARY adjectives

2A Circle three adjectives to complete the sentence:

Cycling in the city is …

convenient   safe
fast
easy   inconvenient
comfortable   slow
dangerous   unhealthy
        uncomfortable
polluting
        difficult
green
    healthy

B Match each adjective to its opposite.
fast – slow

C ▶ 9.4 Listen and check.

D Listen again and underline the stressed syllable.

speakout TIP

Look in your dictionary to find the pronunciation of new words. *Longman WordWise Dictionary* shows the word stress with a ' before the main stress, e.g. /ˈdɪfɪkəlt/ *difficult*. Find *dangerous* in your dictionary. How does it show stress?

3 Work in pairs and take turns. Student A: you like bikes. Student B: you like cars. Talk about which is better and why.
A: *Cars are faster.*
B: *Yes, but they're more dangerous!*

Paris by Citybike

With 20,000 bikes and 1,450 pick-up stations, *Vélib* is Paris's free bike scheme. Cyclists can take a bike from one pick-up station and leave it at any other station in the city.

Yves Guesnon, a businessman, loves travelling to work with the wind blowing in his hair. 'There's a station near my flat and another one twenty metres from my office, so it's perfect. I can get to work in ten minutes. It takes thirty minutes by metro.'

'The scheme is good for everyone, Parisians and tourists,' a city official said. 'The only condition* is that you have to be over fourteen and healthy.'

Users have to pay twenty-nine euros a year and give their credit card details. They don't have to pay for the first thirty minutes. After that, they have to pay one euro for the second half-hour.

The scheme is very popular, but there's one problem. Some people ride the bikes downhill in the morning and then take the metro home in the evening. 'I'm just not fit enough,' one man explained. 'I can't cycle up the hill to my flat.' So every evening, city workers have to bring the bikes back uphill in a lorry!

*condition = rule

READING

4A Look at the photos of Vélib, the citybike system in Paris. Write three questions with *how much*, *how many*, *who* or *where*.
1 How much <u>does it cost to use a bike</u>   ?
2 How many _____?
3 Who/Where _____?

B Read the article. Did you find the answers to your three questions?

C Are the sentences true (T) or false (F)? Change the false sentences so that they are true.
1 You leave the bicycle in the same place you took it.
2 Yves Guesnon uses a bike because it's fast.
3 Tourists can't use the bikes.
4 Small children can use the bikes.
5 It costs one euro for one hour's cycling.
6 City workers ride the bikes uphill in the evening.

D Work in pairs and discuss. Is the Citybike system a good idea for your town/city? Why/Why not?

9.2

GRAMMAR can/can't, have to/don't have to

5A Underline the correct alternative. Then check your answers in the article.
1 You *can/can't* leave the bike at any station in the city.
2 A thirteen-year-old child *can/can't* use the bikes.
3 Users *have to/don't have to* be healthy.
4 Users *have to/don't have to* pay for the first thirty minutes.

B Match sentences 1–4 above with meanings a)–d).
a) It's necessary.
b) It's not necessary.
c) It's OK.
d) It's not OK.

C Complete the table below.

Tourists	can	use	the bikes.
Children	____	____	the bikes.
Users	have	give	their credit card details.
You	____ have to	____	for the first half hour.

D ▶ 9.5 Listen to sentences 1–4. Circle the correct pronunciation.
1 /kən/   /kæn/
2 /kənt/   /kɑːnt/
3 /hæftuː/   /hæftə/
4 /dəʊnthæftuː/   /dəʊnthæftə/

E Listen again and check. Then listen and repeat.
▶ page 132 LANGUAGEBANK

PRACTICE

6A Complete the sentences with *can/can't, have to/don't have to*.
1 You ___can___ go by underground, bus or taxi to get to the airport.
2 You _____ drive on the left in the UK.
3 You _____ drive in the town centre, so come by bus.
4 You _____ be sixteen or over to drive in Canada.
5 You _____ use your mobile when you drive. It's dangerous!
6 You _____ wear a seatbelt in your car – the driver <u>and</u> all the passengers.
7 You _____ wear a helmet on bikes but it's safer if you do wear one.
8 You _____ park here for free between 11 and 3. Other times you _____ pay.

B Work in pairs. Which sentences are true for your town/city?

SPEAKING

7A Work in groups. Student A: look at page 151. Student B: look at page 148. Student C: look at page 149. Complete the table below with information about each city's tourist card.

	'I love Amsterdam' card	The Madrid card	The Prague card
Price			
Transport			
Entry to museums etc.			
Other			

B Work in groups. Ask and answer questions to complete the information about the other cities. Which city has got the best tourist card system?
I think Prague has got the best system because it's the cheapest.

C Work in pairs. Talk about travelling in two or three towns/cities you know.
A: *What's the best way to get around your city?*
B: *You can buy a travelcard for buses and underground trains. But sometimes it's faster to walk!*

9.3 SORRY I'M LATE

FUNCTION | apologising   VOCABULARY | excuses   LEARN TO | tell a long story

VOCABULARY excuses

1 Work in pairs and discuss. Are you often late for work, school or meetings? Why/Why not?

2A Work in pairs and match 1–5 to a)–e) below.

1 I lost   a) broke down.
2 I missed   b) my alarm clock.
3 My car   c) the train.
4 The traffic   d) my keys.
5 I didn't hear   e) was bad.

B Look at the collocations above and write sentences with the words in the box.

| the bus | my ticket | was terrible | the phone | didn't start |

FUNCTION apologising

3A Look at the cartoon and answer the questions. Who are the people? What's the problem? What do you think happened?

B Read the text and check your answers.

> **Train delays**
> Rail services on a busy commuter line into London were late on Tuesday morning when a train hit a cow. The animal got onto the line between two stations and the accident happened at about 7.40a.m. Train services between London and the south were seriously delayed.

4A What did the man say to his boss? Underline the correct alternatives in the sentences below.

1 Look, I'm *really/real* sorry I'm late.
2 I'm *terribly/terrible* sorry I'm late.
3 I feel *terribly/terrible* about it.
4 I'm *afraid/sorry* my train hit a cow!

B ▶ 9.6 Listen and check. Then listen and repeat.

C Look at the responses below. Is the boss happy (✓) or unhappy (✗) about the situation?

1 I don't believe you.
2 It's half past nine!
3 Don't worry about it.
4 That's OK. No problem.
5 Don't let it happen again.

▶ page 132 LANGUAGEBANK

5A Work in pairs. Complete the conversation between a student and a teacher.

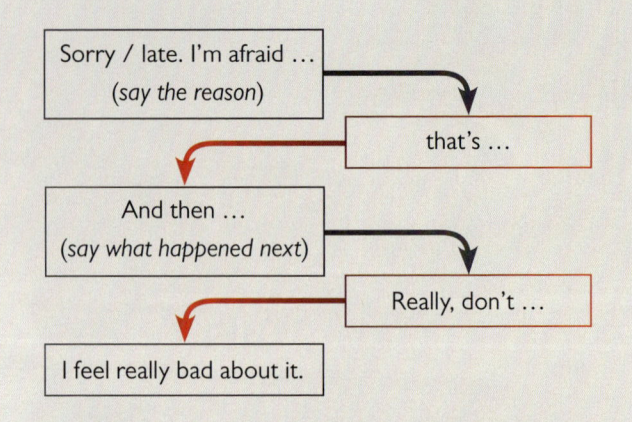

- Sorry / late. I'm afraid … (*say the reason*)
- that's …
- And then … (*say what happened next*)
- Really, don't …
- I feel really bad about it.

B Work in pairs and have another conversation. Apologise for being late. Choose one of the pairs below.

- a student – a teacher
- a friend – a friend
- a worker – the boss
- a child – a parent

C Listen to other students' conversations. Guess their roles.

LEARN TO tell a long story

6A Look at the online diary extracts below. Why was the man late each day?

Day one: _____
Day two: _____
Day three: _____

Monday
The train left fifteen minutes late. But that wasn't the problem – it simply didn't go very fast. We really knew there was a problem when a man on a bicycle went faster than us! I was an hour late for work. The boss wasn't happy … but *she* doesn't take the train.

Tuesday
OK, I didn't hear my alarm so I woke up late and missed my train. I got the next one, but then the train stopped in the middle of nowhere … for twenty minutes! The guard said there was a signal problem and then the air-conditioning stopped working! Imagine, no air-conditioning in the middle of summer! I was two and a half hours late for work and really hot and sweaty. My boss was *very* unhappy.

Wednesday
Service: 0 points. Originality: 10 points. We stopped again, for no reason, but then there *was* a reason – not the signals, not the engine but a cow on the line! Poor thing, we didn't stop in time. This time, I was two hours late for work and my boss didn't believe me …

B ▶ 9.7 Listen to the man talk to a colleague. Which two days does he talk about?

C Listen again. Which two things are different from the online diary above?

92

7A Look at the linkers in the box and circle them in the listening extract below.

> ~~first of all~~   and   but   so   finally   because   then   after that

(First of all,) I got up late because I didn't hear my alarm, so I only woke up at 8.30. I ran to the train station – usually I walk – but I missed the train by two minutes! Then I waited for the next train, the 9.15, and everything was fine until we just stopped – just *stopped* – in the middle of nowhere. The guard said that there was a signal problem. After that, the air-conditioning stopped working. It was like an oven – at least a thousand degrees! Finally, after forty minutes, we started moving … very, very slowly.

B Work in pairs and discuss.
1 Which linkers do you use for the beginning and end of the story?
2 Which two linkers mean next in the story?

speakout TIP

Linkers join sentences in a story and help the listener to follow and understand the story better. When you next tell a story, practise using the linkers in Exercise 7A.

SPEAKING

8A Imagine you are late for an important event/situation, e.g. a wedding, a birthday party, an English lesson, a date with a boy/girlfriend, a meeting, a job interview, the doctor's. Make notes about five things that happened. Use the photos to help. Think about:
- When was it?
- Where were you?
- Who were you with?
- What happened?
- What did you do?
- What happened finally?

B Work in pairs and take turns. Student A: tell your story. Student B: show interest and ask follow-up questions.
A: *First of all, my car broke down …*
B: *Oh no! That's terrible! What did you do?*

9 Write your story using your notes above. Remember to use linkers.

9.4 AIRPORT

DVD PREVIEW

1 Work in pairs and discuss. What are the good and bad things about airports and flying?

2A Put the actions below in the correct order.
a) check in   1
b) the plane takes off
c) go through security
d) wait in the departure lounge
e) get on the plane
f) go to the departure gate
g) do some tax-free shopping
h) go through passport control

B ▶ 9.8 Listen and check. Then listen and repeat.

C Work in pairs and take turns. Student A: say one of the actions in Exercise 2A. Student B: say the next action.
A: You check in and then you … ?
B: Go through security and then you … ?

3 Read the programme information and answer the questions.
1 Why are the planes late at Heathrow Airport?
2 What do you think passengers do while they wait?

▶ DVD VIEW

4A Look at the sentences. Use a dictionary to check the meaning of any new words.
1 People are queuing.
2 Some men are making phone calls.
3 A woman is reading a newspaper.
4 Two men are playing chess.
5 People are sleeping everywhere.
6 A man is arguing at a check-in desk.
7 A family is eating pizza.
8 Some boys are skateboarding.

B Watch the DVD. Tick the activities above you see.

C Watch again and listen to four people talk about the situation. Match the person with the activity.

Woman 1 — is trying to get to Amsterdam.
Man 1 — wants to go to Berlin.
Woman 2 — is there with her grandmother and parents.
Man 2 — thinks everything is very calm, very 'Zen'.
— can't find a place in a hotel.
— is there with her son and daughter.

BBC Airport

Airport is a TV series about day-to-day life at one of the busiest international airports in the world, London Heathrow. In tonight's programme, there's a computer problem in the control tower and flights are delayed for hours. Hundreds of passengers have to wait in the crowded terminal so the programme looks at how people are feeling and how they spend their time waiting.

speakout deal with a problem

5A Work in pairs. Read problems 1–8 below and discuss. Which do you think are the three worst problems?

1. You want to check in, but there are no more seats on the plane.
2. Your baggage is too heavy. You have to pay 200 euros, but you don't have enough money.
3. Your flight is delayed by twenty-four hours. You want the airline to pay for a hotel.
4. You get on a long-distance flight. There's a screaming child in the seat next to you.
5. You ordered a vegetarian meal, but when your food arrives, it's chicken curry.
6. You're on the plane and very tired. The person next to you wants to talk … and talk.
7. You arrive and go to get your luggage. You see your bag but another passenger picks it up.
8. You arrive and go to pick up your luggage. It never comes out.

B ▶ 9.9 Listen to the conversation. Which problem does the passenger have?

C Listen again and tick the key phrases you hear.

keyphrases

I'm sorry, but there's a (small) problem here.

I understand [the situation], but [it's very important that I get on this plane!]

I see, but …

Let me explain [one more time/again].

You don't understand.

It's your job to [find a hotel/bring me a meal/etc.].

Can I speak to the person in charge, please?

D Work in pairs. Choose a problem from Exercise 5A and role-play the situation. Use the key phrases to help.

writeback an email

6A Complete the email below.

To

Hi ¹_____,
Well, I'm finally here in ²_____, but the journey ³_____! I arrived at the airport yesterday at ⁴_____, but when I got there ⁵_____, so I ⁶_____.
At ⁷_____ o'clock ⁸_____ and so I ⁹_____. Then I had a good idea.
I ¹⁰_____ and then I ¹¹_____.
After that I ¹²_____. The plane finally ¹³_____ at ¹⁴_____!
On the plane, I thought everything was fine and then ¹⁵_____. That made me really angry, so I ¹⁶_____.
What a nightmare! I'm trying to get some sleep now. Speak to you soon, ¹⁷_____

B Write an email to a friend. Tell them about a problem you had at an airport/on a plane.

9.5 « LOOKBACK

TRANSPORT

1A What are the adjectives? Add the vowels. Then match them with their opposites.

1 ch e_ a p	easy
2 _nh_ _lthy	fast
3 p_ll_t_ng	safe
4 d_ng_r__s	expensive
5 d_ff_c_lt	green
6 sl_w	healthy

B Work in pairs and take turns. Student A: choose a type of transport. Student B: guess the transport.
B: *Is it fast or slow?*
A: *Fast.*

2 Work in groups. Make a list of the things that:
1 you can ride   *a bike, …*
2 you can drive
3 you can get on and off
4 you do in an airport
5 can go wrong with transport to make you late for work/school

ARTICLES

3A Complete the sentences with *a/an, the* or no article (–).
1 Most of us have to use ___ alarm clock to wake up in ___ morning.
2 Two of us didn't have ___ breakfast this morning.
3 Three of us live in ___ town/city centre.
4 All of us think ___ bikes are better than ___ cars for travelling in the town/city centre.
5 One of us has got ___ motorbike.
6 Half of us took ___ taxi home last weekend.
7 None of us go ___ home by ___ train.

B Work in pairs. Write the questions and ask other students. Was the information above true or false?
A: *Do you have to use an alarm clock to wake up in the morning?*
B: *Yes, I do. I have to use two because I can't wake up!*

CAN/CAN'T, HAVE TO/DON'T HAVE TO

4A Complete the rules with the correct alternatives.

In a library …
1 You *can't/don't have to* talk on your mobile phone.
2 You *can't/don't have to* pay for a book before you take it out.

On a plane …
3 You *can/have to* wear a seat belt when the plane takes off.
4 You *can't/don't have to* smoke.

At home …
5 You *can/have to* do anything you want.
6 You *can't/don't have to* pay to eat.

B Choose three of the places below and write two sentences for each place. Use *can/can't, have to/ don't have to.*

a restaurant    a classroom

a beach 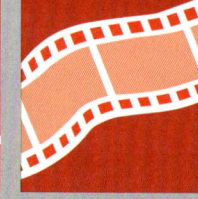   a cinema

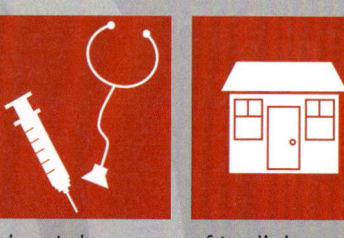

a hospital   a friend's house

C Work in pairs and take turns.
Student A: read out your sentences.
Student B: guess the place.

TELL A LONG STORY

5A Work in pairs and take turns.
Student A: close your book.
Student B: ask your partner to tell you words to put in the spaces 1–10. Write them in the spaces and then read the story.
B: *Tell me an adjective.*
A: *funny*

Today was a ¹_____ day.
(an adjective)
First of all, I got up late because I
didn't hear ²_____ knock
(a student's name)
on my door. Finally, ³_____
(a celebrity's name)
phoned me on my mobile and
woke me up. I went to the
⁴_____, put on
(a room in a house)
my ⁵_____ and
(a piece of clothing)
⁶_____ and ran out of the
(another piece of clothing)
door. Then my ⁷_____
(a type of transport)
didn't start, so I took a
⁸_____. But I got on the
(another type of transport)
wrong one and it went all the way
to ⁹_____. I phoned my
(the name of a city)
boss from there, but he didn't
believe my story, so I lost my job.
That's OK – I never liked working
as a ¹⁰_____.
(a job)

B Work in groups. Read your story to the other students. Which is the funniest?

BBC VIDEO PODCAST
Watch people talking about their journeys to and from work on ActiveBook or on the website.

Authentic BBC interviews
www.pearsonELT.com/speakout

UNIT 10

SPEAKING
> Talk about your future plans/wishes
> Make predictions about situations
> Make suggestions and learn to say *no* politely

LISTENING
> Listen to a radio interview with lottery winners
> Watch an extract from a documentary about the wettest place in Europe

READING
> Read an extract from an instruction book about survival
> Read an article with tips on things to do with your friends

WRITING
> Improve your use of linkers and write a short story
> Write a message board notice about your country

BBC CONTENT
- Video podcast: What are your plans for the future?
- DVD: Wild Weather

the future

▶ Life's a lottery   p98
▶ Survive!   p100 
▶ Let's do something   p102 
▶ Wild Weather   p104

10.1 LIFE'S A LOTTERY

▶ **GRAMMAR** | be going to; would like to   ▶ **VOCABULARY** | plans   ▶ **HOW TO** | talk about future plans/wishes

LISTENING

1A Look at the photo below and read the newspaper extract. What's surprising about the story?

Big Mac couple's lotto win

A couple who work together at McDonald's say they have no plans to stop working after winning £1.3 million on the lottery.

Elaine Gibbs, twenty-eight, and Aled Bevan, twenty-three, from Cardiff, met four years ago at work and learnt about their big win last Thursday. 'We're going to stay here. It's an enjoyable job and they treat us well' said Aled.

B Work in pairs and discuss. How do you think the couple plan to spend their money?

C ▶ 10.1 Listen to a radio interview and check your ideas. Tick the couple's plans.
- move house
- stop work
- get married
- buy a car
- travel around the world
- have a holiday
- buy some clothes
- start a family

D Discuss. What do you think of Elaine and Aled's plans?

GRAMMAR be going to; would like to

2A Look at the sentences. Then underline the correct alternative to complete the rules below.
1 We're going to get married.
2 I'd like to learn to drive.

Rules:
1 Use *be going to* when you *have/don't have* a definite plan.
2 Use *would like to* when you want to do something or when you *have/don't have* a definite plan.

B Look at audio script 10.1 on page 154 and complete the table with the correct forms of *be going to* and *would like to*.

I'____ We'___ He ____	going ____	buy look for buy	some new clothes. a house. a car.

I'____ We'___	like ____		learn to drive. move.

What	_____	you	going _____ like _____	do?

C ▶ 10.2 Listen and check your answers.

D Circle the correct pronunciation of *going to* and *would*. Then listen again and repeat.
1 going /tuː/   going /tə/
2 /wʊd/   /wʊld/

▶ page 134 **LANGUAGEBANK**

PRACTICE

3A Write the sentences in full. Use *be going to* or *would like to*.
1 I / like / move into a big flat / city centre.
   I'd like to move into a big flat in the city centre.
2 I / like / drive / sports car.
3 I / go / have / holiday / in the Caribbean.
4 I / not / go / buy / any presents / my family and friends.
5 I / like / move / to another country.
6 I / go / buy / a boat.
7 I / like / start / my own business.
8 I / not / go / keep / all the money for myself.

B Imagine you won the lottery yesterday. What are your plans? Change the sentences so that they are true for you.

C Work in pairs and compare your answers.

98

10.1

VOCABULARY plans

4A Complete the collocations with verbs from the box.

| ~~have~~ buy go for get move |
| start do go learn stay |

1 _have_ a holiday, a barbecue, a party
2 _____ married, a new suit, a job
3 _____ nothing, a course, a lot of exercise
4 _____ shopping, clubbing, jogging
5 _____ in, with friends, at a hotel
6 _____ Spanish, to drive, to swim
7 _____ a walk, a bike ride, a drink
8 _____ a new job, a family, a new business
9 _____ to another country, house, into a flat
10 _____ a present for a friend, a boat, some jeans

B Work in pairs. Student A: say the verb. Student B: say the phrases that go with the verb.

C Look at the collocations in Exercise 4A again. Add a new phrase to each verb.

speakout TIP

When you study, make lists of words that go together. Cover all the verbs, and try to remember them. Then cover the other words and try to remember the full phrases.

SPEAKING

5A What are you going to do/would you like to do in the future? Complete the table using your own ideas or the photos to help.

	You	Student 1	Student 2
this weekend	shopping	basketball	
next week			
next year			

B Work in groups. Ask and answer questions about your plans/wishes for the future. Make notes in the table.

A: Rafael, what are you going to do this weekend?
B: Well, I'm going to watch a basketball match …

C Tell the class about someone in your group. Can they guess who it is?

A: This weekend, he's going to watch a basketball match and next month he's going to do a course in sports education. Next year he'd like to go to the USA.
C: Is it Rafael?

10.2 SURVIVE!

▶ **GRAMMAR** | will, might, won't   ▶ **VOCABULARY** | phrases with get   ▶ **HOW TO** | make predictions

VOCABULARY phrases with *get*

1A Work in pairs. Look at the four photos and discuss.
1. Where are the people?
2. Which situation is the most dangerous? Why?

B Look at sentences 1–5 below and discuss. Which ones can happen at sea (S) and which can happen in the desert (D)? Which can happen in both (SD)?
1. You don't have enough water so you get thirsty. S D
2. Sharks are swimming around.
3. There are snakes and insects.
4. You fall off your raft.
5. You're hot and you sweat a lot.

C Complete the sentences to make phrases with *get* and the words in the box below.

| ~~hot~~ wet hungry thirsty bored |
| sunburnt lost tired |

1. When I exercise in the gym I get very ___hot___.
2. I didn't drink anything all day so I got _____.
3. I stayed up too late and I got really _____.
4. I forgot my umbrella yesterday and I got _____.
5. I didn't eat breakfast so I'm getting _____.
6. I didn't have a map so I got _____.
7. I stayed out in the sun and I got _____.
8. This exercise isn't very interesting! I'm getting _____.

speakout TIP

The verb *get* has more than twenty meanings in English! It can mean 'become' (*get hungry*), 'arrive' (*get home*), 'obtain' (*get a job*), 'buy' (*get a new car*) and is in many phrases: *get up, get on a plane, get dressed*. When you hear or see the word *get*, think about which meaning it has.

Which meaning does *get* have in these phrases: *get to the airport, get a new haircut, get better, get some chocolate*?

READING

2A Read the survival tips below. Cross out the incorrect alternatives.

B Work in pairs and compare your ideas.

C Work in pairs. Student A: read the text on page 150. Student B: read the text on page 148. Were your ideas correct? Tell your partner.

SURVIVE!

Imagine your boat sinks and you are alone on a raft in the middle of the sea. Or your car breaks down in the desert and you're far away from the nearest town. Could you survive? Here are some tips to help!

At sea:
1. Do/~~Don't~~ sit in the bottom of the raft.
2. Do/Don't sleep a lot.
3. Do/Don't drink sea water.
4. Do/Don't put rubbish in the water.
5. Do/Don't move around too much on the raft.

In the desert:
6. Do/Don't sleep on the ground.
7. Do/Don't take off your shirt.
8. Do/Don't travel in the day.
9. Do/Don't wear shoes.
10. Do/Don't wear gloves.

GRAMMAR will, might, won't

3A Look at the sentences and complete the rules.
1 You'll get wet.
2 You won't get sunburnt.
3 You might sweat too much.

> Rules:
> 1 Which sentence do we use when we think something in the future:
> a) is certain to happen? ____
> b) is possible? ____
> c) is certain not to happen? ____
> 2 What are the full forms of 'll and won't?
> ____

B ▶ 10.3 Listen to the sentences 1–3 above. Then listen and repeat.

C ▶ 10.4 Listen and underline the sentence you hear.
1 You'll get too hot. / You get too hot.
2 We'll fall into the water. / We fall into the water.
3 They'll sweat too much. / They sweat too much.
4 I'll get hungry. / I get hungry.

▶ page 134 LANGUAGEBANK

PRACTICE

4A What can you remember? Complete the sentences below with 'll, won't or might.
1 Don't sit in the bottom of the raft. You 'll get wet.
2 Don't drink sea water. You _____ get thirstier after you drink it.
3 Don't put rubbish in the water. Sharks _____ come because for them it's food.
4 Don't move around on the raft. You _____ fall into the water.
5 Don't sleep on the sand. You _____ get too warm.
6 Always use sun cream. You _____ get sunburnt with it on.
7 Travel at night. You _____ sweat so much.
8 Always wear shoes. You _____ step on a snake, so it's safer to have them on.

B Read the texts on pages 148 and 150 again to check your answers.

SPEAKING

5A Work in pairs. Look at the cartoon below and discuss.
1 What happened to the plane? Why did it crash?
2 How are the people from the plane feeling?
3 What problems might they have?

B Work in pairs. Choose three objects from the box below that might help the people from the plane. Give reasons for your choice.

| ~~chocolate~~ | a radio | a box of matches | a mobile phone |
| sun cream | a knife | a bottle of water | playing cards |

I think chocolate is useful because they might get hungry.

C Think of three other objects that might be useful. Use your dictionary if you don't know the word.

D Work with another pair and compare your objects. Decide which five objects will help the people in the cartoon.

WRITING too, also, as well

6A Look at the sentences. What is the position of *too*, *also* and *as well* in the sentences?
1 Your body loses a lot of water when you sweat, so relax and try to sleep a lot, **too**.
2 Fish is your most important food and it's **also** easy to catch.
3 Most fish are safe to eat and you can drink water from fish eyes **as well**.

B Put *too*, *also* and *as well* into the story.

> We walked all morning and we walked for five hours in the afternoon, *too*. We had a short break for lunch. We stopped for a rest in the afternoon. In the evening, Sam taught us how to kill a snake and how to cook it. I didn't like the smell, but I ate some and Sam ate some.

C Finish the story with your own ideas. Use *too*, *also* and *as well*.

10.3 LET'S DO SOMETHING

▶ **FUNCTION** | making suggestions ▶ **VOCABULARY** | adjectives ▶ **LEARN TO** | respond to suggestions

VOCABULARY adjectives

1A Look at the adjectives in the box. Do they all mean *OK* or *very good*?

> ~~brilliant~~ wonderful amazing fantastic
> great awesome excellent cool lovely

B How many syllables are in each adjective? Write the adjectives in the correct column in the table.

O	Oo	Ooo	oOo
		brilliant	

C ▶ 10.5 Listen and check. Then listen and repeat.

speakout TIP

Some adjectives are very informal, e.g. *cool* and *fantastic*. The *Longman WordWise Dictionary* shows this as:

> **cool** *adjective spoken informal*

Use these words with friends, and not in formal situations, e.g. a job interview.

READING

2A Work in pairs and complete the sentences.

1 When I meet my friends, we usually do
   a) the same old things.
   b) something different each time.
2 We like doing things
   a) indoors.
   b) outdoors.
3 At weekends, we meet
   a) for just a few hours.
   b) for the whole weekend.
4 We need new ideas for things to do.
   a) true
   b) false

B Read the article about how to spend time with friends. Tick five activities that you think are good ideas.

C Work in pairs and compare your ideas.

We're all super-busy these days so it's important that friends make the most of their time together. If you're stuck for ideas, we've got some suggestions …

1 Get some exercise! Go swimming or play tennis or go for a walk in the park.
2 Enjoy a 'movie marathon'. Rent some DVDs, get lots of snacks and spend the day being film critics.
3 Paint a room in your flat. Invite your friends to help you.
4 Go to a club or a concert or a music festival.
5 Go to the zoo. Show each other your favourite three animals.
6 Go to the theatre. Read the play together first.
7 Do some internet shopping. Buy something for each other.
8 Go for a bike ride and have a picnic lunch.
9 Play a card game. First, look in a book of card games (or on the internet) for a new game.
10 Cook something, e.g. a cake, or dinner. Try a new recipe together. Invite some friends and have a food tasting.
11 Play a computer game together or watch a fitness DVD and practise aerobics or yoga.
12 Go to an art gallery. Find a painting you like and talk about why you like it.

FUNCTION making suggestions

3 ▶10.6 Listen to two conversations. Which activities from the article do the friends decide to do?

4A Look at the sentences. Underline four phrases for making suggestions.
1 <u>How about</u> going to an art gallery?
2 What about having a 'movie marathon'?
3 Let's cook something.
4 Why don't we invite Augusto and Carla for lunch?

B ▶10.7 Complete the suggestions below. Then listen and check.
1 How _____ _____ to the zoo?
2 What _____ _____ something more relaxing?
3 Why _____ _____ _____ some internet shopping?
4 _____ _____ to the theatre.

C Listen to the sentences again. Does the speaker sound positive? Does his/her voice start high or low?

D Listen again and repeat.

5A Complete the suggestions.
1 How about _____ swimming?
2 What about _____ a new recipe?
3 Why don't we _____ a picnic lunch?
4 Let's _____ to the cinema.

B Work in pairs and take turns. Student A: make a suggestion. Student B: say *OK* if your partner sounds positive or *no thanks* if he/she doesn't.

LEARN TO respond to suggestions

6A ▶10.8 Listen to the conversations again. Match the suggestions 1–5 with the responses a)–e) below.
1 visiting an art gallery
2 cooking
3 inviting friends for lunch
4 a bike ride
5 going to see a play

a) Ah, fantastic!
b) I don't really feel like doing that.
c) Sounds lovely.
d) That sounds a bit tiring.
e) Brilliant!

B Look at the phrases a)–e) above and decide if they are positive (+) or negative (-).

▶ page 134 LANGUAGE**BANK**

7 Work in pairs and take turns. Student A: choose three weekend activities and make suggestions. Student B: respond to the suggestions. When you respond negatively, give a reason.
A: *Why don't we go for a walk in the park?*
B: *Mmm. I don't really feel like doing that. It's too cold!*

SPEAKING

8A Complete the table with three activities you would like to do. Write a place and a time next to each activity.

	You	Student 1	Student 2	Student 3
Activity 1	zoo Sunday 2p.m.			
Activity 2				
Activity 3				

B Work in pairs and take turns. Student A: phone your partner and suggest an activity for tomorrow. Student B: respond and suggest another activity. Use the flowchart to help you role-play the conversation. Add your partner's information to the table above.

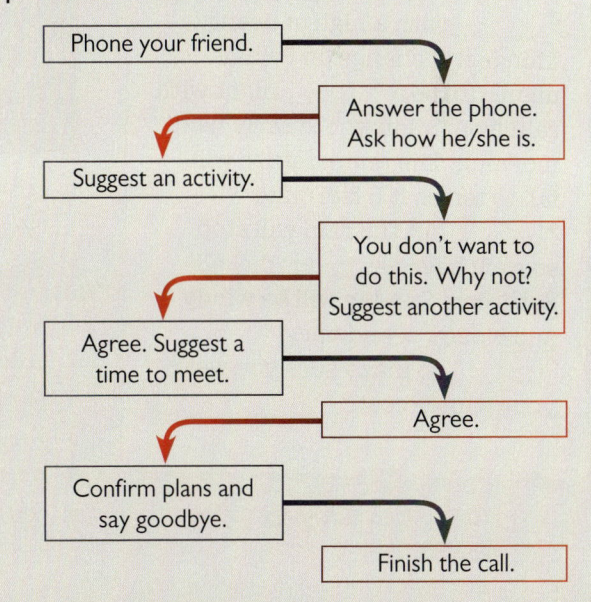

- Phone your friend.
- Answer the phone. Ask how he/she is.
- Suggest an activity.
- You don't want to do this. Why not? Suggest another activity.
- Agree. Suggest a time to meet.
- Agree.
- Confirm plans and say goodbye.
- Finish the call.

C Phone two more students and suggest activities. Add their information to the table above.

D Work in groups. Tell the other students about your plans.
I'm going to play tennis with Alfonso and then I'm going to …

10.4 WILD WEATHER

DVD PREVIEW

1A Match phrases 1–6 with pictures A–F.
1 It's stormy.
2 It's windy.
3 It's snowing.
4 It's sunny.
5 It's cloudy.
6 It's raining.

B Work in pairs and take turns. Student A: point to a photo and ask about the weather. Student B: reply.
A: *What's the weather like?*
B: *It's raining.*

2A Complete the weather forecast with the words from the box.

| ~~hot~~ warm cool cold wet dry |

In Dublin today, it'll be ¹ *hot* and sunny with temperatures up to twenty-five degrees Celsius. Tomorrow will be cloudy but quite ² _____, with a high of twenty. Things will change on Friday night: it'll be a ³ _____ night with rain from midnight to early next morning. The temperature will fall to ten so it'll feel quite ⁴ _____, but the rain will stop so we'll have a ⁵ _____ day all Saturday. Sunday will be windy and cloudy … and very ⁶ _____, so make sure you wear your winter coat!

B ▶ 10.9 Listen and check your answers.

▶ DVD VIEW

3A Read the programme information. Which places do you think the presenter visits for each of the four programmes?

BBC Wild Weather

In *Wild Weather* the presenter, Donal MacIntyre, looks for the wildest weather in the world. He travels to different places and finds answers to the questions: Where does the weather come from? How does it work? There are four programmes: *Hot*, *Wet*, *Wind* and *Cold*. Follow his journey as he finds and experiences dramatic moments of amazing weather.

B Watch the DVD and answer the questions.
1 Which programme is it: *Hot*, *Wet*, *Wind* or *Cold*?
2 The presenter talks to two people. Where do they work?

C Watch the DVD again. Underline the correct alternative.
1 In Bergen it rains *one / two / three* out of three days.
2 There are *two / three / four* types of umbrellas.
3 They sell Bergen rain to tourists in *bottles / cups / cans*.
4 In one year, *105 / 125 / 225* tonnes of rain fall on a family house.
5 The longest period of rain in Bergen was in *1990 / 1992 / 1995*.
6 It rained for *73 / 83 / 93* days.

speakout the weather

4A Make sentences with the prompts below.
1. What / favourite / kind / weather? Why?
2. What / kind / weather / hate? Why?
3. What / be / weather / like on your last holiday?
4. What / favourite / season? Why?
5. What / like / do in (spring/summer/autumn/ winter)?
6. What / best / season / visit your country or city? Why?

B ▶ 10.10 Listen to people answer the questions above. Number the questions in the order you hear the answers.

C Look at the key phrases below. Listen again and tick the ones you hear.

> **keyphrases**
> I love/hate [stormy] weather.
> I really [don't like/like/love/hate] it when it [rains/'s hot].
> The best time to visit [country/city/town] is [month/season] because …
> That's when …
> It's the perfect time to …
> It [rained/was sunny] every day, [but/and] we had a [great/awful] time.

5A Work in pairs. Interview each other using the questions in Exercise 4A. Make notes on your partner's answers.

B Work in groups and compare your answers. What did you find out?

C Tell the rest of the class. How many people talked about the same place?

writeback reply on a message board

6A Read the message from a travel website. Write the name of your town/city/country.

> **Message Board**   02-Feb-09 12.26 pm
>
> I want to visit _____ for two weeks.
> What's the best time of year to come?
> What about clothes?
> Posted by: **Lars, Sweden**
>
> Reply   < Previous Message | Next Message >

B Write a reply. Use the phrases in brackets to help.

> **Message Board**   < 03-Feb-09 11.55 pm
>
> Hi Lars, I'm from _____ and I live
>   (country)
> in _____. The best time to visit is _____
>   (town/city)   (month/season)
> because _____ and also you can _____.
>   (weather)   (activity)
> You _____, too. Bring _____ and
>   (give another idea)   (clothes)
> _____ as well, or you'll be too _____.
> (clothes)   (adjective)
>
> Posted by:
>
> Reply   < Previous Message | Next Message >

10.5 « LOOKBACK

VERB PHRASES

1A Complete the questions with the correct verbs.
1 On your next holiday, do you want to:
 - st_ay_ at home or g___ abroad?
 - st___ in a hotel or with friends?
2 You have a free Saturday. Do you want to:
 - g___ shopping or g___ ___ a walk?
 - in the evening, st___ in and d___ nothing, or h___ a party and then g___ clubbing?
3 Time for some big changes. Do you want to:
 - g___ married or go travelling?
 - m___ to an English-speaking country or stay in your country?

B Work in pairs and take turns. Ask and answer the questions.

GOING TO; WOULD LIKE TO

2A Look at the list. Write sentences using *be going to* and *would like to*.
1 I'd like to have dinner with Gemma, but I can't – she's busy.
2 I'm going to Oxford. I've got my bus ticket.

Weekend wish list
1 dinner with Gemma – she's busy!
2 go to Oxford (bought bus ticket) ✓
3 go to the U2 concert – no tickets!
4 meet Andy for drink (he said OK) ✓
5 Watch 'Gone with the Wind' on DVD (borrowed it from Cindy) ✓
6 sleep a lot – no time!

B Make your own 'Weekend wish list'. Then look at the list and tick the things that are possible. Write reasons for the things that aren't possible.

C Work in pairs and take turns. Tell your partner about your plans for the weekend.

PREDICTIONS

3A You and some friends are going to spend the weekend in a hotel on a high mountain. Read the information.

- It's a beautiful, quiet place.
- It always rains at this time of year.
- Walking in the mountains is beautiful, but very dangerous.
- There are ten beds.
- The hotel has a very good kitchen. Their restaurant can serve meals for twenty-five people maximum.
- Not all the students like 'mountain life'!

B Complete the sentences with *might, might not, 'll* or *won't*.
1 It _____ rain.
2 We _____ get bored.
3 Someone _____ get hurt.
4 Some people _____ like it. I think I _____ like it.
5 There _____ be enough beds for all of us.
6 The food _____ be very good.
7 There _____ be enough food.
8 It _____ be very peaceful.

C Work in pairs and compare your answers.

D Discuss. Would you like to go on this kind of weekend break? Why/Why not?

MAKING SUGGESTIONS

4A Correct the sentences.
1 Why we don't have a party in the school garden?
2 Let's to have 90s music.
3 What about start at 7 o'clock?
4 That a great idea!
5 Sound good.
6 That might be problem.

B Work in groups. Make suggestions for a class party/celebration. Think about the place, food, music, etc. Use the phrases above to help.

C Tell the other groups about your party/celebration. Which one would you like to go to?
We're going to have a barbecue in the park. We're going to bring beef and …

THE WEATHER

5A Rearrange the letters to complete the sentences.
1 When it's __sunny__ (nusny) I often go to the beach.
2 When it _____ (irsan) I usually go running.
3 When it's _____ (dulcoy) I always feel depressed.
4 When it _____ (swons) I never go out.
5 When it's _____ (dinyw) I like going for a walk.
6 When it's _____ (roymts) I feel quite nervous.

B Write four sentences about you and the weather. Begin each sentence with: *When it … I …*

C Work in pairs and compare your ideas.

BBC VIDEO PODCAST
Watch people talking about their ambitions for the future on ActiveBook or on the website.

Authentic BBC interviews
www.pearsonELT.com/speakout

UNIT 11

SPEAKING
> Talk about what to do when you don't feel well
> Discuss cures for the common cold
> Give advice and offer help
> Ask for help in a pharmacy

LISTENING
> Listen to a radio programme about colds and flu
> Watch an extract from a sitcom about a shopping experience

READING
> Read and do a quiz about how fit you are
> Read about a social experiment

WRITING
> Make your stories more interesting
> Write some advice for a health message board

BBC CONTENT
- Video podcast: Do you have a healthy lifestyle?
- DVD: The Two Ronnies

UNIT 11

health

▶ My head hurts   p108
▶ Never felt better   p110 
▶ Help!   p112  
▶ The Optician   p114

11.1 MY HEAD HURTS

▶ GRAMMAR | should/shouldn't　　▶ VOCABULARY | the body; health　　▶ HOW TO | give advice

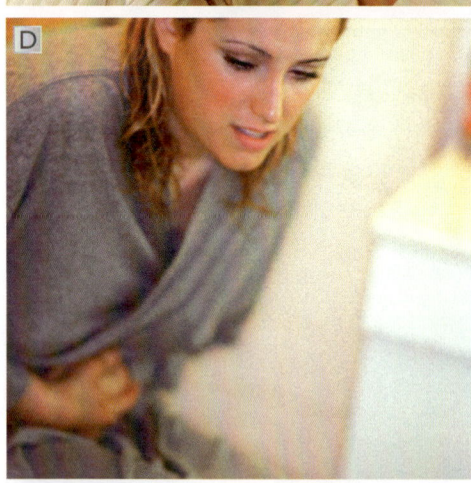

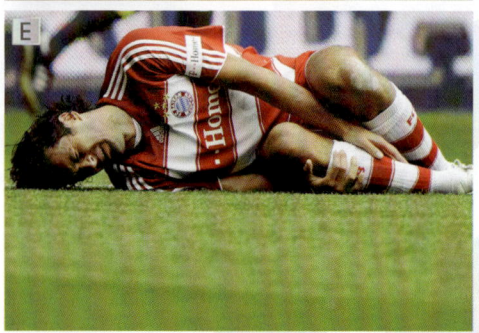

VOCABULARY the body

1A Look at photos A–E. How many parts of the body can you see and name?

➡ page 146 **PHOTOBANK**

B ▶ 11.1 How do you pronounce: *throat, stomach, mouth, shoulder, thumb, toes*? Listen and repeat.

C Work in pairs and take turns. Student A: say a part of the body. Student B: point to it in photos A–E.

LISTENING

2A Work in pairs and discuss.
1 What do you do when you've got a cold? Do you go to work/school, stay at home and rest or go to the doctor/take medicine?
2 When was the last time you were ill? What was the problem? What did you do about it?

B Look at the health problems in the box. Which can you see in photos A–E?

| a runny nose   his/her legs hurt   a sore throat   a cough   a headache |
| a temperature (= a high temperature)   his/her arms hurt   stomach ache |

C Look at the problems above and write the problems in the correct place in the table.

Cold	Flu	Both
a runny nose		

D ▶ 11.2 Listen to a radio programme and check your answers.

E Listen again. Underline the correct alternatives you hear.
1 Flu starts *suddenly/slowly*. You *can/can't* work.
2 A cold starts *suddenly/slowly*. You *can/can't* work.

speakout TIP

Many words in English have a very different pronunciation from their spelling. You can underline problem letters and write the sound underneath, e.g. *cough*　*ache*
　　　　　　　　　　　　　　　　　/f/　　/k/
In your notebook, do the same for *thumb* and *stomach*.

3A Look at the sentences below. Cross out the incorrect alternative. Then add one more word to each group.
1 I've got *an earache / a backache / a throatache*　*a stomach ache*
2 I've got a sore *cough / throat / eye*.
3 My *runny nose / head / back* hurts.
4 I feel *tired / temperature / better*.

B Work in pairs and take turns. Student A: choose a problem and mime it. Student B: guess what's wrong.

11.1

cold cures around the world

This month, we asked readers from around the world, 'What's the best thing to do when you've got a cold?' Here are some of their answers:

- Jean from France: 'You should drink lots of water and get lots of sleep. Nothing else helps.'
- Sun-Do from Korea: 'We eat kimchi – a dish made from cabbage. You should try it. The cabbage is full of vitamin C and the spices in kimchi also help.'
- Sam from South Africa: 'No medicine – you shouldn't take antibiotics for a cold – that's crazy. Your body can fight the cold virus.'
- Ana-Maria from Spain: 'You should eat fruit, lots of it, especially things like oranges.'
- Mary from Scotland: 'You should drink herbal tea with honey and lemon in it and you should relax. You shouldn't go to work.'
- Doug from the USA: 'That's easy. You should have a bowl of my grandmother's chicken soup. That's the perfect cure. I don't care what anybody says – there's nothing better.'

READING

4A Read the article about cold cures. Which ideas in the text are in the pictures?

B Read the article again. Which person do you agree with most? What do people do in your country when they've got a cold?

C Work in pairs and compare your ideas.

GRAMMAR should/shouldn't

5A Look at the sentences and underline the correct alternative to complete the rules.
1 You should get lots of sleep.
2 You shouldn't go to work.

> Rules:
> 1 Use *should* for something that is *necessary/a good idea*.
> 2 Use *shouldn't* for something that is *unnecessary/a bad idea*.

B Complete the table. Use the article to help.

You	should	_____	lots of water.
		_____	fruit.
	_____	take	antibiotics.

C ▶ 11.3 Listen and check. Then listen and repeat.

➡ page 136 LANGUAGEBANK

PRACTICE

6A Look at problems 1–4 and advice a)–h). For each problem, write advice with *should/shouldn't*.
1 I'm tired.
  You should get more sleep.
  You shouldn't go to bed so late.
2 I'm hungry.
3 It's raining and I have to go.
4 I feel ill.

a) be here in the lesson
b) eat something
c) ~~get more sleep~~
d) go home
e) go out now
f) ~~go to bed so late~~
g) take an umbrella
h) miss breakfast

B Work in pairs and take turns. Cover the advice a)–h) above. Student A: say one of the problems. Student B: give advice with *should/shouldn't*.

SPEAKING

7A Work in groups. What are your 'five tips for good health'? Make a list. Think about the things in the box.

| sleep   food   exercise   drink   smoking   other |

You should go to bed early.

B Work with another group. Compare your lists and decide on the top five tips.

109

11.2 NEVER FELT BETTER

▶ GRAMMAR | adverbs of manner   ▶ VOCABULARY | common verbs   ▶ HOW TO | talk about how you do things

Healthy body, healthy mind

1 Can you ___swim___ 100 metres in a pool?
   a) Yes, easily.   b) Yes, but only slowly.   c) No chance!
2 Can you _____ 400 metres without stopping?
   a) Yes, easily.   b) Yes, I can, but not very fast.   c) No, I can't.
3 Can you _____ up four sets of stairs?
   a) Yes, no problem.   b) Yes, but it's really hard!   c) I always take the lift.
4 Can you _____ a car number from fifty metres?
   a) Yes, clearly.   b) Yes, just.   c) No, I have to wear glasses.
5 Can you _____ and _____ someone talking to you in a noisy room?
   a) Yes, easily.   b) Yes, but not very well.   c) If they speak *very* loudly.
6 Can you _____ on something (e.g. your homework) for thirty minutes without a break?
   a) Yes, I can.   b) Yes, but not easily.   c) No, I can't.
7 Do you _____ everything you ate the day before yesterday?
   a) Yes, perfectly.   b) Yes, but not easily.   c) No, not really.
8 Do you often _____ your bank PIN number or a computer password?
   a) No, never.   b) Not often, but sometimes.   c) All the time!

KEY
a = 3 points   b = 2 points   c = 1 point

16–24 points:
Well done! You are very fit and healthy in mind and body. You do regular exercise, you eat well and get enough sleep, so your mind and memory are clear. Don't stop! And tell your friends how they can do things to feel better.

9–15 points:
You are quite fit and healthy in mind and body. Do you want to be fitter? Then maybe you should do more exercise. Thirty minutes three times a week keeps your mind and body young. Eat more fruit and vegetables and have oily fish once a week. Join a brain gym or look for one on the internet.

1–8 points:
Maybe you should do some exercise for your body and mind. Start small! You don't have to go to the gym. Walk more. You can get off the bus or tram one stop before work/school and walk the rest of the way. Try to eat healthily, too and get enough sleep – this will help your mind as well as your body.

VOCABULARY common verbs

1A Complete the quiz with the verbs in the box.

| ~~swim~~ run remember forget hear |
| understand read climb concentrate |

B Work in pairs. Ask and answer the questions. Add up your partner's score and read the results in the key.

C Work in pairs and take turns. Student A: say a verb from Exercise 1A. Student B: say the verb phrase. Then think of other possible nouns.
A: *forget*
B: *forget your PIN number*
A: *forget people's names*
B: *forget …*

▶ page 127 **IRREGULAR VERBS**

GRAMMAR adverbs of manner

2A Look at the sentences and the rule. Underline the correct alternatives to complete them.
1 Can you swim 100 metres? Yes, but only *slow/slowly*.
2 Can you run 400 metres? Yes, *easy/easily*.

Rule: Use adverbs of manner to say *how/when* we do something.

B Complete the table. Use the quiz and key to help.

Adjective	Adverb
easy	easily
slow	
clear	
fast	
loud	
perfect	
good	
healthy	

▶ page 136 **LANGUAGE BANK**

PRACTICE

3A Complete the sentences and make them true for you. Use the correct form of one of the words in brackets.
1 It's _easy_ for me to remember new words in English. (easy/hard)
2 I like it when the teacher speaks English _____. (quick/slow)
3 I think I speak English _____. (good/bad)
4 I've got a _____ memory. (good/bad)
5 When I have lunch or dinner, I usually eat _____. (fast/slow)
6 I think I usually eat _____. (healthy/unhealthy)
7 I can't concentrate when it's _____. (quiet/noisy)
8 I'm usually quite _____. (lazy/energetic)

B Work in pairs and compare your sentences.

WRITING adverbs in stories

4A Look at pictures A–D. What do you think happened? Put them in the correct order. Use the prompts 1–4 to help.

1 Saturday / Ken / get up / have breakfast / got on / bike
2 he / ride / down the road / not / look / ahead / cat / run / in front / him
3 he / fall off / bike / broke / arm
4 evening / he / sit / at home / with / broken arm

B Use the prompts to write the story. Remember to use linkers.
1 On Saturday, Ken got up, had breakfast and …

C Change the adjectives in the box below into adverbs. Then use three to add to your story in Exercise 4A.

| quick   careful   careless   dangerous   early   fast   late   sad   slow |

On Saturday, Ken got up late, had breakfast quickly …

D Write the next part of the story with three more adverbs. Start with '*Six weeks later, on Saturday morning, Ken got up …*'

E Work in pairs and exchange your stories.

SPEAKING

5A Work in pairs and discuss. Look at two pages from Julie's diary. Did she have a healthy weekend? Why/Why not?

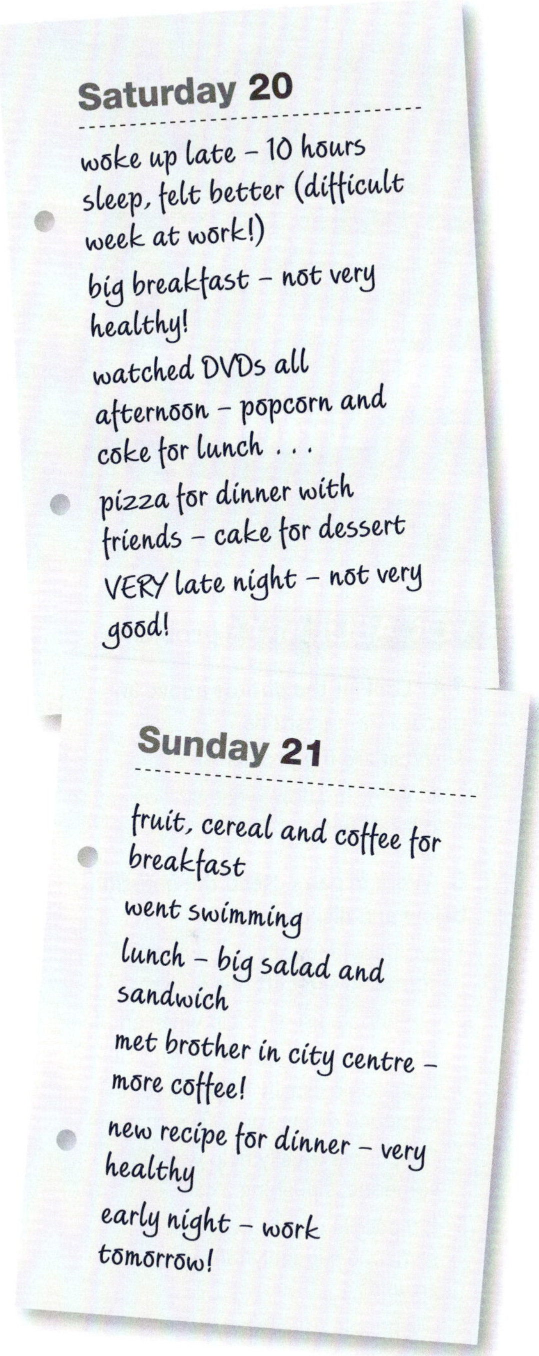

Saturday 20
- woke up late – 10 hours sleep, felt better (difficult week at work!)
- big breakfast – not very healthy!
- watched DVDs all afternoon – popcorn and coke for lunch …
- pizza for dinner with friends – cake for dessert VERY late night – not very good!

Sunday 21
- fruit, cereal and coffee for breakfast
- went swimming
- lunch – big salad and sandwich
- met brother in city centre – more coffee!
- new recipe for dinner – very healthy
- early night – work tomorrow!

B In your notebook, write a 'health diary' for last weekend. Make notes about:
- food and drink
- exercise
- sleep
- relaxing

C Work in groups and compare your answers. Who had the healthiest weekend? What three things can you do differently next weekend?
Last weekend I didn't have a healthy weekend because …

11.3 HELP!

▶ FUNCTION | offering to help ▶ VOCABULARY | problems ▶ LEARN TO | thank someone

VOCABULARY | problems

1A Look at the photos above and discuss the questions.
1 What are the problems?
2 In each situation, what can you say to offer to help?

B Work in pairs. Read the questions below and discuss.
1 Do people usually help when someone **can't lift** heavy luggage?
2 Do people usually help when an older person is **standing** on a train or bus?
3 Do people usually help when someone **drops** some files or papers?
4 Do people usually help when someone is **pushing** a car?
5 Do people usually help when someone suddenly **falls** to the ground?
6 Do people usually help when someone **cuts** his/her hand?

READING

2A Read the article quickly. Number pictures A–C in the correct order.

B Read the article more carefully. In which situation does the person get help?

When someone sees a person in trouble, do they stop and help, or just 'walk on by'?
BBC reporter Michael Coombes wanted to find out. With his assistant, Kitty Dann, he chose three situations to test how quickly people help or if they help.

In the first situation, Kitty dropped some papers. After a few seconds, Brian McCann came and helped her. He said 'I saw her drop everything and I wanted to help her. Most people don't help these days.'

In the next situation, Kitty tried to move a heavy sign on the street outside a shop. She pushed and pulled it, but no one helped her.

In the final situation, Michael fell to the ground in the street. He stayed there for several minutes, but no one came to help.

Later, he asked some people why they didn't help. One woman, Claire, said, 'I thought maybe you were drunk or dead. People are afraid of helping these days because they don't know what's going to happen to them.'

Eighty-two-year-old Paul Weston said, 'You don't know if it's real or not. You have to be very, very careful these days. The world is different now.'

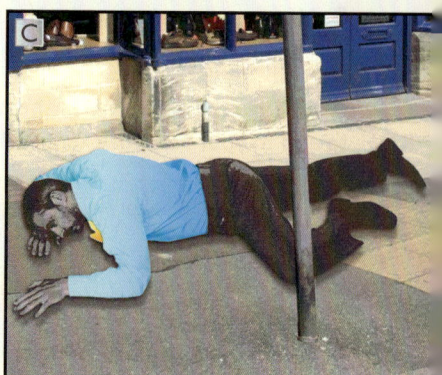

11.3

LEARN TO thank someone

5A Look at audio script 11.4 on page 155 and complete the sentences.

Conversation 1:
Man: Here, let me help. What a mess!
Woman: Thank ¹_____.
Man: No ²_____.

Conversation 2:
Woman: Are you all right? Shall I call an ambulance?
Man: No … Yes … Uh … Thanks ³_____.
Woman: That's ⁴_____.

Conversation 3:
Man: Oh, look. I'll do that for you. Where do you want it?
Woman: Just over here, in front of the window … Thanks ⁵_____. That's ⁶_____.
Man: You're ⁷_____.

B Underline the ways of thanking someone. How can you respond when someone thanks you?

➡ page 136 **LANGUAGEBANK**

6A Look at the flowchart below and put the conversation in the correct order.

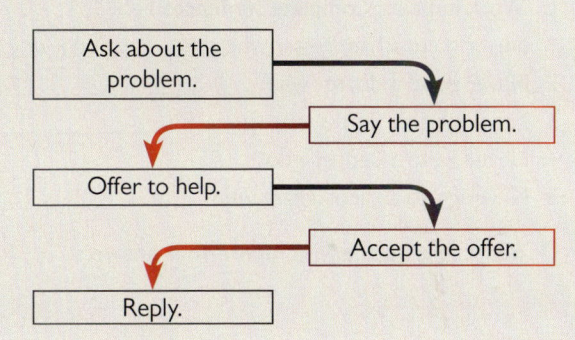

```
Ask about the
   problem.
                      →  Say the problem.
Offer to help.  ←
                      →  Accept the offer.
   Reply.       ←
```

1 A: That's OK.
2 B: Thanks a lot.
3 A: I'll make you a sandwich.
4 A: Are you OK?
5 B: No, I'm really hungry.

B Work in pairs and take turns. Student A: look at page 150. Student B: look at page 150. Use the flowchart to help and role-play the conversation.

SPEAKING

7A ▶ 11.6 Listen to the situations. What's happening?

B Work in pairs. Listen again and offer to help.

1 _____
2 _____
3 _____
4 _____
5 _____
6 _____

FUNCTION offering to help

3A ▶ 11.4 Listen and match each conversation with pictures A–C.

B Listen again and complete sentences 1–3 below.
1 _____ me help.
2 _____ I call an ambulance?
3 I _____ do that for you.

C ▶ 11.5 Listen to the pronunciation of the offers. Then listen and repeat.

4A Match problems 1–5 with offers a)–e).

1 I can't open the window.   a) I'll get it for you.
2 I'm hungry.   b) Let me carry it.
3 I can't reach the dictionary.   c) I'll make you a sandwich.
4 I can't lift this bag.   d) Shall I open the window?
5 It's hot in here.   e) Let me try … Ooh, it's stuck.

B Work in pairs and take turns. Student A: say a problem. Student B: offer to help.
A: I can't open the window.
B: Let me try … Ooh, it's stuck.

speakout TIP

When you see someone who needs help, you often <u>start</u> the conversation with *Are you OK?* or *Are you all right?* and <u>then</u> offer to help.

113

11.4 THE OPTICIAN

DVD PREVIEW

1A Look at the photos A–F. What does each person do?
Photo A is an optician. He/She checks someone's eyes.

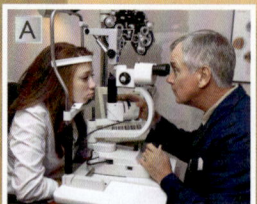

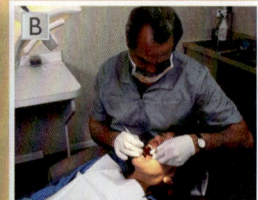

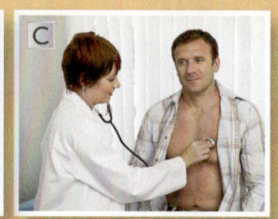

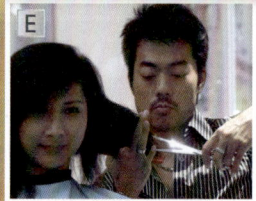

B Work in pairs. Look at the phrase and discuss. Do you think it's good advice?

> Never go to an optician who wears glasses.

C Work in pairs. Complete sentences 1–5.
1 Never go to a hairdresser who ____ *hasn't got any hair* ____.
2 Never go to a doctor who _____.
3 Never go to a fitness instructor who _____.
4 Never go to a dentist who _____.
5 Never go to an accountant who _____.

D Work in groups and compare your answers.

▶ DVD VIEW

2A Read the programme information. Why is the programme called *The Two Ronnies*?

BBC The Two Ronnies

The Two Ronnies are the stars of one of the longest-running comedy shows on British television. They both wear glasses, they're both called Ronnie and together they can make a simple situation very complicated … and very funny! In this sketch, Ronnie Corbett (the short one) has a problem and goes into a shop to ask for help from Ronnie Barker (the tall one).

B Watch the DVD and answer the questions.
1 Where is the man?
2 Where does he think he is?
   a) at a greengrocers
   b) at a baker's
3 What's the problem with both of the men?
   a) they can't hear very well
   b) they can't see very well
4 Which letter <u>doesn't</u> the man say?
   a) Y.
   b) H.
5 Why are the two men happy at the end?
   a) They don't need glasses..
   b) They can both see better.

3 Watch the DVD again. Number the sentences below in the order you hear them.
a) Hello. Anybody there? *1*
b) Is that better or worse?
c) Could I have two pounds of potatoes, please?
d) What do you see with?
e) No, you're reading all the furniture!
f) They're mine! They're mine!
g) Try the next line on your own.

speakout at a pharmacy

4A Work in pairs and answer the questions.

1 Do you go to a pharmacy, a doctor's, a dentist's or a hospital in these situations?
   a) You ate some fish last night. This morning you've got an awful stomach ache.
   b) You broke a glass and cut your thumb badly.
   c) You woke up this morning with earache.
   d) Your eyes are really sore.
   e) You've got terrible toothache.
   f) You stayed out in the sun too long this morning. Now you've got bad sunburn.

2 Can you remember a time when you had any of these problems? Where were you? What did you do?

B ▶ 11.7 Listen to the conversation in a pharmacy. What's the problem? What does the pharmacist advise?

C Look at the key phrases below. Listen again and tick the phrases you hear.

> **keyphrases**
> Can you help me? I've got [bad toothache/a problem with my eye].
> Have you got anything for [a headache/an earache/sore eyes]?
> When did it start?
> Take [this medicine/these tablets/some painkillers].
> Put [these drops in your …/this cream on your …].
> You [should see a doctor/shouldn't go out in the sun].

D Work in pairs. You are on holiday in another country. Choose a problem from Excercise 4A or use your own idea and role-play the situation. Use the key phrases to help

E Work in groups and take turns. One pair: role-play your conversation. Other students: listen and guess the problem.

writeback a website message

5 Work in pairs. Read the two questions from a health message board. Choose one and complete Message 3 to give some advice. Use the key phrases to help.

Message 1   < posted yesterday >

Help! I started working from home three weeks ago. Now I've got terrible backache and my eyes hurt. I'm on the computer for about eight hours every day. Any advice?

Posted by: **YuchenChi, China**

Reply   < Previous Message | Next Message >

Message 2   < posted yesterday >

I stopped smoking a year ago and now I'm overweight. I often feel stressed and unhappy. I think I might start smoking again but I don't want to. What can I do?

Posted by: **Great Amigo, Mexico**

Reply   < Previous Message | Next Message >

Message 3   < posted today >

Hi, _____. The same thing happened to _____. Don't worry! The best thing is to _____. Also you should _____. Why don't you _____ as well? Don't _____ and you shouldn't _____.
All the best, _____.

Reply   < Previous Message | Next Message >

11.5 « LOOKBACK

HEALTH PROBLEMS

1A Complete the poems.

A: What's the matter? What's wr _ _ _ with you?

B: I've got a terrible co_ _ _ ,
– a runny n_ _ _ , a bad s_r_
thr_ _ _ …
I can't stay here. I'm off!

A: My a_ _ _ hurt, my l_ _ _ hurt,
I think I've got the fl_ .

B: Have you got a t_mp_r_t_ _ _?

A: Yes, what can I do?

A: I've got an awful h_ _d_ _ _ _.

B: My f_ng_ _ _ hurt a lot.

A: My e_ _ _ are t_r_d.

B: My b_ck_ _ _ _'s bad.

A & B: We don't know what we've got!

B Work in pairs. Read the poems.

ADVERBS

2A Write the opposite adverbs.

1 calmly *angrily*
2 loudly
3 slowly
4 badly
5 carelessly

B Complete the sentences with the words in the box below and your own ideas.

| speak(s)   eat(s)   talk(s) |
| drive(s)   walk(s) |

1 I _____ too _____ (adverb).
2 My teacher sometimes _____ too _____ (adverb).
3 My closest friend _____ too _____ (adverb).
4 Everyone _____ too _____ (adverb).

C Work in groups and take turns. One student: say one of your sentences. Other students: give advice or say your opinion using *should/shouldn't*.

A: *Everyone talks too loudly on their mobiles.*
B: *Yes, they should speak quietly.*

COMMON VERBS

3 Work in pairs. Match phrases 1–6 with a)–f). Then ask and answer the questions.

1 Can you read   c)
2 Do you remember
3 Did you hear
4 Can you concentrate
5 Do you understand
6 Did you ever climb

a) with the TV or radio on in the same room?
b) trees when you were younger?
c) music?
d) the first day of this English class?
e) films in English?
f) the news this morning?

SHOULD/SHOULDN'T

4A Read the situations and make a note of what the person *should/shouldn't* do.

A
My arm hurts so I can't use my computer. I have to finish a report by tomorrow.

B
I've got a terrible backache. I'm going on holiday tomorrow and I've got two heavy bags to carry.

C
I've got a headache and a bad sore throat. I've got an important interview for a new job tomorrow.

D
My leg hurts so I can't walk very far. I'm going out tomorrow night and I want to dance.

B Work in pairs and take turns. Role-play the four situations using your ideas above.

OFFERING TO HELP

5 Work in pairs. What can you say in each situation?

1 You're at a friend's house and she breaks some glasses.
2 You're walking down the street and someone falls off his bicycle.
3 You're on a train and a woman next to you becomes ill.
4 You're in a restaurant and the waiter pours hot coffee on your friend's clothes.
5 Your friend is cutting vegetables and cuts his finger badly.
6 Your friend wants a coffee, but she doesn't have enough money to buy one.

6A Complete the conversation with the words in the box.

| ~~Shall~~   me   a   're   you |

A: Good morning. Can I help you?
B: Yes, the shower in my room doesn't work.
A: I ~~Shall~~ send someone to look at it.
B: Thank. And when does the City Museum open?
A: Let ____ look on the computer … It opens at 10.00 today.
B: Thanks. And can ____ get me a taxi … to go to the museum?
A: No problem. I phone for one now?
A: In about an hour, please.
B: Certainly.
A: Thanks ____ lot.
B: You ____ welcome.

B Work in pairs. Practise the conversation.

BBC VIDEO PODCAST
Watch people talking about their lifestyles on ActiveBook or on the website.

Authentic BBC interviews

www.pearsonELT.com/speakout

UNIT 12

SPEAKING
- Talk about unusual experiences
- Describe movement from one place to another
- Phone someone about a problem

LISTENING
- Listen to people talking about their experiences
- Watch an extract from a documentary about sharks

READING
- Read about a dangerous job

WRITING
- Write a postcard
- Write about an exciting/frightening experience

BBC CONTENT
- Video podcast: What's the most exciting thing you've ever done?
- DVD: Shark Therapy

UNIT 12

experiences

▶ Unforgettable   p118
▶ Afraid of nothing   p120 
▶ I've got a problem   p122 
▶ Shark Therapy   p124

12.1 UNFORGETTABLE

▶ **GRAMMAR** | present perfect   ▶ **VOCABULARY** | outdoor activities   ▶ **HOW TO** | talk about experiences

VOCABULARY outdoor activities

1A Complete the phrases below with the words in the box. Use the photos to help you.

ride   swim   go   sail   climb   watch

1 _____ an elephant / a horse
2 _____ a volcano / a mountain
3 _____ a small boat / down the Nile
4 _____ fishing / camel trekking
5 _____ in a river / in a thermal spa
6 _____ an opera / a play outdoors / birds

B Work in pairs. Look at photos A–E and discuss the questions.
1 Which of the activities above can you see in the photos?
2 Which activities would you like to do? Why?
3 Which activities would you <u>not</u> like to do? Why not?

LISTENING

2A ▶ 12.1 Listen to a survey. In what order do people talk about the activities in photos A–E? Which two activities don't they talk about?

B Listen again. Tick the activities the speakers have done.

	Speaker 1	Speaker 2	Speaker 3
ridden elephants			
sailed down the Nile			
climbed a volcano			
swum in a thermal spa			

118

12.1

GRAMMAR present perfect

3A Look at the sentence and underline the correct alternatives to complete the rules.

> I've been to Guatemala and I've climbed that volcano.

> Rules:
> 1 Use the present perfect to talk about past events *when you know the exact time/don't know when* the event happened.
> 2 Use the present perfect to emphasise *what/when* the action happened.

B ▶ 12.2 Listen and complete the table.

I	_____	sailed	down the Nile.
	haven't	_____	to Iceland.

_____	you ever	ridden	an elephant?
No,	I	_____	.

C Listen again and check. Then listen and repeat.
➡ page 138 **LANGUAGEBANK**

PRACTICE

4A Complete the table with the correct infinitive.

infinitive	past participle
1 _drive_	driven
2 _____	flown
3 _____	had
4 _____	met
5 _____ / _____	been
6 _____	seen
7 _____	slept
8 _____	swum

B Use four of the past participles above to write sentences about you. Two sentences should be false.
I've driven a Ferrari.

C Work in pairs and take turns. Student A: say your four sentences. Student B: guess which two are false.

speakout TIP

Many past participles are similar. Look for patterns to help you remember. In your notebook, complete the verb patterns and add another verb to each group:
meet – met, keep …
speak – spoken, break …
grow – grown, know …
drive – driven, give …
swim – swum, drink …

SPEAKING

5A Complete the questions with your own ideas.
1 Have you ever been to _____?
2 Have you ever slept in a _____?
3 Have you ever had _____?
4 Have you ever _____?
5 Have you ever met _____?

B Work in groups. Ask and answer the questions above. Who has done most things in your group?
A: *Have you ever been to a festival?*
B: *Yes, I have.*
C: *No, I haven't, but I'd like to.*
D: *No, I haven't and I don't want to.*

WRITING postcard phrases

6A Read the postcard from Oliver and Kristina. Which country are they visiting?

> Luxor, 12th May
> Hi everyone,
> Having a great time. It's very hot here in the day and cold at night. We sleep in tents, or sometimes on the boats and every day we get up at 6 o'clock and have breakfast next to the river. We've seen the temples in Kom Ombo and Edfu and we've taken lots of pictures. We haven't seen the Pyramids – that's Saturday. Must go now! See you soon.
> Wish you were here!
> Oliver and Kristina

> The Wilson Family
> 434 Church Street
> Pleasantville,
> NY 10570
> USA

B Look at the postcard again and complete the information.
1 Write the _name_ and _____ on the right-hand side.
2 You can write the _____ and _____ at the top.
3 You can start a postcard with _____.

C Underline four typical postcard phrases in the postcard. What's missing from each phrase? Write the phrases in full.
<u>We're</u> having a great time.

D Cross out words to make more postcard phrases.
1 ~~We're~~ staying in a fantastic hotel.
2 I have to stop now.
3 I'll speak to you soon.
4 I hope you're all OK.

7 Work in pairs. Write a postcard to your class. Use the ideas above to help. Don't write the name of the place. Then exchange postcards with another pair and guess the place.

12.2 AFRAID OF NOTHING

▶ **GRAMMAR** | present perfect and past simple　▶ **VOCABULARY** | prepositions　▶ **HOW TO** | talk about past experiences

Vic ARMSTRONG is afraid of nothing. He has fallen out of windows, jumped off bridges, ridden a motorcycle through fire, climbed up the outside of a skyscraper and driven into a wall – because that's his job.

Vic is a stunt double in films and does things that most of us think are crazy.

Vic was Harrison Ford's stunt double in all three early Indiana Jones films. He has also worked on many James Bond films including *Die Another Day*. 'A job on a Bond film is the most fun for a stuntman – I try out the cars,' says Vic.

His most famous stunt was when he jumped from a horse onto a German tank in one of the Indiana Jones films. Movie viewers voted this 'one of the ten best stunts of all time'.

Vic has broken some bones, but he says that it's part of the job. He now spends more time as a stunt director, directing other stuntmen. In 2002 he worked on *Gangs of New York* with one of his favourite directors, Martin Scorsese. Vic says it was 'great fun'.

Now, after forty years of stunt work, the man without fear feels the same way. Vic still thinks it's the best job in the world: 'I enjoy my work now as much as when I started,' he says. 'And now, as a stunt director, I tell other people to fall and jump. And the money is very, very good.'

> " A job on a Bond film is the most fun for a stuntman … "

READING

1A Read the definition of *stunt* below. Can you think of any famous stunts?

Stunt[1] /stʌnt/ noun A dangerous thing that someone does to entertain people, especially in a film: *There's a great stunt in which his car has to jump across a 15 metre gap.*

From Longman Wordwise Dictionary.

B Read the article and list the stunts the man has done.

C Read the article again. Are sentences 1–7 true (T) or false (F)?

1 Vic played Indiana Jones when Harrison Ford was ill.
2 He likes working on Bond films because he can drive the cars.
3 Steven Spielberg is one of his favourite directors.
4 He started doing stunt work over forty years ago.
5 Vic has sometimes hurt himself in his job.
6 He doesn't like working on films very much any more.
7 Vic gets a lot of money for his work.

D Find five movement verbs in the first paragraph of the text. Write the verb, past simple and past participle.

(fallen) – fall　fell　fallen

12.2

GRAMMAR present perfect and past simple

2A Look at the sentences. Underline the correct tense of the verbs.
1 He has worked on many James Bond films. (*past simple/present perfect*)
2 In 2002 he worked on *Gangs of New York*. (*past simple/present perfect*)

B Underline the correct alternatives.

Rules:
1 With the present perfect, you *say/don't say* the exact time.
2 With the past simple, you *say/don't say* the exact time.

➡ page 138 **LANGUAGEBANK**

PRACTICE

3A Write the questions in full. Use the present perfect.
1 meet / a famous person?
   Have you ever met a famous person?
2 break / your arm?
3 eat / anything unusual?
4 watch / a live football match?
5 make / something to wear?
6 go / to a really hot or cold country?

B Work in pairs and take turns. Ask and answer the questions above. Remember to ask and answer follow-up questions using the past simple.
A: *Have you ever met a famous person?*
B: *Yes, I have. I met a famous actor last year.*
A: *Really? Who did you meet?*

4A Work in pairs. Write the past participles of the verbs in the box next to the correct sound below.

| ~~sleep~~ ~~sing~~ ~~speak~~ ~~drive~~ ~~buy~~ meet |
| write think fly win read do give |
| choose bring |

/e/	/ʌ/	/əʊ/	/ɪ/	/ɔː/
sl<u>e</u>pt	s<u>u</u>ng	sp<u>o</u>ken	dr<u>i</u>ven	b<u>ou</u>ght

B ▶ 12.3 Listen and check. Then listen and repeat.

VOCABULARY prepositions

5A Look at the pictures below. What is the man doing?

B Match the prepositions in the box with the pictures A–J.

| down   through   up   out of   under   towards |
| away from   across   over   into |

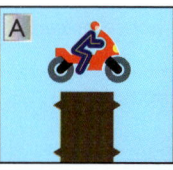

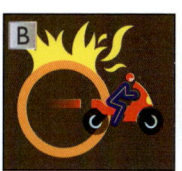

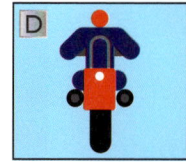

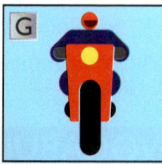

C Some of the prepositions have opposites. Look at the pictures again and find the opposites of these prepositions: *down, over, away from, out of.*

6 Complete the situations with a preposition of movement. More than one might be possible.
1 going *up/down* the outside of a building in a glass lift
2 walking _____ a big dog
3 going _____ a bridge when a train is going _____ the bridge
4 walking _____ a big park alone
5 riding a bike fast _____ a big hill
6 walking _____ customs at an airport
7 driving _____ a very long tunnel
8 walking _____ a room full of new people

SPEAKING

7A Work in pairs. Make a list of some dangerous/exciting/scary situations.

B How do you feel about the situations? Write one of the phrases in the box below next to each one.

| I love it.   It's not a problem. |
| I really don't like it.   I'm afraid of it. |
| I've never done it.   I'm not keen. |

C Work in pairs and discuss your answers.
A: *How do you feel about going across a river on a rope bridge?*
B: *I really don't like it.*
A: *Why? Have you had a bad experience?*
B: *Yes, two years ago I was …*

12.3 I'VE GOT A PROBLEM

▶ FUNCTION | telephoning ▶ VOCABULARY | telephoning expressions ▶ LEARN TO | say telephone numbers

SPEAKING

1 Work in pairs and take turns. Ask and answer questions 1–5.
1 Have you ever lost your keys/passport/credit card/mobile phone? What happened?
2 Have you ever locked yourself out of your house or car? What happened?
3 Have you ever missed the last train or bus home? What happened?
4 Have you ever been very late for a meeting/appointment? What happened?
5 Have you ever got lost in a city? What happened?

VOCABULARY telephoning expressions

2A Complete the sentences with phrases from the box.

> ~~take a message~~   leave a message   call   answer   ring back

1 You answer the phone. It's a call for Patricia but she's not in the office today so you ___take a message___ for her.
2 You phone Mark but he's not at home so you _____ on his answerphone.
3 You want Mark to _____ you _____ this evening.
4 It's the evening. You _____ Mark, but he's having a shower.
5 Ten minutes later the phone rings and you _____ it. It's Mark.

B Work in pairs and compare your answers.

FUNCTION telephoning

3A ▶ 12.4 Listen to three conversation extracts. Which situations from Exercise 1 are they?

B Listen again. In which conversation(s) do the people know each other?

4A ▶ 12.5 Complete the extracts with words from the box. Then listen and check.

> ~~it's~~   check   moment   tell   ask   there   ring
> number   message   back   leave   speak   call

Extract 1
B: Hi, Sean. ¹___It's___ Debbie.
A: Hi, Debbie. What's up?
B: ²Is Kevin _____?
A: No, he's not. He went out about ten minutes ago.

Extract 2
B: ³Could I _____ a _____ for him?
A: Of course.
B: ⁴Just _____ him to _____ me.

Extract 3
B: Hello. ⁵Could I _____ to customer services, please?
A: ⁶Just a _____.
C: Customer services.
B: Hello, I've got a problem.

Extract 4
B: ⁷Could you _____ me back?
C: Of course. ⁸Could you give me the _____ there?
B: Just a moment … It's 34 for Spain, 91 for Madrid, then 308 5238.
C: ⁹Let me _____ that. 34 91 308 5238.
B: That's right.
C: Fine. Put the phone down – ¹⁰I'll call you _____ straight away.

B Match the conversation extracts 1–4 with descriptions a)–d) below.
a) Asking someone to call back 4
b) Calling a business
c) Calling a friend
d) Leaving a message

C Underline the key stressed word in telephoning phrases 1–10 in Exercise 4A.

D ▶ 12.6 Listen and check. Then listen and repeat.
➡ page 138 LANGUAGEBANK

12.3

LEARN TO say telephone numbers

6A ▶ 12.7 Complete the phone number. Then listen and check.
3114020 = Three _____ one four _____ two _____

B Listen again. Draw a line between the words where you hear a short break.

> **speakout TIP**
>
> In telephone numbers:
> • say 'oh' for the number zero.
> • when there are two of the same number, e.g. 77, say 'seven seven' or 'double seven'.
> • say the last seven numbers of a telephone number in two groups. First, three numbers and then four, e.g. 926 5173.

7A Work in pairs. Practise saying the numbers.
1 7996072
2 9954270
3 8013005
4 5807713

B Work in pairs and take turns. Student A: look at page 148. Student B: look at page 151.

SPEAKING

8A Work in pairs. Choose a situation from Exercise 1. Write key words for your conversation in the flowchart below. Then practise together.

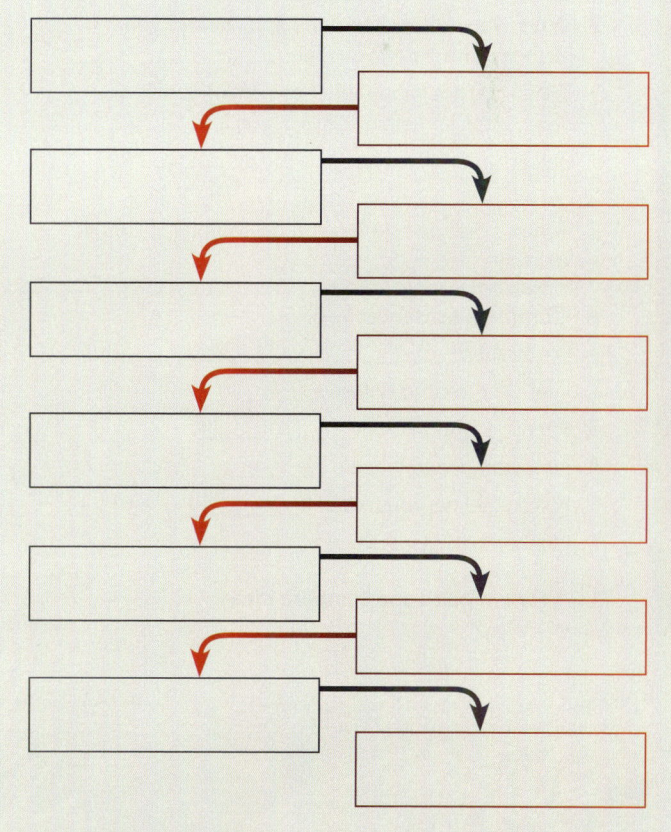

B Work with another pair. Exchange flowcharts and act out their conversation.

5A Work in pairs. Look at the flowchart and write the conversation in full.

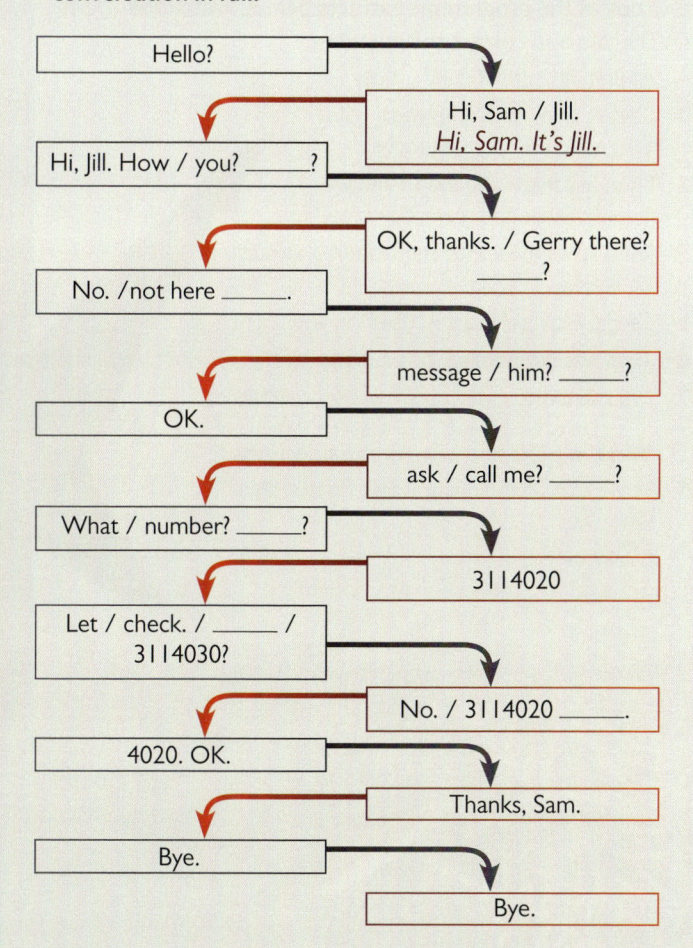

- Hello?
- Hi, Sam / Jill. *Hi, Sam. It's Jill.*
- Hi, Jill. How / you? _____?
- OK, thanks. / Gerry there? _____?
- No. /not here _____.
- message / him? _____?
- OK.
- ask / call me? _____?
- What / number? _____?
- 3114020
- Let / check. / _____ / 3114030?
- No. / 3114020 _____.
- 4020. OK.
- Thanks, Sam.
- Bye.
- Bye.

B Work in pairs. Read out your conversation.

12.4 SHARK THERAPY

DVD PREVIEW

1 Work in pairs. Look at the photos and answer the questions.
1 Are you afraid of any of these animals? Which ones? Why?
2 How do most people feel about sharks? Is it safe to swim with them?

2A Complete the sentences with words from the box.

| ~~frightened~~   proud   excited   afraid |
| nervous   embarrassed |

1 Some people are _frightened_ or _____ of the dark.
2 When you are positive and happy before your birthday or a party, you feel _____.
3 When you are happy about something you've done, often something difficult, you feel _____.
4 Before an exam or going to the dentist, you feel _____.
5 When other people see you do something stupid, you feel _____.

B Complete sentences 1–6.
1 I'm afraid of _____.
2 I get very excited before _____.
3 I'm not frightened of _____.
4 I felt very proud when I _____.
5 I often feel nervous when I _____.
6 I feel embarrassed when I _____.

C Work in pairs and compare ideas.

DVD VIEW

3A Read the programme information. Why does Tanya go to the Bahamas?

BBC Shark Therapy

Tanya Streeter is a world-famous diver but she's got one *big* problem. She's afraid of sharks! To overcome her fear, she needs help or 'therapy' and travels to the Bahamas to get it. Here, she learns how to swim with them … and comes face to face with the dangerous tiger shark.

B Watch the DVD. Underline the correct alternatives.
1 It's safer to wear a *black/green/shiny* swimsuit.
2 Tanya uses a *knife/stick/gun* to protect herself from the sharks.
3 *No/One/Two* shark(s) try to bite Tanya.

C Look at the programme extracts below. Watch the DVD again and correct the mistakes.
1 'At first, it isn't ~~difficult~~.'   *easy*
2 'I didn't think that they were going to be … quite so … friendly.'
3 'I noticed the mask and I think we should change the mask completely.'
4 'Jim throws meat into the water to attract the sharks.'
5 'Tanya, look behind you over on your right.'
6 'That was frightening! Tanya did great.'
7 'I've started to overcome my very real feeling.'

D Work in pairs and answer the questions.
1 At the end of the programme do you think Tanya was:
   a) frightened?
   b) embarrassed?
   c) proud?
2 Would you like to try what Tanya did? Why/Why not?

speakout a frightening experience

4A Think about an exciting or frightening experience you've had. Look at the questions below and make notes:
- How old were you?
- Where was it?
- What happened? (write the verb phrases)
- How did you feel?
- What happened in the end?
- How did you feel in the end?

B ▶ 12.8 Listen to a man talk about an experience. Was it exciting or frightening? What happened?

C Listen again and tick the key phrases you hear.

key phrases
This happened in [time/place] when I was (age).
One day, … Then, … After that, …
I felt [excited/afraid/frightened] …
In the end, …
It was (one of) the most [exciting/frightening] experiences I've ever had.

D Work in groups and take turns. One student: talk about your experience. Use the key phrases and your notes to help. Other students: listen and ask two questions about each event.

writeback a story

5A Before he talked about his experience, the man made some notes. Look at the notes below and number the events in the correct order.

> went for a walk   1
> one dog bit my arm
> didn't move, didn't look at the dogs
> remembered advice
> dogs ran towards me
> heard some dogs
> realised I didn't know where I was
> dogs jumped and barked

B Work in pairs and compare your answers.

C Use your notes from Exercise 4A and write about your experience in 80–100 words. Remember to use some of the key phrases to help.

12.5 ◀◀ LOOKBACK

OUTDOOR ACTIVITIES

1A What are the activities? Add the vowels.
1 g_ tr_kk_ng
2 r_d_ an _l_ph_nt
3 sw_m _n a r_v_r
4 cl_mb a m__nt__n
5 g_ sc_b_ d_v_ng
6 t_k_ a b__t d_wn the N_l_
7 w_tch a pl_y __td__rs
8 g_ f_sh_ng
9 sw_m _n a th_rm_l sp_
10 cl_mb a v_lc_n_
11 w_tch b_rds
12 r_d_ a h_rs_

B Work in pairs and discuss.
1 Which activities above can you do in your country? Where can you do them?
2 Which activities above do you think are fun/boring/exciting?
3 Which activities above do you want to do/try? Why?

PRESENT PERFECT

2A Write the sentences in full.
1 I / never / eat / fish eyes.
2 I / never / go to / an art gallery.
3 I / never / see / a sunrise.
4 I / never / drive / a Mercedes.
5 I / never / drink / tea with milk for breakfast.
6 I / never / play / golf.
7 I / never / cook / dinner for my parents.
8 I / never / speak / English on the phone.
9 I / never / be / to an outdoor festival.
10 I / never / hear / Oasis live.

B Change the last part of each sentence so that it is true for you.
I've never eaten cabbage.
I've never been to an art gallery, but I'd like to.

C Work in pairs and compare your answers.

PRESENT PERFECT AND PAST SIMPLE

3A Complete the questions. Use the correct form of the verb in brackets.
Have you ever …
1 _ridden_ a horse? (ride)
2 _____ an overnight train? (take)
3 _____ in a small plane? (fly)
4 _____ across a river? (swim)
5 _____ a long distance? (cycle)
6 _____ on a train? (sleep)
7 _____ a mountain? (climb)

B Work in pairs and take turns. Ask and answer the questions in Exercise 3A and ask follow-up questions.
A: Have you ever … ?
B: Yes, I have.
A: Oh, when was that?

PREPOSITIONS

4A Look at the word webs and cross out the place/thing which does not go with the preposition.

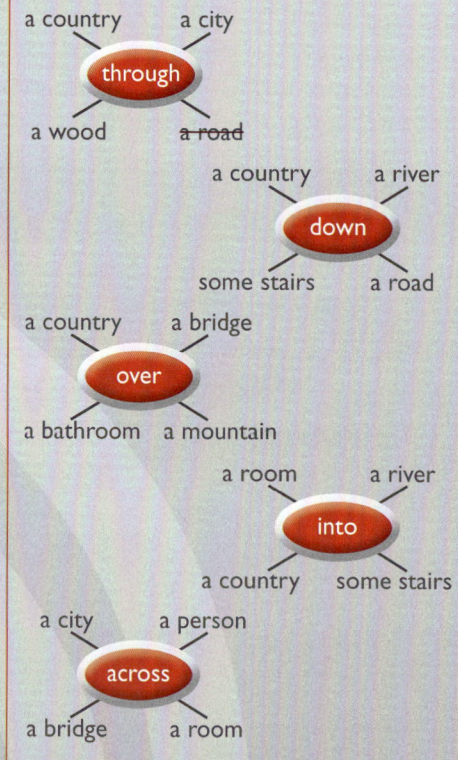

a country — a city
 \ /
 through
 / \
a wood — a road

a country — a river
 \ /
 down
 / \
some stairs — a road

a country — a bridge
 \ /
 over
 / \
a bathroom — a mountain

a room — a river
 \ /
 into
 / \
a country — some stairs

a city — a person
 \ /
 across
 / \
a bridge — a room

B Work in pairs. Student A: choose one of the prepositions. Say three things that can come after it. Student B: guess the preposition.
A: A country, a building, a bridge
B: Over?

ADJECTIVES

5A Unjumble the letters and find six adjectives below.
pypha = happy
1 dupor
2 xeectid
3 fiarda
4 onreuvs
5 amebearrssd
6 freghtinde

B Find five more words from Unit 12. Write them as jumbled words.

C Work in pairs. Exchange papers and unjumble the words.

TELEPHONING

6A Complete the telephone conversation.
A: Hello, the Learn English Centre.
B: Hello, ¹_____ Sofia Mitsotakis. ²_____ my teacher, Rachel, please?
A: Just a moment. ³_____ check … I'm afraid she's in class at the moment. ⁴_____ in about half an hour?
B: Oh, that's difficult. ⁵_____ a message for her?
A: Sure. Go ahead.
B: Could you ⁶_____ me this afternoon?
A: Yes, could you ⁷_____ number?
B: It's 0853 58230.
A: Fine. ⁸_____ her to call you. And it's Sofia … ?
B: Mitsotakis. Thank you very much.

B Work in pairs and role-play the conversation. Student A: you want to speak to your English teacher. Phone the school. Student B: you are the receptionist. The teacher can't come to the phone. Continue the conversation with your ideas.

BBC VIDEO PODCAST
Watch people talking about recent experiences on ActiveBook or on the website.
Authentic BBC interviews
www.pearsonELT.com/speakout

IRREGULAR VERBS

VERB	PAST SIMPLE	PAST PARTICIPLE
be	was	been
become	became	become
begin	began	begun
bite	bit	bitten
blow	blew	blown
break	broke	broken
bring	brought	brought
build	built	built
buy	bought	bought
catch	caught	caught
choose	chose	chosen
come	came	come
cost	cost	cost
cut	cut	cut
do	did	done
draw	drew	drawn
drink	drank	drunk
drive	drove	driven
eat	ate	eaten
fall	fell	fallen
feel	felt	felt
find	found	found
fly	flew	flown
forget	forgot	forgotten
freeze	froze	frozen
get	got	got
give	gave	given
go	went	gone
grow	grew	grown
have	had	had
hear	heard	heard
hide	hid	hidden
hit	hit	hit
hold	held	held
hurt	hurt	hurt
keep	kept	kept
know	knew	know
learn	learned/learnt	learned/learnt
leave	left	left

VERB	PAST SIMPLE	PAST PARTICIPLE
lend	lent	lent
let	let	let
lie	lay	lain
lose	lost	lost
make	made	made
mean	meant	meant
meet	met	met
pay	paid	paid
put	put	put
read	read	read
ride	rode	ridden
ring	rang	rung
run	ran	run
say	said	said
see	saw	seen
sell	sold	sold
send	sent	sent
shine	shone	shone
show	showed	shown
shut	shut	shut
sing	sang	sung
sit	sat	sat
sleep	slept	slept
smell	smelled/smelt	smelled/smelt
speak	spoke	spoken
spend	spent	spent
spill	spilled/spilt	spilled/spilt
stand	stood	stood
swim	swam	swum
take	took	taken
teach	taught	taught
tell	told	told
think	thought	thought
throw	threw	thrown
understand	understood	understood
wake	woke	woken
wear	wore	worn
win	won	won
write	wrote	written

7 LANGUAGE BANK

GRAMMAR

7.1 comparatives

adjective		comparative	rule
one-syllable adjectives	cold	colder	+ -er
some two-syllable adjectives	quiet	quieter	
adjectives: ending in -e	large	larger	+ -r
ending in -y	noisy	noisier	y + -ier
ending in a consonant + vowel + consonant	hot	hotter	double the final consonant
many two-syllable adjectives	boring	more boring	more + adjective
all longer adjectives	expensive	more expensive	
irregular adjectives	good	better	
	bad	worse	

Use comparatives (+ *than*) to compare things and people.
Use *than* not *that* with comparatives: *A restaurant is quieter **than** a disco.* NOT *A restaurant is quieter that a disco.*

7.2 superlatives

adjective	comparative	superlative	rule
cold	colder	the coldest	*the* + -est
nice	nicer	the nicest	*the* + -st
friendly	friendlier	the friendliest	*the y* + -iest
big	bigger	the biggest	double the final consonant
boring	more boring	the most boring	*the most* + adjective
interesting	more interesting	the most interesting	
good	better	the best	
bad	worse	the worst	

Use superlatives to talk about the number one thing in a group: *Maria's spelling is **the best in the class**.*
Note: The spelling rules for superlatives are the same as for comparatives.

7.3 asking for/giving directions

Go	straight on. /ahead.	
	down/past	the High Street. /the bank.
Turn	left/right	into East Avenue.
Take	the first/second/third	left. /right.
It's	on the left/right.	

Use imperatives (e.g. *turn*, *take*, *go*) to give directions.
In speaking, it is also possible to add *You*: **You** *go past the cinema and turn left.*
To ask for directions, use *Can you tell me the way to* + place: **Can you tell me the way to** *the sports centre?*
When speaking, check information by repeating what you hear: *The **third** right? So, I take the **next** left?*
Correct information by stressing the correction: *No, the **first** right. No, the next **right**.*

128

PRACTICE

7.1

A Write the comparative of the adjectives.

1. fast — *faster*
2. close — _____
3. big — _____
4. beautiful — _____
5. easy — _____
6. cheap — _____
7. important — _____
8. happy — _____

B Complete the sentences with comparatives. Use the adjectives in brackets to help.

1. A café is *quieter* than a nightclub. (quiet)
2. Travelling by train is _____ _____ flying. (slow)
3. A nightclub is _____ _____ a café. (noisy)
4. It's _____ in India _____ in England. (hot)
5. Eating at a café is _____ _____ eating in a restaurant. (cheap)
6. The weather is _____ in autumn _____ in summer. (bad)

7.2

A Write the superlative of the adjectives.

1. great — *the greatest*
2. quiet — _____
3. comfortable — _____
4. close — _____
5. noisy — _____
6. cheap — _____
7. interesting — _____
8. hot — _____
9. fast — _____
10. crowded — _____

B Complete the sentences. Use the superlative of the adjectives in the box.

| ~~long~~ busy big high good old deep popular |

1. *The longest* bridge in the world is the Pearl Bridge in Japan. It's 1,991 metres.
2. _____ tourist destination in Europe is Disneyland Paris. Over twelve million people visit it in a year.
3. _____ and _____ lake in the world is Lake Baikal, in southern Siberia, Russia. It's 1,600 metres deep and over twenty-five million years old.
4. _____ jungle (rainforest) in the world is the Amazon. It's four million square kilometres.
5. _____ mountain in the USA is Mount McKinley. It's 6,194 metres. _____ view is at the top.
6. _____ train station in the world is the Shinjuku Station in Tokyo. Over three million people use it every day and it has over 200 exits.

7.3

A Read the conversation. Add six more missing words.

A: Excuse ^me^. Can you tell me way to the beach?

B: Yes, you right at the cinema. Then go straight for about five minutes.

A: Five minutes?

B: Yes, and then turn left Menier Avenue and then take second street on right. I think it's Grand Avenue. You can see the beach straight ahead.

A: Thank you very much.

8 LANGUAGE BANK

GRAMMAR

8.1 Present continuous

+	I	'm	having	a great time.
	He/She/It	's	sitting	on the balcony.
	You/We/They	're	waiting	for a train.
−	I	'm not	enjoying	this food.
	He/She/It	isn't	working	at the moment.
	You/We/They	aren't	doing	anything.

?	Am	I	leaving?	Yes,	I	am.
					you/we/they	are.
	Are	you/we/they		No,	I	'm not.
					you/we/they	aren't.
	Is	he/she/it	working?	Yes,	he/she/it	is.
				No,		isn't.

Use the present continuous to speak about something happening now/at this moment.

In speaking, usually use the contracted form: **I am not** = I'm not. NOT ~~I am not~~.

In the negative, also use: He's **not** working. They'**re not** doing anything.

Spelling -ing

Most verbs + -ing	wait do	waiting doing
Verbs ending in -e, ~~e~~ + -ing	write take	writing taking
Most verbs ending in a consonant–vowel–consonant, double the final consonant	swim run	swimming running

8.2 Present simple and present continuous

Mario often	wears	a jacket and tie.
Now he	's wearing	jeans and a T-shirt.

What	do	you	do?	I'm a police officer.
	are		doing?	I'm writing down your number!

Use the present simple to talk about habits or routines: **We often watch** DVDs on Friday evenings.

Also use it to talk about things which are always true or true for a long time: **Elinor works** in the city centre.

Use the present continuous to speak about something happening at this moment: Sorry, I can't chat now. **I'm watching** a new DVD.

8.3 Asking for a recommendation

What do you recommend?	
Do you think I'd like	this DVD? it?

Giving a recommendation

What kind of	films	do you like?
I think I don't think	you'd like	Gold River. it.
There's a good	film	called Impact.

130

PRACTICE

8.1

A Write the -ing form of the verbs.
1. live _____
2. go _____
3. come _____
4. put _____
5. feel _____
6. make _____
7. get _____
8. stand _____
9. drive _____
10. meet _____

B Write a phone conversation using the prompts below.

Bruno: Hi, Gerald. It's me. you / sleep? *Are you sleeping?*
Gerald: No, I'm at work. I / read.
Bruno: What / you / read?
Gerald: I / read some reports. What / you / do?
Bruno: Karl and I / play cards and listen / to music.
Gerald: Hey, why / you / not / work?
Bruno: I / take a break.
Gerald: Uh-oh. I / talk on the speaker phone. The boss / listen.
Bruno: you / joke?
Boss: No, he / not / joke!

8.2

A Complete the sentences with the verbs in the box in the correct form.

> wear (x2)   listen to (x2)   write   have (x2)
> phone   stay (x2)   watch (x2)

1. I ___wear___ glasses but I ___'m not wearing___ them now.
2. I don't normally _____ TV, but I _____ it now.
3. We usually _____ salad for lunch, but today we _____ sandwiches.
4. I _____ my mother an email at the moment – usually I _____ her.
5. We often _____ classical music in the office, but today we _____ pop.
6. He usually _____ in a five-star hotel, but now he _____ in a self-catering apartment.

B Complete the questions with the verbs in brackets. Use the present simple or the present continuous.

1. ___Do___ you ___study___ English every day? (study)
2. _____ you _____ English now? (study)
3. _____ your best friend _____ every day? (work)
4. _____ your best friend _____ at the moment? (work)
5. _____ your teacher _____ blue today? (wear)
6. _____ your teacher often _____ blue? (wear)
7. _____ you usually _____ grammar exercises alone? (do)
8. _____ you _____ this exercise alone? (do)
9. _____ you _____ to English shows/music a lot? (listen to)
10. _____ you _____ to English shows/music at the moment? (listen to)

8.3

A Read the conversation and correct the mistakes.

Ines: I'd like to watch a good DVD. What recommend?
Pedro: What films you like?
Ines: Action films, mostly. Yes, and comedies.
Pedro: It's a good film called *Rush Hour*.
Ines: Who in it?
Pedro: Jackie Chan and Chris Tucker.
Ines: What's about?
Pedro: Jackie Chan is a detective and he comes to New York to help a friend.
Ines: You think I like?
Pedro: Yeah, I think so. I'll bring it tomorrow and you can borrow it.

9 LANGUAGE BANK

GRAMMAR

9.1 articles

no article		
usually use no article	before plural nouns when we speak in general	I like cats, but I don't like dogs. Sweets are bad for you.
	before cities and countries	Shanghai is in China. I went to Russia last year.
	in some phrases	go by car/train/bus/taxi go on foot go home, go to work/school be at home/work/school have breakfast/dinner/lunch

a/an		
usually use a/an	before singular nouns	It's a Ferrari. I've got a younger brother.
	before jobs	My sister's a teacher.

the		
usually use the	before nouns when there's only one	The president visited us last year. Can you close the door, please?
	in some phrases	In the morning/afternoon/evening at the weekend in the town/city centre on the right/left

With countries, use *the* with groups: **the** United States, **the** United Arab Emirates.

With times, use *in the* morning/afternoon/evening but use *at night* (no article).

9.2 can/can't, have to/don't have to

I/You/He/ She/We/They	can	use	the bikes for free.
	can't	park	in the city centre.
I/You/We/ They	have to	pay	ten euros.
He/She/It	has to		
I/You/We/ They	don't have to	pay	anything – it's free.
He/She/It	doesn't have to		

Use *can* when something is OK/permitted.
Use *can't* when something is not OK/not permitted.
Use *have to* when something is necessary/obligatory.
Use *don't have to* when something is not necessary/obligatory.
Compare:
*You **can't** come to the party.* (You didn't get an invitation.)
*You **don't have to** come to the party.* (You got an invitation, but it's OK to stay at home.)

9.3 apologising

Apologising		Responding
Sorry I'm late. I'm really/very sorry. I'm terribly/so sorry. I feel bad/terrible about this.	+	That's OK. No problem. Don't worry about it. No, really. It's fine.
I'm afraid Sorry, but	(+ reason) I missed the bus. I didn't hear my alarm clock. I lost my keys.	–	I don't believe you. Don't let it happen again.

When speaking:
- to emphasise how sorry you are, use an adverb *so* + *sorry*: *I'm terribly/so sorry*.
- to show how it makes you feel, use *feel* + adjective: *I feel terrible about the mess!*
- reply with *No, really. It's fine* when someone apologises again: **A:** *I'm so sorry.* **B:** *Don't worry about it.* **A:** *But I feel terrible …* **B:** *No, really. It's fine.*
- Use *Don't let it happen again* only when you're really angry.

PRACTICE

9.1

A Complete the text with *a/an*, *the* or no article (–).

Lucio is from ¹ _Italy_ and he's ² _____ doctor. He was born and grew up in ³ _____ Venice but now he lives just outside ⁴ _____ small town in the south. Every day, early in ⁵ _____ morning, he leaves ⁶ _____ home and drives to his clinic in ⁷ _____ town centre. He usually has ⁸ _____ lunch with ⁹ _____ colleagues and sometimes teaches in ¹⁰ _____ afternoon. At ¹¹ _____ weekend, he often visits his brother's family. They live in the countryside, about two hours away by ¹² _____ car.

B Complete the sentences with *a/an*, *the* or no article (–).

1 I think — cars are safer than motorbikes.
2 I'd like ____ scooter for my birthday.
3 It's the best airline in ____ world.
4 I rode ____ bike to school when I was younger.
5 I hate ____ boats. I'm always sick!
6 I live in a small village and walk to ____ train station every day.

C Read the conversation. Find and correct six mistakes with *the*. (Two are correct.)

Pedro: Mrs Thorpe. Where can I buy **the** dictionary?

Mrs T: There's **the** bookshop in South Street. I think they sell **the** dictionaries. What kind do you want?

Pedro: I need **the** English–Spanish dictionary for my English class. **The** teacher said we have to get one. **The** only problem is that **the** books are very expensive here.

Mrs T: Maybe you can borrow one. Does your school have **the** library?

Pedro: Yes, it does. Good idea. I can ask there.

9.2

A Look at signs A–F. What do they mean? Underline the correct alternative.

1 Motorbikes *don't have to/can't* go here. They *have to/don't have to* go on another road.
2 You *can/have to* park here for free. You *can't/don't have to* pay for fifteen minutes parking.
3 Bikes *have to/can* keep left. People on foot *don't have to/can't* walk on the left.
4 You *can/can't* catch the bus here. You *have to/don't have to* wait more than ten minutes.
5 You *can't/don't have to* ride your bike. You *can/have to* get off and walk.
6 You *can/can't* take a taxi here. You *can/can't* park here.

B Complete the conversations. Use the correct form of *can/can't*, *have to/don't have to* and the verb in bold.

Conversation 1

A: You ¹_have to wear_ (wear) a jacket and tie to this dinner. It's a very formal party.

B: But it's so hot!

A: Well, you ² _____ (wear) your light jacket.

Conversation 2

A: You ³ _____ (come) to the meeting. It's not very important.

B: That's good because I ⁴ _____ (come) – I'm too busy.

Conversation 3

A: I ⁵ _____ (get) a birthday present for Sandra. I completely forgot yesterday.

B: It's OK. You ⁶ _____ (get) anything. I bought her a present from both of us.

A: Thanks! What did you buy?

9.3

A Read the conversation and correct the six mistakes.

Teacher: Can I have your homework?

Student: Oh, I really sorry. I'm afraid of left it at home.

Teacher: Don't worry it. Did you do it?

Student: Yes, of course.

Teacher: Which part did you think was difficult?

Student: Sorry, both I don't remember.

Teacher: Did you *really* do it?

Student: Er … I afraid I forgot to do it.

Teacher: Don't left it happen again!

10 LANGUAGE BANK

GRAMMAR

10.1 be going to

+	I	'm	going to	be there	soon.
	He/She/It	's		eat	tonight.
	You/We/They	're		practise	tomorrow.
−	I	'm not			
	He/She/It	isn't			
	You/We/They	aren't			

Use *be going to* + verb to talk about plans and intentions: **I'm going to do** my homework **tonight**.

In the negative, also use *is/are not going to*: We **aren't going to go** to the concert.

With *be going to* + *go*, you don't need to repeat *go*: She **'s going** (to go) to the post office.

It is possible to use *be going to* with future time phrases, e.g. *tomorrow, soon, this weekend, next week, next month, next year, in two years*. **In two weeks** (time) **I'm going to be** on holiday!

?	Am	I	going to	speak to Eva today?
	Is	he/she		
	Are	you/we/they		

+	Yes,	I	am.
		he/she/it	is.
		we/you/they	are.
−	No,	I	'm not.
		he/she/it	isn't.
		we/you/they	aren't.

would like to

| + | I/You/He/She/It/We/They | would 'd | like to | go. |
| − | | wouldn't | | |

| ? | Would | I you he she it we they | like to | drink some tea? |

| + | Yes, | I you he she it we they | would. |
| − | No, | | wouldn't. |

Use *I'd like to* + infinitive to talk about what you want to do: *It's hot.* **I'd like to go** *for a swim.*

You can also use *want to* + infinitive for the same idea: *I* **want to go** *to the gym.*

Note: *I'd like to* is more polite than *I want*.

10.2 will/might (not)/won't

| + | I/You/He/She/It/We/They | 'll (will) | go shopping. visit some friends. |
| − | | might might not won't (will not) | |

| ? | Will | I/you/he/she/it/we/they | win? |

| + | Yes, | I/you/he/she/it/we/they | will. |
| − | No, | | won't. |

Use *might* + infinitive to predict the future if you are not certain: *I* **might see** *Yuki tonight* (= it's possible, but I'm not sure).

It is also possible to use *will, might, might not,* and *won't* with *there*: *I think* **there will be** *a lot of people at the party.*

Use *will* + infinitive and *won't* + infinitive to predict the future when you are certain about it.

10.3 making suggestions

How about	going	to the zoo?
What about		
Why don't I/you/we	go	internet shopping?
Let's	cook	something.

Use *How/What about* + verb + *-ing* in questions: **What about** having lunch now?
Use *Why don't* + subject + verb in questions: **Why don't we watch** a film?
Use *Let's* + verb in positive sentences: **Let's go** to the beach.

responding to suggestions

| + | Great/Brilliant! (That's a) good idea. Sounds interesting. OK. |
| − | I don't really feel like going. That/It doesn't sound very good. That might be a problem. |

PRACTICE

10.1

A Complete the sentences with the correct form of *be going to*. Use the verbs in brackets.

1 I _____ the cinema tonight. (go)
2 We _____ a flat next weekend. (look at)
3 _____ ready in time? (you / be)
4 We _____. (not wait)
5 They _____ a new car. (buy)
6 When _____ to Rome? (Steve / go)

B Underline the correct alternative.

1 I *'d like to go / 'm going* to the theatre, but there are no more tickets.
2 I *'d like to go / 'm going* to a concert tonight. I've got the tickets here.
3 We *'d like to / 're going to* buy a bigger flat, but we don't have enough money.
4 I *'d like to / 'm going to* take a trip to Zurich tomorrow. My train leaves at 7a.m.

C Complete the sentences with the words in the box.

like (x2)   don't   'd (x2)   would (x2)   want

A: Would you ¹_____ to go to the party?
B: Yes, I ²_____, but I've got too much work.
A: Would you ³_____ to dance?
B: No, thanks. I ⁴_____ like to sit down for a minute!
A: What ⁵_____ you like to do on your birthday tomorrow?
B: I don't know, I ⁶_____ want to think about it. I feel quite old!
A: Do you ⁷_____ to have dinner with me tonight?
B: I ⁸_____ love to!

10.2

A Complete the conversation with *'ll*, *will*, *won't* or *might*.

A: Oh, no. The dog ran away again!
B: Don't worry – he ¹_____ come back.
A: Are you sure he ²_____?
B: OK, he ³_____ not come back today – that's possible. But I'm sure he ⁴_____ come back tomorrow.
A: I don't believe you! He ⁵_____ come back. We ⁶_____ never see him again – I'm sure.
B: Oh, look … Here he is now!

B Circle the two correct alternatives.

1 He (will) / (won't) / might eat it – I'm sure!
2 It *might / 'll / won't* rain, so bring an umbrella.
3 There *might not / won't / might* be enough time to finish the whole film, so let's not start.
4 I *might not / 'll / won't* go by train. It's quicker by car.
5 She *might / won't / 'll* phone tomorrow so please take a message.
6 We *might / 'll / won't* be late, so don't wait for us.

10.3

A Put the words from the box in the correct places in the conversation.

~~about~~   problem   idea   don't   like   how   have

Sam: I'm tired. How ∧*about* having a break now?
Jim: I don't feel stopping.
Sam: Oh, come on! Let's a coffee.
Jim: Why *you* make some coffee? I'll go on working.
Sam: That's a good. about a sandwich?
Jim: No thanks – I want to finish this.
Sam: Mmm. That might be a. You work, I'll have lunch.
Jim: It's not a problem for *me*!

11 LANGUAGE BANK

GRAMMAR

11.1 should/shouldn't

+	I/you/he/she/it/we/they	should	go to bed.
			drink lots of water.
−		shouldn't	take antibiotics.
			work.

| ? | Should | I/you/he/she/it/we/they | go | to the doctor? | Yes, | I/you/he/she/it/we/they | should. |
| | | | | | No, | | shouldn't. |

Use *should* + infinitive to give advice: You **should take** an aspirin
and to recommend: You **should see** that film.
Note: You **should try** this soup. NOT ~~You should to try this soup.~~

11.2 adverbs

	adjective	adverb
Most adjectives, add -ly	bad	badly
	loud	loudly
	careful	carefully
Adjectives ending in -y, -y + -ily	easy	easily
	angry	angrily
Adjectives ending in -le, change to -ly	terrible	terribly
Irregular adverbs	good	well
	fast	fast NOT ~~fastly~~
	hard (= difficult)	hard NOT ~~hardly~~
	early	early
	late	late

Use adverbs of manner to say how you do something: I can swim **well**. She spoke **quietly**.

Use adverbs of time to say when you did something: I went to bed **early**. She had lunch **late**.

Use adverbs with verbs: He **drives** badly.
BUT with *be* and *feel*, use adjectives: The film **was** terrible. I **feel** terrible.
Use adjectives with nouns: He's a bad **driver**.

Adverbs often go after the verb: I **arrived** early. She **drove** quickly to the shops.
or after the verb phrase: I **started work** early. She **drove her car** quickly.
or at the end: I **arrived** at work **early**. She **drove** to the shops **quickly**.

11.3 offering to help

Problems	Offers		Thanking	Responses
I can't lift this case	I'll	do it.	Thanks a lot.	You're welcome.
It's hot in here	Let me	try.	That's kind of you.	No problem.
	Shall I	do it?	Thanks. I'm very grateful.	That's OK.
		try?		

Use *I'll* (NOT ~~I will~~), *Let me* and *Shall I* + infinitive to offer help.

LB 11

PRACTICE

11.1

A Complete questions 1–6. Then match them with replies a)–f).

1. I don't have much time. _Should I_ send Kirsten an email? _d)_
2. Ben doesn't like the colour of his mobile. _____ get a new one?
3. Look at my hair – it's a mess! _____ get a haircut?
4. Some students never say anything in class. _____ speak more?
5. My daughter wants to travel in South America. _____ learn Spanish?
6. There are so many words we don't know. _____ buy an electronic dictionary?

a) Yes, you should. It's too long.
b) Yes, they should. It's important to practise.
c) No, he shouldn't. The old one is fine.
d) No, you shouldn't. Phone her – it's quicker.
e) Yes, she should if she has enough time.
f) Yes, you should get an English–English one.

B Complete the sentences with *should* or *shouldn't* and a verb from the box.

~~get~~ go have stay try wear change

1. My camera's very old. I _should get_ a new one.
2. You _____ this drink. It's delicious!
3. Do you think I _____ my money here or at the airport?
4. You _____ black. I think it doesn't look good on you – sorry!
5. They _____ by taxi. It's too expensive.
6. She looks tired. She _____ a holiday.
7. We _____ out in the sun too long. We'll get sunburnt.

11.2

A Complete the sentences. Use the adjective or adverb form of the word in brackets.

1. The teacher was very _____. She spoke to the students _____. (angry)
2. She dances _____. She's such a _____ dancer. (beautiful)
3. I passed the exam _____. It was _____. (easy)
4. Shhh – be _____. The baby's sleeping. We have to talk _____. (quiet)
5. She's a _____ teacher. She teaches _____. (good)
6. I sing _____. I'm a _____ singer. (terrible)

B Complete the story. Use the adverb forms of the adjectives in the box.

~~early~~ late easy quick angry slow

The other morning, I woke up ¹_early_ because the neighbours were shouting ²_____. I didn't want to stay at home, so I made some breakfast ³_____ and ran out of the door to work. I forgot to take an umbrella and it started raining so I got very wet. I got to the station at 7.50 and caught the eight o'clock train ⁴_____. I was surprised when I looked round because the train was empty. Because of the rain, the train went very ⁵_____ so I arrived at the office ⁶_____. There was no one there. Then I realised that it was Sunday, and I didn't have to work!

11.3

A Complete the five conversations below. Use the verbs in brackets to help.

Conversation 1
A: I can't find the information anywhere.
B: I'_____ _____ on the computer. (check)

Conversation 2
A: I don't understand this homework.
B: _____ me _____ a look. (have)

Conversation 3
A: My hands are full. I can't carry all these things.
B: _____ I _____ something for you? (carry)

Conversation 4
A: The radio is too loud.
B: _____ I _____ it down? (turn)

Conversation 5
A: The top on this bottle is too tight.
B: _____ me try to _____ it. (open)

137

12 LANGUAGE BANK

GRAMMAR

12.1 present perfect

Use the present perfect to talk about past experiences in your life. Usually you don't know or say *when* exactly these things happened.

+	I/You/We/They	've	climbed	a volcano.
	He/She/It	's	travelled	around the world.
−	I/You/We/They	haven't	worked	in different countries.
	He/She/It	hasn't	studied	lots of languages.

Ever = 'in your life'. In the negative you can use *never*: *I've **never** played golf.*

?	Have	I/you/we/they	(ever) worked	in Australia?	Yes, No,	I/we/you/they	have. haven't.
	Has	he/she/it			Yes, No,	he/she/it	has. hasn't.

Make the present perfect with *have/has* + past participle.

For regular verbs, the past participles are the same as the past simple.

Many common verbs have an irregular past participle form. Look at the list on page 127.

I/You/We/They	've	been to	the Bahamas.
He/She/It	's	seen	Mount Fuji.

Go has two past participles: *been* and *gone*:

*She's **gone** to India.* = She went there and she's there now.

*She's **been** to India.* = She went there in the past and she came back.

12.2 present perfect or past simple

Use the present perfect to talk about past experiences in your life. You don't say exactly *when*: *I've travelled in South America.*

Use the past simple if you say *when* something happened: *I travelled in Poland in May 2008.*

When speaking, it is possible to start a conversation by asking a question in the present perfect and then asking about more details in the past simple:

A: **Have** you **ever been** to the USA?
B: Yes, I have. I **went** there two years ago.
A: **Did** you **like** it?
B: Yes, it **was** great!

I've travelled in South America.

in South America

The past — — — — — — — — — — — — — NOW

I travelled in Poland in May 2008.

went to Poland

The past — — — — — May 2008 — — — — NOW

12.3 telephoning

Calling a friend	Hi, Philippe. It's Debbie. Is Lise there?
Calling a business	Hello. This is Carla Rimini. Could I speak to Alan Jones, please?
Calling back	Could you ring back? Just ask him/her to call me. I'll call you back.
Leaving/taking a message	Could I leave a message for him/her? Could you give me the number? Let me check that.

Use *It's* + name (informal) or *This is* + name (formal) NOT ~~I am~~: Hello, **this is** Ali Hassan.

PRACTICE

12.1

A Write sentences in the present perfect.
1. you / ever / eat / Japanese food?
2. I / eat / Japanese food two or three times
3. we / never / sleep / in a hotel before
4. they / drive / across Europe many times
5. he / ever / go / to England?
6. she / have / three husbands
7. I / spend / too much money
8. She / learn / Arabic, Spanish and Chinese
9. you / ever / climb / a mountain?
10. My parents / never / use / an iPod

B Correct ten mistakes in the conversation.
A: You have ever been to Australia?
B: No, I have. And you?
A: Yes, I've.
B: And have you gone to China, too?
A: No, but I been to Korea.
B: You've travel in many countries in your life …
A: Yes, I has. I've meeted a lot of people and I've try a lot of interesting food.
B: But you haven't learn to speak English perfectly!
A: Not yet …

12.2

A Read the email and underline the correct alternatives.

Hi Renata,

Thanks for the email. Lucky you … going to Italy next month! You asked me about Venice. Yes, ¹*I've been/went* there. ²*I've been/went* there for a long weekend last year. ³It *has been/was* beautiful. ⁴*I've loved / loved* all the bridges and old squares. ⁵*I've also visited/also visited* Rome. ⁶We *have been/were* there in 2006. It's busier than Venice, but I know you like old buildings and churches, so maybe you'd like Rome better. ⁷*I've never travelled/never travelled* in the Italian countryside but my friend Emily ⁸*has driven/drove* around the south and she says it's lovely, but very hot at that time of year. Anyway, I'm sure you'll have a great time! Send me some photos.

Simone

B Complete the sentences using the prompts in brackets.
1. *Have you seen* Gangs of New York? (you / see)
   Yes, I ____saw____ it a few years ago.
2. _____ Sarah? (you / meet)
   Yes, we _____ last year.
3. _____ to Spain? (Lea / go)
   Yes, she _____ there last summer.
4. _____ an accident on his motorbike? (Paolo / ever have)
   Yes, he _____ a small accident a month ago.
5. _____ Anna Karenina? (you / read)
   Yes, I _____ it at university.
6. _____ school? (your children / finish)
   Yes, they _____ a long time ago.

12.3

A Complete Judy's sentences. Then write the correct response from Dan.

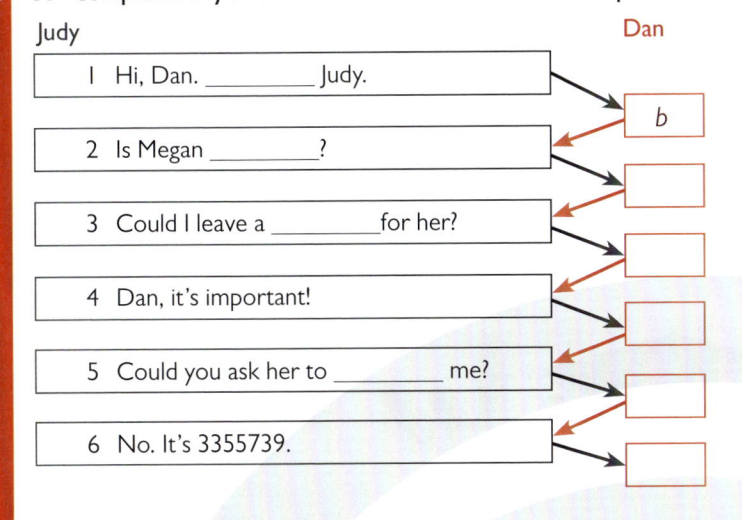

Judy
1. Hi, Dan. _____ Judy.
2. Is Megan _____?
3. Could I leave a _____ for her?
4. Dan, it's important!
5. Could you ask her to _____ me?
6. No. It's 3355739.

Dan
1. b
2. ___
3. ___
4. ___
5. ___
6. ___

a) 3355739. OK, got it. I'll tell her.
b) Oh, hi Judy.
c) No, she's gone out somewhere.
d) Has she got your number?
e) Let me just look … OK, I've got one.
f) A message … ? Oh, I can't find a pen. Could you ring me back?

PHOTO BANK

COUNTRIES AND NATIONALITIES

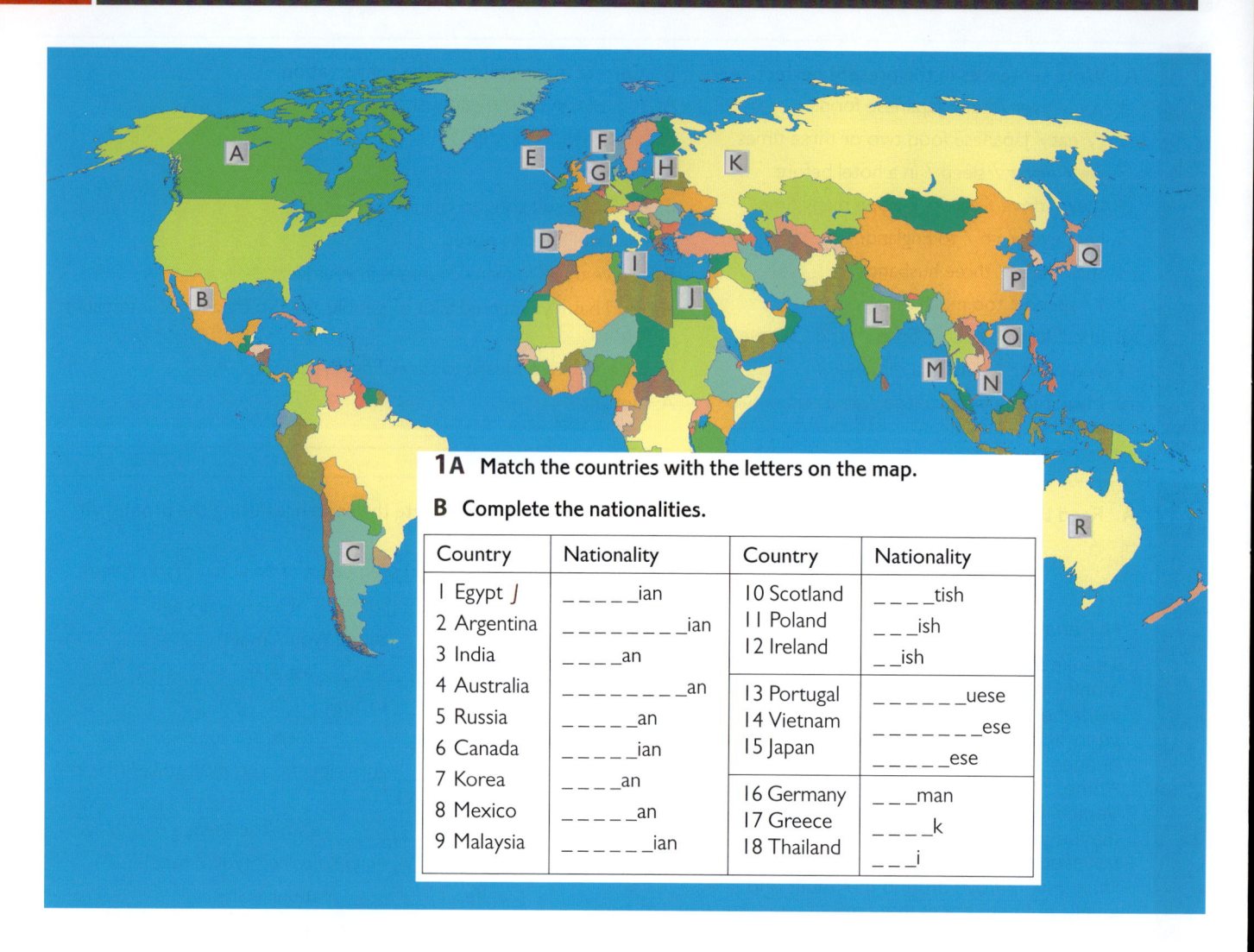

1A Match the countries with the letters on the map.

B Complete the nationalities.

Country	Nationality	Country	Nationality
1 Egypt J	_ _ _ _ ian	10 Scotland	_ _ _ tish
2 Argentina	_ _ _ _ _ _ _ ian	11 Poland	_ _ _ ish
3 India	_ _ _ an	12 Ireland	_ _ ish
4 Australia	_ _ _ _ _ _ _ an	13 Portugal	_ _ _ _ _ uese
5 Russia	_ _ _ _ an	14 Vietnam	_ _ _ _ _ _ ese
6 Canada	_ _ _ _ ian	15 Japan	_ _ _ _ ese
7 Korea	_ _ _ an	16 Germany	_ _ _ man
8 Mexico	_ _ _ _ an	17 Greece	_ _ _ _ k
9 Malaysia	_ _ _ _ _ ian	18 Thailand	_ _ _ i

EVERYDAY OBJECTS

1A Match the everyday objects with the photos.

B Complete the gaps with *a*, *an* or —.

1 *a* dictionary   A
2 _—_ stamps
3 ____ identity card
4 ____ sweets
5 ____ file
6 ____ tissues [pocket pack]
7 ____ umbrella
8 ____ glasses
9 ____ wallet
10 ____ comb
11 ____ driving licence
12 ____ coins
13 ____ chewing gum
14 ____ batteries
15 ____ credit card

140

JOBS

1A Match the jobs with the pictures.

B Complete the gaps with *a* or *an*.

1 ____ lawyer
2 ____ teacher
3 ____ accountant
4 ____ police officer
5 ____ engineer
6 ____ politician
7 ____ hairdresser
8 ____ shop assistant
9 ____ chef
10 ____ doctor
11 ____ receptionist
12 ____ nurse
13 ____ personal assistant (PA)
14 ____ waiter/waitress
15 ____ sportsman/sportswoman
16 ____ actor/actress
17 ____ businessman/businesswoman

PHOTO BANK

FAMILY

A Frank Jackson B Maggie Jackson

C Ann Barnes D John Barnes E Elizabeth Jackson F Robert Jackson

G Katy Barnes H Jake Barnes I Mark Jackson J Amy Jackson

1A Look at the family tree and write the people in the correct space below.

1 _____ are Jake's grandfather and grandmother.
2 _____ are Jake's father and mother (parents).
3 _____ is Elizabeth's husband.
4 _____ is John's wife.
5 _____ are Elizabeth and Robert's son and daughter.
6 _____ is Jake's sister.
7 _____ is Amy's brother.
8 _____ are Katy's aunt and uncle.
9 _____ are Mark's cousins.
10 _____ are Ann's nephew and niece.

B Choose one person from the family tree. Then use the words in the box to write how he/she is related to the other people.

father   mother   wife   husband   parents   grandfather grandmother   son   daughter   brother   sister   uncle aunt   cousin   niece   nephew

Robert is Maggie's son. He's Elizabeth's …

142

ROOMS AND FURNITURE

1A Match the names of the rooms and places with the photos.

1. garage
2. balcony
3. hall
4. kitchen
5. dining room
6. living room
7. stairs
8. home office
9. bedroom
10. bathroom
11. upstairs
12. downstairs

B Now label the items of the furniture using the words in the box below.

| armchair bath bed carpet cupboard |
| desk lamp plant rug shower sink |
| sofa table wardrobe washbasin |

2 Look at the pictures for thirty seconds. Then close your book and make a list of the furniture in each room.

PHOTO BANK

SHOPS

1 Match the names of the shops with the photos.

1 baker's
2 bookshop
3 butcher's
4 clothes shop
5 dry-cleaner's
6 electronics shop
7 greengrocer's
8 hairdresser's
9 internet café
10 pharmacy/chemist's
11 newsagent's
12 shoe shop
13 sports shop
14 supermarket

FOOD

1A Write countable (C) or uncountable (U) next to each word.

1 tomatoes
2 potatoes
3 onions
4 beans
5 peas
6 a cabbage
7 a lettuce
8 corn on the cob
9 a pepper
10 an orange
11 a pear
12 cake
13 crisps
14 biscuits
15 rolls
16 sugar
17 rice
18 pasta
19 cereal
20 herbs
21 spices
22 oil
23 yoghurt
24 beef
25 lamb
26 prawns

B Match the names of the food with the photos.

PHOTO BANK

APPEARANCE AND CLOTHES

1A Label the photos using the words in the box.

| tall   short   slim*   overweight** |
| bald   straight hair   curly hair |
| long hair   short hair |

* also use *thin*, but *slim* is more positive

** *fat* is also possible, but is very negative

B Match the names of the clothes with the photos.

1 socks
2 jeans
3 suit
4 jacket
5 trousers
6 shirt
7 tie
8 top
9 skirt
10 sweater
11 shorts
12 dress
13 T-shirt
14 coat

2 Write which words are adjectives (adj), uncountable nouns (U), countable singular nouns (C sing), countable plural nouns (C pl).

BODY PARTS

1 Match the names of the body parts with the photos.

1 arm
2 back
3 ear
4 eye
5 face
6 finger
7 foot
8 hand
9 head
10 knee
11 leg
12 elbow
13 neck
14 nose
15 shoulder
16 mouth
17 thumb
18 toe

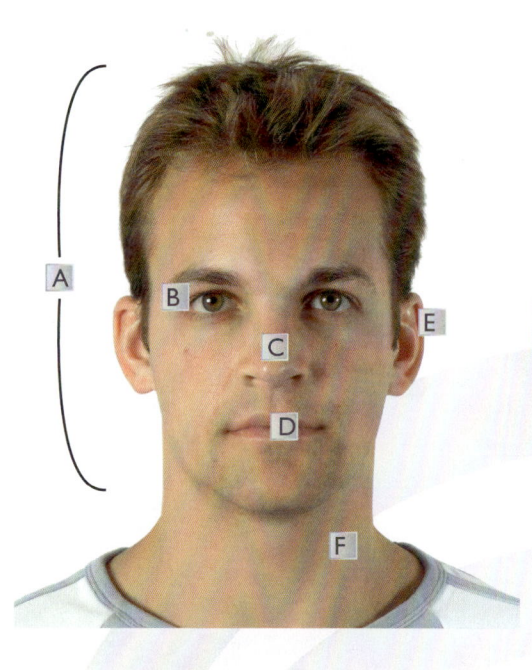

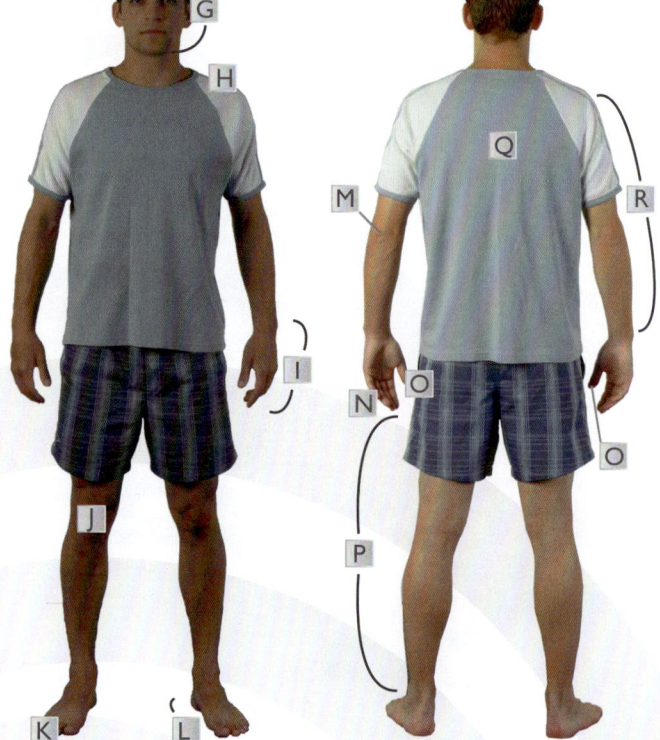

2 What do you have one, two, eight and ten of? Make a list.

1 = *head, face, nose …*

146

TRANSPORT

1 Match the types of the transport with the photos.

1. a bike
2. a boat
3. a bus
4. a car
5. a ferry
6. a helicopter
7. a lorry/a truck
8. a motorbike
9. a plane
10. a scooter
11. a ship
12. a taxi
13. a train
14. a tram
15. an underground/ a subway train
16. a van

2 Put the words into the following transport groups:

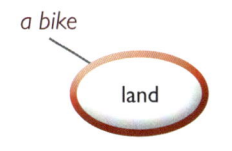

- land (*a bike*)
- sea
- air

COMMUNICATION BANK

9.2

7A Student B

Madrid
- 58 euros for 72 hours
- no public transport but free bus tour
- over 50 museums, and Madrid Fun Fair, Zoo, Aquarium

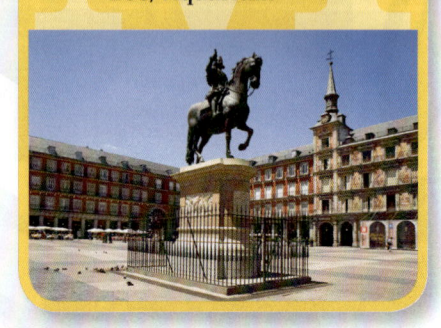

10.2

2C Student B

SURVIVE IN THE DESERT!

In the desert, the temperature can change a lot. It can be very hot in the day, up to 55°C and then go down to 10°C at night. In the day, try to stay out of the sun and always put something between your body and the hot ground. Don't sleep on the ground – your body will get too warm from the hot sand. Wear a hat and a shirt to cover your head and arms. Remember to use sun cream and you won't get sunburnt.

You need to stay cool so drink water every hour. If you have food but no water, don't eat or your body will use too much water to digest your food. Try not to move or travel in the day when it's really hot – you might sweat too much.

There are many different types of small animals in the desert, so always wear shoes and gloves and look when you walk or before you put your hands down anywhere. When you get up after sleeping, always check your shoes and clothes. You don't want to step on a snake!

9.1

6B Student B: look at the information about the Lightning Bug. Use a dictionary to check the meaning of any new words. Tell your partner about it. Why is it better than the Horseless Sulky?

- an American invented it in the 1930s
- it's completely safe – impossible to crash, it can't turn over
- there isn't any glass, only plastic windows
- it can stop faster than a car
- it can go up to 65 kilometres per hour

12.3

7B Student A: ask Student B for the telephone numbers. Answer Student B's questions.

A: *What's Sam's phone number?*
B: *It's … What's Ahmed's phone number?*
A: *It's …*

Sam	
Ahmed	5823031
Nina	
Chen	3662149
Simon	
Fatima	0870 1642513
Yuko	
Penny	00 281 5955427

8.1

5 Student A: Ask and answer questions to compare your picture with Student B's. Don't look at Student B's picture. Find eight differences in the pictures.

What's Mike doing? What's he wearing?

9.2

7A Student C

Prague
- 790 crowns (32 euros) for 4 days
- free entry to over 50 museums and sights
- unlimited travel on Prague transport system (for an extra 330 crowns or 13 euros)

7.3

6C Student A: check this information. Read it to Student B.
1. Kris lives in North Road.
2. His house is five minutes from here.
3. It's on the left.

D Now listen to Student B. Use the information below to correct any mistakes.
1. The bank's in East Street.
2. It's on the right.
3. Take the number 9 bus.

COMMUNICATION BANK

11.3

6B Student B

Problem 1
I'm really tired.

Problem 2
I can't see the whiteboard. It's too dark in here.

Problem 3
I'm really thirsty, but I haven't got any money for a coffee.

9.1

6B Student A: look at the information about the Horseless Sulky. Use a dictionary to check the meaning of any new words. Tell your partner about it. Why is it better than the Lightning Bug?

- an Italian invented it in the 1930s
- it's easy to get into and out of
- it's easy to see things on the left and right
- it's easy to turn
- it can go up to 190 kilometres per hour

10.2

2C Student A

SURVIVE AT SEA!

Surviving at sea is difficult. The biggest problems are the weather, food and drink. In cold weather, try to stay dry and never sit on the bottom of the raft – there's usually water there and you'll get wet. In hot weather, wear a hat and a shirt to cover your head and arms. Remember to use sun cream and you won't get sunburnt.

Drinking water is the most important thing. With water only and no food, you can live for ten days or longer. Your body loses a lot of water when you sweat, so relax and try to sleep a lot, too. If you don't have water, don't eat because your body will use too much water to digest your food. Never drink seawater. It is too salty and you'll get thirsty.

In the open sea, fish is your most important food and it's also easy to catch. Most fish are safe to eat and you can drink water from fish eyes as well. But never put rubbish into the water – sharks might come! Try not to move around too much because you don't want to fall off the raft with sharks near.

11.3

6B Student A

Problem 1
It's cold in here.

Problem 2
This computer doesn't work.

Problem 3
It's too noisy. The music's too loud and I can't concentrate.

7.3

6C Student B: listen to Student A. Use the information below to correct any mistakes.
1 Kris lives in North Avenue.
2 His house is ten minutes from here.
3 It's on the right.

D Now check this information. Read it to Student A.
1 The bank's in West Street.
2 It's on the left.
3 Take the number 5 bus.

8.1

5 Student B: ask and answer questions to compare your picture with Student A's. Don't look at Student A's picture. Find eight differences in the pictures.

What's Mike doing? What's he wearing?

12.3

7B Student B: answer Student A's questions. Ask Student A for the telephone numbers.

A: What's Sam's phone number?
B: It's ... What's Ahmed's phone number?
A: It's ...

Sam	9240473
Ahmed	
Nina	7886301
Chen	
Simon	0463 3739912
Fatima	
Yuko	00 44 2816933
Penny	

9.2

7A Student A

'I love Amsterdam'

* 53 euros for 72 hours
* all public transport
* free entry to over 25 museums
* 2 free boat tours
* 1 free cup of coffee

AUDIO SCRIPTS

UNIT 7 Recording 2
M=Man W=Woman

M: So, how do you usually travel? By plane or train?
W: Train. I think travelling by train's more comfortable than flying. And I don't like flying.
M: I put 'plane' because flying is faster than going by train.
W: Not always! OK, next question. Where do you like to stay: in a hotel or a self-catering apartment?
M: In an apartment. And you?
W: In a hotel.
M: Oh. But a hotel is more expensive than an apartment!
W: Yeah, but it's more comfortable. Hmm …. next question. What do you prefer to do: go sightseeing or relax on a beach?
M: Oh, that's easy! I hate beach holidays! Boring!
W: OK – there's one we answered the same. So we agree about that.
M: Yeah, sightseeing's definitely more interesting!
W: Right. When do you like to go: in spring or summer?
M: In spring – I don't really like hot weather. Tourist places are more crowded in summer.
W: True. But the weather's better. Summer is hotter than spring. I love hot weather.
M: Well, we don't agree there. Anyway, next question. What do you like to eat: local dishes or the food you usually eat?
W: Local dishes, I think. You?
M: Definitely! That's two answers the same!
W: Hmm, interesting. Next … what do you like to do in the evening? Go to a club or go to a restaurant?
M: Well, go to a restaurant.
W: Oh, good. Me, too. It's much quieter than a club.
M: Yes, I agree. Restaurants are quieter … more relaxing.
W: And the last question … how long is your perfect holiday?
M: Three months.
W: You can't have *three* months! The answer is either a week or a month.
M: OK, a month then.
W: Me, too!
W: So we've got four answers the same!
M: Maybe we *can* travel together …

UNIT 7 Recording 5
I=Interviewer P=Passenger

I: So, Jeff. A few questions about the trip. What was the coldest place you visited?
P: The coldest place was Mount Everest. We stayed at Everest base camp and the temperature was minus thirty.
I: Really? And what was the hottest place?
P: Well, it was hot in Pakistan, but the Red Desert in Australia was hotter.
I: Ah, was it? And what was the friendliest place?
P: That's an impossible question. I can't say. We met so many fantastic people. Everyone was wonderful.
I: OK. What was the longest you travelled in one day?
P: One day we travelled about 400 kilometres in Pakistan. That was a long day!
I: Very! So, what was the most beautiful building you saw?
P: There were some great ones in Nepal and Bali, but my favourite building was the Taj Mahal in India. I think it's the most beautiful building in the world.
I: Yes, it is. So, what was the most amazing experience of the journey?
P: Seeing a tiger in the tiger reserve in the Himalayas. A-ma-a-a-zing!

UNIT 7 Recording 6
A: Excuse me. Can you tell me the way to the Pier, please?
B: Yeah, you go down West Street until the end.
A: Straight on?
B: Yeah. And then turn left and you'll see the Pier.
A: Thanks very much.

UNIT 7 Recording 8
A: You go out of this car park and turn right. So that's right into Church Street. Then take the third right, I think it's called New Road.
B: The first right.
A: No, the third right. And you go straight on until the end of the road and then turn left. After about one minute you'll see it on the left. You can't miss it!
B: So third right, erm, left at the end of the road and then … ?
A: It's on the left.
B: On the left.
A: Yeah.
B: Fine. Thanks a lot.
A: You're welcome.

UNIT 7 Recording 10
M=Man W=Woman

M: We want to talk about Rimini, an old city on the Adriatic coast in Italy. It's got a beautiful beach and you can swim in the sea in the summer. One of the most important places in Rimini is the cathedral, and also the Arch of Augustus.
W: Ah, but for me the most important place is the beach.
M: Yes, for me, too. And at night, the bars on the beach. You can go dancing – it's really good fun …
W: And what about the food? Well, a typical food from Rimini is *puntarelle* or pasta with fresh vegetables, but the fish is really amazing. The city is by the sea so the fish is very fresh.
M: So, we think Rimini is a beautiful, relaxing place. You can sit on the beach all day, eat great food and dance all night.

UNIT 8 Recording 3
Conversation 1
A: Is it a man or a woman?
B: A woman.
A: What does she look like?
B: I think she's in her thirties. She's got long, dark hair and dark eyes. She's wearing make-up.
A: Hmm. Is it Michelle Yeoh?
B: Yes.

Conversation 2
A: Is it a man or a woman?
B: A man.
A: What does he look like?
B: He's got short, dark, curly hair. He's got a beard and a moustache. He's black.
A: Oh, I know … it's Will Smith.
B: Sure is!

UNIT 8 Recording 4
I=Interviewer

I: Hello and welcome to *Fashion Now*, with me, Dan Taylor. In today's programme, we ask the question, 'What is Beauty?' Do men today *really* like women with blonde hair and blue eyes? And do women like the James Bond look – tall, dark and very masculine, or do they like something different now? Are ideas about beauty changing? We went out to see what you *really* think …

UNIT 8 Recording 5
I=Interviewer W1=1st woman
W2=2nd woman W3=3rd woman
M1=1st man M2=2nd man

I: Excuse me, ladies. Do you have a moment?
W1: Yes?
I: Just a quick question. Research says that these days women prefer men with feminine faces …
W1: Really?
I: Yes. It's true … honestly!
W1: I don't agree at all. I like masculine faces …
I: Can I show you some photos?
W1: Sure.
I: So which of these guys do you like best?
W1: Sean Connery. He's definitely the best looking man here. And he's tall, isn't he? Yeah … I like tall men. And I like a man with a beard.
I: Uh-huh. What about you?
W2: Mmm. I'm not sure. I like this one, what's his name?
I: It's Gael García Bernal. He's a Mexican film star.
W2: Yeah? Well, he's got quite a feminine face and he's very good-looking. I like his eyes – he's got dark brown eyes and I like men with dark eyes and black hair. But I

think it's more in the personality ... in the smile ... so I like this one best. Will Smith. He's got a really nice smile.

I: Thank you. And here's another lady. Excuse me. Have you got a moment?

W3: Well …

I: I'm doing a survey about the changing face of beauty. Can I ask you some questions?

W3: Yes, OK. Yes.

I: I've got some photos here. Can you tell me which of these people you like? Do you think any of them are good-looking?

W3: Well, I don't really like any of them …

I: No? So what sort of man *do* you like?

W3: What sort of man do I like? Well, my husband's over there. I think he's good-looking. I like his hair. I love guys with red hair.

I: Which one? The one looking in the shop window?

W3: No, he's over there. He's wearing a white T-shirt and he's talking to … that blonde woman … Excuse me …

I: And then I talked to some men to find out if they really prefer blondes – just like they did fifty years ago. Do you think it's true that men prefer blondes, sir?

M1: What? No, not at all! Beauty comes in all shapes and sizes and ages. Look at this photo of Judi Dench. She's lovely. She isn't young, but she's got beautiful grey eyes and she always wears beautiful clothes. She looks kind and intelligent.

M2: Yeah, she does. But I still prefer blondes, you know … like Scarlett Johansson. She's lovely … slim, blonde hair, blue eyes – that's the sort of woman I like.

M1: Scarlett Johansson, *slim*?

M2: Well, OK … but she's not *fat*.

M1: No, that's true…

I: OK, guys. Thanks for talking to us …

UNIT 8 Recording 6

Conversation 1
M=Man W=Woman

W: OK … what do you feel like watching?

M: Hmm. I don't know really. What do you recommend?

W: Erm, … Well, how about *French Kiss*? Do you know it?

M: No, I don't think so. What's it about?

W: Well, it's a romantic comedy. It's about an American woman. She goes to France and meets a French guy and … they fall in love. It's quite old, but it's really funny.

M: Sounds OK, I suppose. Who's in it?

W: Meg Ryan and Kevin Kline.

M: Oh, I like Meg Ryan. Mmm. Do you think I'd like it?

W: Yeah, I think so. You like comedies, don't you? And it's very funny.

M: Yeah, OK. Why don't we get it then?

W: Great. Excuse me. Can we have this one, please?

Conversation 2
W=Woman M=Man

W: What was the last DVD you saw?

M: Erm, Let me think. Oh – I know, it was *Speed*.

W: *Speed*? Is it new? What's it about?

M: No, a bit old actually. It's an action film. It's about a bus and it can't stop. It has to go at top speed or … or it explodes. It's great!

W: Right. Who's in it?

M: Sandra Bullock and … the guy is, the actor is, er … Keanu Reeves.

W: Mmm. Do you think *I'd* like it?

M: Well, do you like action films?

W: Not really. I prefer romantic films and dramas.

M: Oh, then I *don't* think you'd like it …. Er, well. Oh, I know. I think you'd like that French film, you know, with the actress Juliette Binoche. What's it called? Oh, yeah: *Chocolat*.

W: *Chocolat*? Do I know it?… Oh …with Johnny Depp? Mmm! Now that *is* a good recommendation. Have you got the DVD?

UNIT 8 Recording 7

1 What do you recommend?
2 How about *French Kiss*?
3 Do you think I'd like it?
4 I don't think you'd like it.
5 I think you'd like that French film.

UNIT 8 Recording 9

Recently I went to a concert in the park with my boyfriend and some other friends … It was in City Park … We went because we all like the band, Double-X, and we listen to their music all the time.
The concert only lasted two hours, but we took a picnic with us and went out early in the afternoon – it was a free concert, you see, so there were already a lot of people sitting out in the park in front of the stage. We got a really good place, close to the stage. We chatted and lay in the sun all afternoon … and then in the evening more and more people came and it got quite crowded. Then the concert started and well, it was … fantastic! Double-X is an amazing band … and better *live*! I really liked the concert because everyone was dancing and singing – we had a great time.

UNIT 9 Recording 1

G=Guide V1=1st visitor
V2=2nd visitor V3=3rd visitor

G: So, ladies and gentlemen … Let's move into the transport section now. Could you all come over this way? Let's look at these photos. As you can see, these early methods of transport have two things in common … they're all great ideas, great ways to travel through the air rather than on the ground … but they weren't successful! There was a big problem with each one.

V1: But the monorail – that was successful …

G: Well, yes and no…. Look at this photo on the left. It's from the World Fair in Seattle. That was in 1962. Monorails were a very popular idea in America at that time. People wanted to leave their cars at home and go to work by public transport. But they weren't successful – monorails are difficult to build and expensive to keep in good condition. So you're right. There are some monorails in the world … but not very many!

V2: Hey … Look at this photo. Is that a car under a plane?

G: Oh, yes. This was a very interesting idea. People wanted to fly from Los Angeles to New York … and then drive straight into the city centre from the airport.

V2: No way! How?

G: Well, the idea was that the car came off the bottom of the plane and then … you got in and drove away. This was in the 1940s. Ah, yes. Look … here's the date: 1948. It was a nice idea – no airports or waiting around – but it wasn't successful.

V2: Why not?

G: There was an engineering problem … the car was too heavy and small planes weren't strong enough to carry them.

V3: What's this? A helicopter in the garage?

G: Yes, indeed. We laugh at this now, but people were very serious about it at the time. People wanted to leave home in the morning, say goodbye to the family and go to work by private helicopter. The idea was very popular … but of course, it was impossible. Helicopters are very difficult to fly … and can you imagine the traffic problems in the sky … So noisy!

V2: Yes. Very noisy … There's far too much traffic these days in my opinion.

G: I agree. People should go to work by bike … or on foot. By far the best way to travel …

UNIT 9 Recording 3

1 There was a problem.
2 It was a good idea.
3 The photo on the left.
4 In the city centre.

UNIT 9 Recording 5

1 Tourists can use the bikes.
2 Children can't use the bikes.
3 Users have to give their credit card details.
4 You don't have to pay for the first half hour.

UNIT 9 Recording 7

L=Liam K=Kamal

K: Hey, Liam. Did you stay in bed too long this morning?

L: Ha-ha! It's these trains – they're terrible!

K: Why? What happened *this* time?

L: Well, first of all, the train was late leaving the station, but only about a quarter of an hour or so. After that, it just went at walking speed – all the way to London. Really! There was a guy on a bike on the road next to us

153

AUDIO SCRIPTS

… I think he got to London before we did!

K: Well, you're two hours late … and the boss wants to see you.

K: Hey, Liam. The boss wants to see you. Whoa! What happened to you? You're all wet!

L: Believe me, it's a *long* story. First of all, I got up late because I didn't hear my alarm, so I only woke up at 8.30. I ran to the train station – usually I walk – but I missed the train by two minutes! Then I waited for the next train, the 9.15, and everything was fine until we just stopped – just *stopped* – in the middle of nowhere. The guard said that there was a signal problem. After that, the air-conditioning stopped working, so it was like an oven – at least a thousand degrees! Finally, after forty minutes, we started moving … very, very slowly. What could I do? Uh-oh, there's the boss.

K: Yeah. She's not happy. Two and a half hours late, Liam … Good luck!

UNIT 9 Recording 9

A=Attendant P=Passenger

A: Your meal, sir.
P: Thank you. Erm, excuse me.
A: Yes, can I help you?
P: Hope so! I'm sorry, but there's a small problem here … I ordered a vegetarian meal – but this is meat.
A: Oh, just a moment … I checked and we don't have a record of your order.
P: What?! But I *always* order vegetarian. I'm a frequent flyer.
A: I understand, sir, but we don't have any more vegetarian meals.
P: I don't believe it! You always have extra meals in business class.
A: Yes, but this is economy class.
P: You don't understand. Let me explain one more time. I don't eat meat. I ordered vegetarian. I can't fly to Tokyo without dinner. It's your job to bring me a meal. A business class vegetarian meal is fine.
A: Just a moment. Here you are, sir. A vegetarian meal.
P: Thank you … but this is already open. And it's cold. Urm, can I speak to the person in charge, please?

UNIT 10 Recording 1

I=Interviewer E=Elaine A=Aled

I: Elaine and Aled, the luckiest couple in Britain today … welcome to the programme!
E/A: Thank you.
I: So Elaine, tell us about that moment when you found out.
E: I saw the winning numbers on television and I phoned Aled straight away!
A: I didn't believe her at first. I thought 'You're lying!'
E: I didn't believe myself! I was in shock!
I: And is it true that you're *not* going to stop working?

A: That's right. We enjoy our jobs and we've got lots of friends here. I don't like doing nothing. I think hard work's good for you.
E: Definitely. People think working in a fast food restaurant is boring … but it's not. We have a lot of fun. It's an important part of our life.
I: So what are you going to do with the money?
E: Well, first of all, we're going to get married this summer. We already had plans to get married before we won the lottery, maybe in two years, but now we can do it this summer.
I: Congratulations!
A: Or next summer.
I: Ah …
E: *This* summer.
A: And we'd like to move. At the moment I'm living with my parents and Elaine's living with hers. So we're going to look for a house to buy.
E: By the sea.
A: Yes, maybe by the sea, or …
I: Are you going to take a break? Travel around the world maybe?
A: No, I don't think so, but we're going to have a holiday. We're going to the Canary Islands.
I: Fabulous. And have you got any other plans? Maybe a new car … or clothes?
E: Yeah, I'm going to buy some new clothes. I'm going shopping with my mum and sister this weekend. Cars …? Well, Aled doesn't drive so no, he isn't going to buy a car.
A: Right … not now … but I'd like to learn to drive and then maybe in the future …
I: What would you like to drive?
A: I'd like a Mercedes … or maybe, or maybe a Ferrari.
E: But we haven't got plans to buy a car now.
I: OK – great! Thanks very much for talking to us today. Oh, just one last question … How did you celebrate when you first heard the news?
E: Well … we went out and had a burger!

UNIT 10 Recording 6

Conversation 1
M=Man W=Woman

W: Hi, Sergio. Let's do something different tomorrow. It's Saturday.
M: OK … How about going to an art gallery? There's a new exhibition on at the Tate.
W: Ur, I don't really feel like doing that. I'd like to stay in. What about having a 'movie marathon'? You know, we could just sit at home all day and watch films, eat junk food …
M: Mmm … Do we have to? I saw a film last night. I don't want to sit around all day anyway. I know! Let's cook something. Or *I* can.
W: Sounds lovely. Why don't we invite Augusto and Carla for lunch?
M: Brilliant! I'll try a new recipe and we can have a food tasting.

Conversation 2
M=Man W=Woman

W: Hey, Tom. Are you busy this weekend?
M: Er … No, I don't think so.
W: Great. Let's do something!
M: OK. What do you want to do?
W: Well … How about going for a bike ride and having a picnic?
M: A bike ride? That sounds a bit tiring … Why don't we play computer games?
W: You're joking!
M: No, really. Why not?
W: Well … because, I sit in front of my computer all week – I'm not going to turn it on tomorrow! Look, let's go to the theatre. Actually, there's a Shakespeare play on in the park: *Romeo and Juliet*.
M: Hmm. I can never understand Shakespeare plays …
W: OK, well, why don't we read it together first?
M: Oh, but can we get tickets?
W: Yes. It's free.
M: Ah, fantastic! Come on then …

UNIT 10 Recording 7

1 How about going to the zoo?
2 What about doing something more relaxing?
3 Why don't we do some internet shopping?
4 Let's go to the theatre.

UNIT 10 Recording 9

In Dublin today, it'll be hot and sunny with temperatures up to twenty-five degrees Celsius. Tomorrow will be cloudy, but quite warm, with a high of twenty. Things will change on Friday night: it'll be a wet night with rain from midnight to early next morning. The temperature will fall to ten so it'll feel quite cool, but the rain will stop, so we'll have a dry day all Saturday. Sunday will be windy and cloudy … and very cold, so make sure you wear your winter coat!

UNIT 10 Recording 10

1 Oh, I think spring is the best. I love it when the flowers come out and the birds start singing … that's when everything is so fresh. It's the perfect time to take a walk along the Danube.

2 It rained every day, but we had a great time. We went to museums, sat in cafés and played cards.

3 In winter I love skiing … getting up early to spend the whole day on the mountain skiing – fantastic! I love having a hot chocolate in a local café at the end of the afternoon – it's the perfect time to do that.

4 I really don't like it when it's very hot, especially in the city. There are so many tourists about – I get so hot and tired … it's awful!

5 Oh, I really like it when it's hot and then there's a big summer storm, with lots and lots of rain … I love the way the air cools down and it feels fresher.

6 Well, definitely not in the rainy season! I think the best time to visit Malaysia is May to September because after that it gets really wet – it feels like it never stops raining!

UNIT 11 Recording 2
P=Presenter D=Doctor

P: And this week in Health Matters, we're talking about colds and flu. What's the difference, and more importantly, how to cure them? With me in the studio is Dr Elizabeth Harper. Dr Harper … How is flu different from a common cold?

D: Well, flu starts very suddenly. One minute you're fine, the next minute you feel terrible. You've got a headache – often a very bad headache – and a cough. You've got a sore throat and your arms and legs hurt. You're very hot. Usually you've got a temperature of over thirty-eight degrees centigrade and you're too ill to do anything. You can't work. You just want to go home and go to bed. Sometimes you have to stay in bed for a week or more.

P: Awful. I see, yes. And what about a typical cold?

D: A cold starts slowly. Maybe it takes two or three days to start. It's a cold when you've got a sore throat … or a cough and a runny nose and you don't feel very well. But – and here's the big difference – if you can get up and go to work, then you've probably got a cold, *not* flu. After a week you feel better. After flu, you often feel very tired for a very long time, maybe two or three weeks!

P: Mmm. OK, so the next question …

UNIT 11 Recording 4
W1=1st woman W2=2nd woman
W3=3rd woman M1=1st man
M2=2nd man M3=3rd man

Situation 1
W1: Oh, no. My papers!
M1: Here, let me help. What a mess!
W1: Thank you very much.
M1: No problem.

Situation 2
W2: Er … Excuse me … sir?
M2: Uhhh …
W2: Are you all right? Shall I call an ambulance?
M2: No … Yes … Uh… Thanks so much …
W2: That's OK.

Situation 3
W3: Hmm … Uh … Mmm …
M3: Oh, look. I'll do that for you. Where do you want it?
W3: Just over here, in front of the window … Thanks a lot. That's kind of you.
M3: You're welcome.

UNIT 11 Recording 7
P=Pharmacist C=Customer

P: Hello, can I help you?
C: Yes, have you got anything for an earache?
P: An earache? Hmm … When did it start?
C: Yesterday afternoon. I took some paracetamol, but it didn't help.
P: And do you have any other pain?
C: No, just my ear.
P: Do you often have earaches?
C: No, it's the first time, but it hurts a lot.
P: OK. I'm going to give you some ear drops. They're very mild.
C: Sorry, I don't understand. Mild?
P: They're not very strong. Put these drops in your ear, three times daily.
C: Three times a day?
P: That's right. When you get up, at lunch and just before you go to bed. If it doesn't get better, you should see a doctor.
C: Thank you. How much is that?

UNIT 12 Recording 1
I=Interviewer S1=1st speaker
S2=2nd speaker S3=3rd speaker

Interview 1
I: Excuse me. Do you have a second? We're asking people about experiences of a lifetime … for a survey.
S1: Oh … Er, yes, if it's quick.
I: Great! Could you look at this list? Have you done any of these things?
S1: Hmm … Yes, yes, I have actually. Well, one of them! I've been to Guatemala and I've climbed that volcano, I think.
I: Anything else?
S1: No, no, I don't think so. Sorry, I have to run …

Interview 2
I: Excuse me …
S2: What?
I: Have you ever ridden an elephant?
S2: What? Why? Uh, no, No, I haven't …
I: We're doing a survey on experiences of a lifetime. Can I show you this list? Have you done any of these activities?
S2: Oh, OK. OK. Let's see … Er … No, no, no, no. Oh, I've sailed down the Nile … so that's one thing. In fact I went to Egypt last year, with the wife … our wedding anniversary …

Interview 3
I: Excuse me. We're doing a survey … about experiences of a lifetime.
S3: Right …
I: Two minutes. Could you just look at this list? Have you done any of these things?
S3: OK. Well … I don't travel that much, so … I haven't been to Iceland … but it looks nice – swimming in a thermal spa looks fun.
I: And the other things?
S3: Hmm … no … well, I've seen some of them on TV. Is that OK? Does that count?

UNIT 12 Recording 4

Conversation 1
A: Hello.
B: Hi, Sean. It's Debbie.
A: Hi, Debbie. What's up?
B: Is Kevin there?
A: No, he's not. He went out about ten minutes ago.
B: Oh …
A: What's up?
B: Well, I locked the keys in the car. Kevin has the spare key.
A: Oh, what a drag!
B: Could I leave a message for him?
A: Of course.
B: Just ask him to call me.
A: On your mobile?
B: No, that's in the car … I'll give you a number.
A: Hold on … OK, go ahead.
B: OK, let's see … It's 3-double 2, 6-3, 2-8.
A: Got it. I'll tell him.
B: Thanks, bye.
A: Bye.

Conversation 2
A: Berkley Bank.
B: Hello. Could I speak to customer services, please?
A: Just a moment.
C: Customer services.
B: Hello, I've got a problem. I think I've lost my credit card.
C: I see. I'm sorry, this line is very bad. Where are you calling from?
B: I'm in Madrid, actually. In fact I'm calling from a public phone and I've only got one minute on this card. Could you ring me back?
C: Of course. Could you give me the number there?
B: Just a moment … It's 34 for Spain, 91 for Madrid, then 308 5238.
C: Let me check that. 34 91 308 5238.
B: That's right.
C: Fine. Put the phone down – I'll call you back straight away.
B: Thank you.

Conversation 3
A: Hello?
B: Oh, thank goodness. Hello, uh … Who's this?
A: My name's Marianne.
B: Thanks for picking up.
A: Well, the phone rang so I picked it up.
B: Yes, well, that's my cell phone. And you found it.

AUDIO SCRIPTS

A: Oh, OK … It's yours. Do you want to get it back?
B: Yes, thanks. Where are you?
A: Central Park, by the fountain. It was here in the grass.
B: Ah, yes … I thought it might be.
A: So where are you?
B: Not far away. I can be there in ten minutes.
A: OK, I'll wait here.
B: Great. Thanks a lot!

UNIT 12 Recording 8

This happened in Australia … when I was about twenty-five. I spent a few days at a hotel in Alice Springs and went to Ayers Rock and … well, anyway, one day, I went out for a walk … in the outback.

It was a lovely day so I walked and walked … and then I realised I didn't really know where I was. I was a bit stupid, really… because I decided to go further … I guess I thought I'd find the way back. Urm … anyway, after that I heard some dogs.

First I heard them barking, and then I saw them … there was a group – maybe five or six dogs, wild dogs, coming towards me. I felt really frightened, but I remembered some advice I, er … urm, I read in my guidebook: Don't move, and don't look at the dogs. So I froze, like a statue …. I didn't move … and I looked at a tree, not at the dogs, and didn't move my eyes. The dogs were all around me, jumping and barking … I thought they were going to bite me. Then one dog *did* bite my arm, just a little, but still I didn't move.

In the end, after about twenty minutes, the dogs went away. I stayed there for a few more minutes and then luckily found my way back to the hotel. It was the most frightening experience I've ever had!

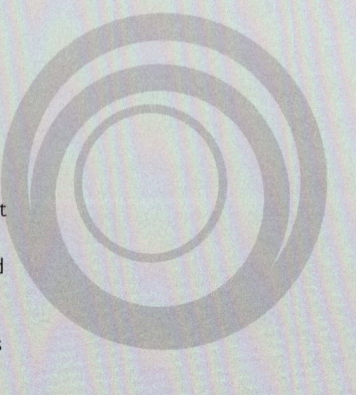

Frances Eales
Steve Oakes

speakout

Elementary
Workbook with key

BBC

CONTENTS

7 HOLIDAYS — PAGE 41

7.1 GRAMMAR | comparatives
VOCABULARY | travel
READING | travel partners

7.2 GRAMMAR | superlatives
VOCABULARY | places (1)
LISTENING | an audio diary
WRITING | checking and correcting

7.3 FUNCTION | giving directions
VOCABULARY | places (2)
LEARN TO | check and correct directions

8 NOW — PAGE 46

8.1 GRAMMAR | present continuous
VOCABULARY | verbs with prepositions
LISTENING | phone conversations
WRITING | pronouns

8.2 GRAMMAR | present simple/continuous
VOCABULARY | appearance; clothes
READING | the T-shirt

8.3 FUNCTION | recommending
VOCABULARY | types of film
LEARN TO | link words

9 TRANSPORT — PAGE 51

9.1 GRAMMAR | articles
VOCABULARY | transport collocations
READING | commuting

9.2 GRAMMAR | can/can't, have to/don't have to
VOCABULARY | adjectives (1)
LISTENING | the balancing scooter

9.3 FUNCTION | apologising
VOCABULARY | excuses; airport
LEARN TO | tell a long story

Review and Check 3 — PAGE 56

10 THE FUTURE — PAGE 59

10.1 GRAMMAR | *be going to*; *would like to*
VOCABULARY | plans
READING | a lottery winner

10.2 GRAMMAR | *will, might, won't*
VOCABULARY | phrases with *get*
LISTENING | survival
WRITING | *too, also, as well*

10.3 FUNCTION | making suggestions
VOCABULARY | adjectives (2); weather
LEARN TO | respond to suggestions

11 HEALTH — PAGE 64

11.1 GRAMMAR | *should/shouldn't*
VOCABULARY | the body
READING | walking – the perfect sport?

11.2 GRAMMAR | adverbs of manner
VOCABULARY | common verbs
LISTENING | what's your real age?
WRITING | adverbs in stories

11.3 FUNCTION | offering to help
VOCABULARY | problems
LEARN TO | thank someone

12 EXPERIENCES — PAGE 69

12.1 GRAMMAR | present perfect
VOCABULARY | outdoor activities
READING | a travel blog
WRITING | postcard phrases

12.2 GRAMMAR | present perfect and past simple
VOCABULARY | prepositions
LISTENING | fear or fun?

12.3 FUNCTION | telephoning
VOCABULARY | telephoning expressions; feelings
LEARN TO | say telephone numbers

Review and Check 4 — PAGE 74

AUDIO SCRIPTS PAGE 77   ANSWER KEY PAGE 80

7.1 HOLIDAYS

VOCABULARY travel

1A Rewrite the sentences using the words in the box. You do not need two of the words.

| empty noisy cheap boring |
| uncomfortable slow expensive quiet |
| fast comfortable crowded interesting |

1 There were no visitors in the museum.
   The museum was _empty_ .

2 This bed's very hard – I can't relax on it.
   This bed's _____ .

3 The train travels at 165 kilometres an hour.
   The train is very _____ .

4 There were a lot of people on the beach.
   The beach was _____ .

5 The book's good and has a lot of useful information.
   The book's _____ .

6 The hotel is perfect – no cars outside, no children around, so I can sleep all day.
   The hotel is _____ .

7 The car was $35,000 so he didn't buy it.
   The car was too _____ for him.

8 I didn't like the film. I slept for most of it.
   The film was _____ .

9 These jeans didn't cost a lot.
   These jeans were quite _____ .

10 I can't sleep because of the party in the flat below.
   The party is very _____ .

B ▶ 7.1 Listen and repeat the adjectives from Exercise 1A.

C Listen again and write the adjectives in the correct place according to the stress.

1 O	2 Oo
cheap	empty
3 Ooo	**4 oOo**
5 oOoo	

GRAMMAR comparatives

2 Correct the mistakes in the sentences.
1 Hondas are popular than Suzukis.
   Hondas are more popular than Suzukis.

2 South Africa's hoter than Italy.
   _____

3 I'm more old than my brother.
   _____

4 Indian food is spicyer than English food.
   _____

5 Lena's intelligenter than me.
   _____

6 Cola is sweeter than lemonade.
   _____

7 Chinese is more difficult that English.
   _____

8 Crisps are badder for you than chips.
   _____

3 Complete the article with the comparative form of the adjectives in brackets.

Either ... or...?

We ask singer and actress Sonia Haig to choose. Which is better ... ?

Q: Singing or acting?
A: Singing. Singing is ¹ _easier_ (easy) for me than acting.

Q: Healthy food or junk food?
A: Junk food. I know healthy food is ² _____ (good) for me, but after a concert all I want is a pizza or a hamburger and chocolate!

Q: Relaxing on a beach or visiting an art gallery?
A: Oh, visiting an art gallery because it's ³ _____ (interesting). Sitting on a beach is boring.

Q: Dinner at a restaurant or dinner at home?
A: That's a difficult question. I like cooking, but I like having dinner at a restaurant because it's ⁴ _____ (romantic) than eating at home.

Q: Family or friends?
A: Family. I'm ⁵ _____ (close) to my sister than to my friends and I phone my parents every day.

Q: Summer or winter?
A: Well, I love looking at snow ... but winter is ⁶ _____ (cold) and I prefer being hot. OK, summer.

Q: New York or Paris?
A: I love Paris, but I love New York more because it's ⁷ _____ (big) than Paris and I like all the shops. I have an apartment near Central Park.

Q: Cats or dogs?
A: Dogs. They're ⁸ _____ (friendly) than cats!

7.1

READING

4A Read the emails. Are Tim and Mike good travel partners?

Hi Dan,

Mike and I arrived in Barcelona on Saturday. The first night we were in a self-catering apartment near the beach. I didn't sleep well because it was too noisy, so yesterday I moved to a hotel in the city centre. Mike stayed at the apartment because it's quite cheap. My hotel's very comfortable and quiet and it's got Spanish TV, so I can practise my Spanish in the evenings.

Yesterday Mike came with me to the Picasso Museum. I thought it was fantastic, but he wanted to leave after an hour. He said it was boring, so we went to the beach and met some local people and he talked to them for almost three hours ... that was boring! Of course, he spoke in English because he doesn't know much Spanish.

Last night I wanted to go to a restaurant to try the local food, but Mike said it was too expensive. We went to a cheap snack bar and the food was awful.

Hope you're well.

Tim

Hi Lucy,

Tim and I are here in beautiful Barcelona. I'm in a self-catering apartment near the beach. It's not very comfortable, but I only go there to sleep. The first night there was a party next door and I danced until 3a.m. Tim said it was too noisy and he moved into a hotel in the city centre. He stays in his room in the evenings and watches TV! Can you believe it – watching TV on holiday!?

Yesterday we went to the Picasso Museum. Well, it was OK ... for about an hour ... but Tim wanted to stay there all day! You know me ... I like relaxing on the beach and meeting people – yesterday I met some great people from Madrid and we chatted all afternoon.

Tim always wants to eat in expensive places, but I like buying food from shops and eating it on the beach. Last night we went to a snack bar. The food was terrible.

Mike

B Who do you think says sentences 1–8? Write Tim (T), Mike (M) or both (TM).

1 I haven't got much money.   M
2 A good night's sleep is important for me.
3 When I visit another country I try to learn some of the language.
4 We don't enjoy the same things.
5 I love going to art galleries and museums.
6 I talked to some Spanish people on the beach yesterday.
7 I don't like eating expensive food.
8 The food in the snack bar wasn't good.

C Read the emails again and answer the questions.

1 Which is more expensive: the apartment or the hotel?
   the hotel

2 Which is further from the city centre: the apartment or the hotel?

3 Which is noisier in the evenings: the apartment or the hotel?

4 Which is more comfortable: the apartment or the hotel?

5 Who is more talkative: Tim or Mike?

6 Who is more serious: Tim or Mike?

7 Who is better at speaking Spanish: Tim or Mike?

8 Who is more laid back: Tim or Mike?

7.2

VOCABULARY places (1)

1 Complete the puzzle and find what you have when you go on holiday.

1. lake

You have _____ !

GRAMMAR superlatives

2A Read adverts A–C. Which holiday is good for:

1 a family?
2 people who like relaxing?
3 people who like active holidays?

A

LUXURY WEEKEND

A relaxing weekend at the beautiful 5-star Hanover Hotel. Swim in the warm sea and relax on the beach all day! Tennis courts and bicycles are available. The perfect laid-back holiday.

(3 nights – €1,490 per person)

B

MOUNTAIN ADVENTURE

Mountain biking in the Indian Himalayas – spend the day biking and sleep in tents at night. Prepare for temperatures of –10°C! A real adventure for the sporty holidaymaker.

(10 days – €2,490 per person)

C

FAMILY FUN

Camp Family has everything your children need to have a good time – a lovely blue lake, an adventure playground, mini-golf and go-karts. Stay in a self-catering apartment. Sit back, relax and let us give your children the holiday of a lifetime!

(6 days – €990 per family)

B Write sentences about the holidays using the superlative of the adjective.

1 expensive — *The most expensive is Mountain adventure.*
2 cheap
3 comfortable
4 noisy
5 long
6 easy
7 difficult
8 short
9 uncomfortable
10 cold

3A Write the questions.

1 What / long / word in this sentence?
   What's the longest word in this sentence?
2 What / short / word on this page?
3 Which / interesting / text in units 1–6 of this book?
4 Which / good / exercise on this page?
5 What / difficult / grammar point in English?
6 Who / happy / person in your family?
7 Who / friendly / person in your English class?
8 Which / bad / restaurant in town?

B Answer the questions in Exercise 3A.

7.2

LISTENING

4A ▶ 7.2 Look at the map and listen to Nick's audio diary. Does his train go to or from Moscow?

B Read sentences 1–8 below and check any new words in your dictionary.
1 The Trans-Siberian train journey takes nine days. F
2 The compartment is for two people.
3 Anton doesn't speak much English.
4 Nick can see snow, forests, villages, and lakes out of the window.
5 Nick and Anton buy food from women on the train.
6 They drink a lot of coffee on the train.
7 On the last evening of the journey, Nick went to a party.
8 Nick loved the Trans-Siberian train journey.

C Listen to Nick's diary again. Are sentences 1–8 true (T) or false (F)?

D Correct the false sentences.
1 *The Trans-Siberian train journey takes seven days.*

WRITING checking and correcting

5A Read the extracts from Nick's blog. Underline and correct ten more mistakes. Check:
- the spelling
- past tense forms
- singular and plural

Hi, it's Nick again. We started the day with a surprise – but not a good one. Anton and I ~~goed~~ *went* to the dining car for brekfast and there wasn't any food. That wasn't a big problem because I had some biscuit and we drinked some tea, but then we went back for lunch and it was the same situation. The waiter telled us that there's a station where they usually get food, but the food truck wasn't there.

Nobody on the train was worried about this becaus almost everybody broght their own food. A guy called Egor gaves us half of his roast chicken and a Chinese couple gave us some bread. Peoples were so kind. Anton and I talked about how to thank them ... so I tought them some English songs and it were really just a big party. My best day on the train!

B Write a short text about one day on a journey. It can be a real journey or an imaginary one. Write 80–100 words. Use the questions to help you.
- Where were you?
- How did you travel?
- What happened?
- Was it a good day?

C Check and correct any mistakes.

7.3

VOCABULARY places (2)

1 Add the missing vowels to make places in towns.

1 sq _ _ r _
2 c _ r p _ rk
3 sw _ mm _ ng p _ _ l
4 th _ _ tr _
5 l _ br _ ry
6 b _ s st _ t _ _ n
7 _ rt g _ ll _ ry
8 t _ _ r _ st _ nf _ rm _ t _ _ n
9 p _ rk
10 m _ s _ _ m

FUNCTION giving directions

2 Look at the map of Dublin, Ireland, and complete the conversation. Speaker A is at Pearse Street station (START) and wants to go to the Tourist Information Office (TI).

A: Excuse me. Can you tell me the ¹ _way_____ to the Tourist Information Office, please?

B: Sure. Go down here and ² _____ right into Lincoln Place and then right again into Nassau Street.

A: OK.

B: Then go ³ _____ on down Nassau Street. Go ⁴ _____ Kildare Street and ⁵ _____ Street.

A: OK, so I stay on Nassau Street.

B: Yes, until the end but then don't turn right ⁶ _____ Grafton Street.

A: Not Grafton Street, OK.

B: Go straight ⁷ _____, into a small street ... I forget the name ... and the Tourist Information Office is on the ⁸ _____.

A: Great. Thank you!

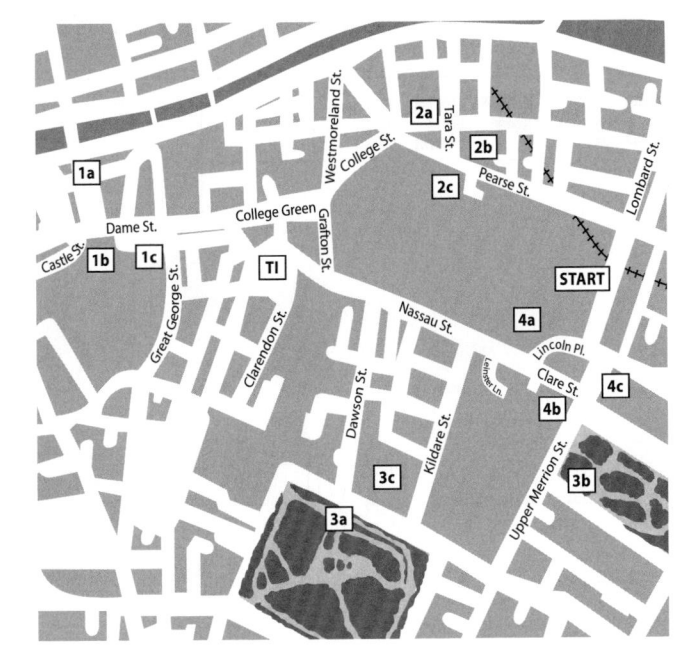

3 Read the information and look at the map. Circle the correct number of the destination.

Walking tours of Dublin

1 To Dublin Castle
From the Tourist Information Office, go to College Green and turn left. Go down College Green and Dame Street, and turn left into Castle Street. It's on the left and number 1a /(1b)/ 1c on your map.

2 From Dublin Castle to Trinity College
Go back to Dame Street and into College Green and then left into College Street. Turn right into Pearse Street, and then take the first right. It's number 2a / 2b / 2c on your map.

3 From Trinity College to St. Stephen's Green
Go back to Pearse Street and turn left, then left into College Street and then Grafton Street, and finally Nassau Street. Turn right into Dawson Street, and go straight ahead until the end. You can see it in front of you. It's number 3a / 3b / 3c on your map.

4 From St. Stephen's Green to the National Gallery
Come out of St. Stephen's Green and go down Kildare Street. At the end, turn right, and go straight on down Clare Street. The National Gallery is on your right, number 4a / 4b / 4c on your map.

LEARN TO check and correct directions

4A Look at the map and correct A's information in sentences 1–6.

1 A: So, the park's between the cinema and the pharmacy.
   B: No, it's _behind_____ the cinema and the pharmacy.

2 A: So the supermarket's between the cinema and the pharmacy.
   B: No, it's between _____.

3 A: So, the cinema is the fourth building on the left.
   B: No, it's _____.

4 A: So, the café is the fourth building on the left.
   B: No, it's _____.

5 A: So, the post office is opposite the bank.
   B: No, it's opposite _____.

6 A: So, the town hall is opposite the bank.
   B: No, it's _____ the bank.

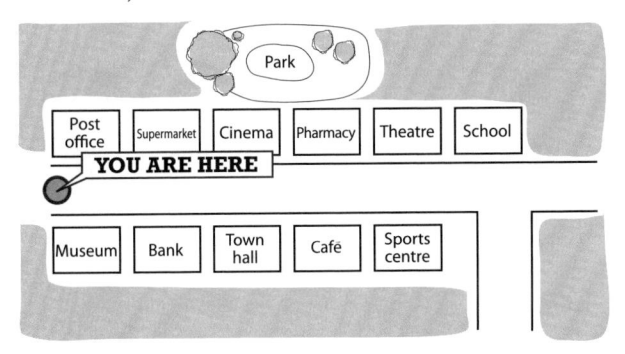

B Circle the stressed word in each of B's answers.

1 B: No, it's (behind) the cinema and the pharmacy.

C ▶ 7.3 Listen and check. Then listen and repeat.

8.1 NOW

GRAMMAR present continuous

1 Write the *-ing* form of the verbs.
1. do — *doing*
2. have — _____
3. run — _____
4. stay — _____
5. swim — _____
6. sleep — _____
7. write — _____
8. try — _____
9. begin — _____
10. give — _____

2A Complete the sentences with the present continuous form of the verbs.
1. Jake *'s playing* (play) the guitar and *singing* (sing).
2. Wesley _____ (take) a photo of Jake.
3. Jo and Sam _____ (stand) near Jake and _____ (listen) to him.
4. Roger _____ (walk) near Jake but he _____ (not listen) to him.
5. Megan _____ (sit) and _____ (drink) a coffee.
6. Paolo and Zoe _____ (chat) with each other. They _____ (not) watching Jake.
7. Lisa _____ (look) at some bags.
8. Philip _____ (sell) a bag to Kalila.

B Look at the picture and use the information in Exercise 2A to label the people.

C Write the questions.
1. What / Megan / read?
   What's Megan reading?
2. Who / Zoe / talk to?
   _____
3. Where / Zoe and Paolo / sit?
   _____
4. How many bags / Jo and Sam / carry?
   _____
5. Who / Wesley / take / a photo of?
   _____
6. What / Roger / do?
   _____
7. Who / laugh?
   _____
8. What / Zoe / drinking?
   _____

D Look at the picture below and answer the questions from Exercise 2C.
1. *She's reading a magazine.*
2. _____
3. _____
4. _____
5. _____
6. _____
7. _____
8. _____

3 Put the words in order to make questions. Then write short answers about you.

1 you / are / shoes / wearing?
Are you wearing shoes? Yes, I am. / No, I'm not.

2 your / is / ringing / phone?
_____

3 are / pen / a / with / exercise / this / doing / you?
_____

4 room / other / the / sitting / are / people / in / any?
_____

5 music / is / room / the / in / playing?
_____

6 exercise / enjoying / are / this / you?
_____

7 teacher / is / your / writing / the / board /on?
_____

8 your / drinking / classmates / coffee / are?
_____

VOCABULARY   verbs with prepositions

4 Complete the sentences with prepositions.

1 Kim's over there. He's chatting *to* Joan.
2 I'm waiting _____ the train.
3 Diana, can you take a photo _____ the class?
4 What are you listening _____?
5 We read _____ the wedding yesterday in the newspaper.
6 I can't come at the moment. I'm _____ the phone.
7 Hazel is on holiday. At the moment she's lying _____ a beach in Goa.
8 Harry looked _____ his watch. Jean was thirty minutes late.

LISTENING

5A ▶ 8.1 Listen and match phone conversations 1–5 with the correct places a)–e).

Conversation 1 → a) tennis match
Conversation 2   b) fashion show
Conversation 3   c) art gallery
Conversation 4   d) concert
Conversation 5   e) ticket office

B Listen again and underline the correct alternative for each conversation.

1 The man *really likes / doesn't like* the paintings.
2 Nellie *wants / doesn't want* to go to the concert.
3 The woman is *in / going into* a concert.
4 Felicity says she *wants / doesn't want* to meet for a coffee.
5 *All / Some of* the people are wearing black.

WRITING   pronouns

6A Read the story. Who took Julia's phone?

On Friday night, David, Julia and I went to the Rock Club. ¹Julia and David are fun and I like ²Julia and David a lot. The club was busy, but ³David, Julia and I found a table.

Julia put her mobile phone on the table, but after an hour ⁴Julia saw that ⁵Julia's phone wasn't there, and she was very angry. Then I had a good idea. I phoned ⁶Julia's number, and ⁷Julia, David and I heard ⁸Julia's phone ringing.

David started laughing, and then ⁹David took Julia's phone out of ¹⁰David's pocket and gave ¹¹Julia's phone back to ¹²Julia. David thought this was funny, but Julia was very angry with ¹³David, so she took ¹⁴David's phone and threw ¹⁵David's phone out of the window! Now ¹⁶David and Julia aren't speaking to each other.

B Replace the underlined nouns in the story with pronouns.

1 *They*
2 _____
3 _____
4 _____
5 _____
6 _____
7 _____
8 _____
9 _____
10 _____
11 _____
12 _____
13 _____
14 _____
15 _____
16 _____

8.2

VOCABULARY appearance

1A Read sentences 1–6 below and label the men in the picture.

A ____ B ____ C ____ D ____ E ____ F ____

1 William's got long dark hair. He's very slim.
2 Tom's got long dark hair and a moustache. He's slim.
3 Mike's got short dark hair and a moustache. He's slim.
4 Sam's got very short dark hair and a beard. He isn't very slim.
5 Robert's got short dark hair, a moustache and a beard. He's very slim.
6 Bruce's got short dark hair. He isn't very slim.

B Describe the women in the picture.
1 Meg_'s got long blonde hair and she's slim._
2 Belinda ____
3 Jay ____
4 Keira ____

GRAMMAR present simple/continuous

2 Underline the correct alternatives.

Gerald: Hi, Bruno. It's me, Gerald. What ¹*do you do / are you doing?*
Bruno: I ²*have / 'm having* a coffee with Carla. What about you?
Gerald: I ³*sit / 'm sitting* at my desk as usual. So you ⁴*don't work / aren't working* today.
Bruno: I am, but I ⁵*don't usually start / 'm not usually starting* work before ten o'clock.
Gerald: How's Carla?
Bruno: OK, but she ⁶*doesn't like / isn't liking* her job at the hospital.
Gerald: Oh, why not?
Bruno: Well, she ⁷*works / 's working* from 11a.m. till midnight every day.
Gerald: That sounds hard. ⁸*Does she look / Is she looking* for a new job?
Bruno: Yes, I think so. She ⁹*looks / is looking* in the newspaper and on the internet every day.
Gerald: Really? Because ¹⁰*I phone / I'm phoning* about a job opening here. Office work, not very interesting but the money isn't bad. Perfect for Carla.
Bruno: Hey, Carla – good news, it's Gerald ...

3 Complete the conversations with the present simple or present continuous form of the verbs in brackets.

Conversation 1
A: So who does the housework in your family?
B: We all ¹ _do_ (do) it. In fact my wife ² ____ (cook) dinner right now, and my daughter ³ ____ (help) her.
A: And what ⁴ ____ you ____ (do) to help at the moment?
B: I ⁵ ____ (watch) TV! There are too many people in the kitchen.

Conversation 2
A: Why ⁶ ____ (wear) black today? You ⁷ ____ (not usually wear) black.
B: What do you mean? I always ⁸ ____ (wear) it!

Conversation 3
A: Hi, Geoff. It's me. Where are you?
B: I ⁹ ____ (stand) on the train.
A: Why? You ¹⁰ ____ usually ____ (not stand).
B: No, I usually ¹¹ ____ (get) a seat, but this is a later train. Where are you?
A: I ¹² ____ (wait) at the station.
B: Oh, sorry. I forgot to tell you I'm late!

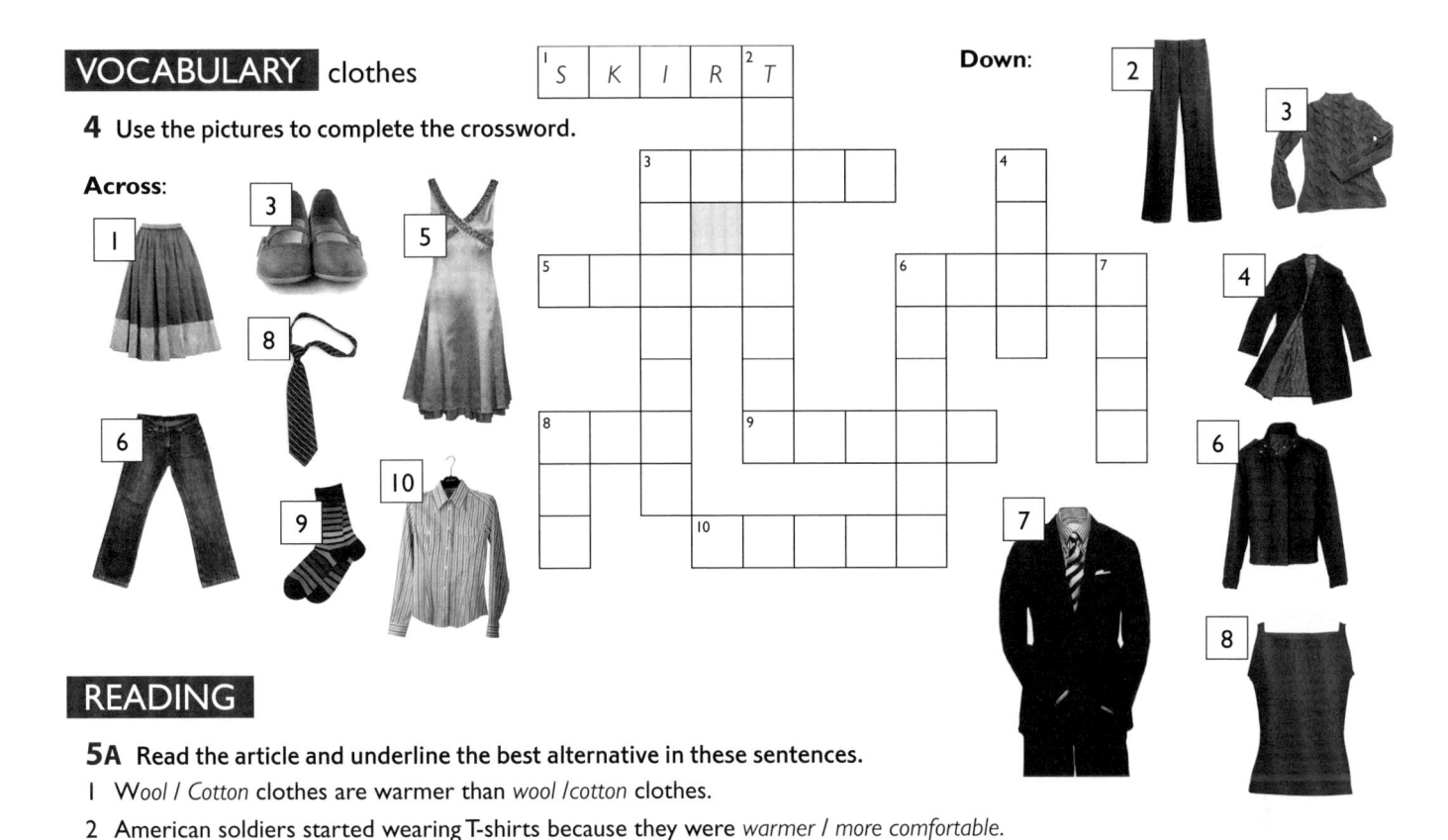

8.2

VOCABULARY clothes

4 Use the pictures to complete the crossword.

Across:

1 S K I R T

Down:

READING

5A Read the article and underline the best alternative in these sentences.
1 *Wool / Cotton* clothes are warmer than *wool /cotton* clothes.
2 American soldiers started wearing T-shirts because they were *warmer / more comfortable*.
3 Now people wear T-shirts because they're *comfortable and cheap / popular all over the world*.

THE T-SHIRT IS HERE TO STAY

It's hard to think of life without T-shirts. But the word 'T-shirt' only became a word in the English dictionary in the 1920s, and the style only became popular in the 1960s.

In the Second World War, American soldiers wore wool uniforms, and they were very hot and uncomfortable in the European summers. The American soldiers saw that European soldiers weren't hot because they wore a light cotton vest under their shirt. After that, all the soldiers in the American army started wearing cotton vests.

So men wore T-shirts under their shirts – T-shirts were underwear. Then in the 1950s, three American film stars (John Wayne, Marlon Brando and James Dean) surprised everyone by wearing their 'underwear' in films.

In the 1960s, it became easier to put words and pictures on T-shirts. By the late 60s, rock and roll bands and sports teams started to make big money selling T-shirts with their logos and team names on them.

After that, T-shirts became popular not just in the USA, but all over the world. People wear T-shirts to express themselves with words and slogans and because they are comfortable, cheap and can be fun. T-shirts will be popular for a long, long time.

B Are the sentences true (T) or false (F)?
1 T-shirts became popular in the 1920s.   F
2 American soldiers brought T-shirts to Europe.
3 For many years T-shirts were underwear.
4 American movie stars surprised people when they took their T-shirts off.
5 Putting pictures on T-shirts started in the 1980s.
6 T-shirts are popular all over the world.

C Match the words from the article with their definitions.

1 uniform
2 light
3 vest
4 logo
5 to express
6 slogan

a) a piece of underwear that people (often men) can wear under a shirt or top
b) special clothes that people wear for a job or school
c) to show your feelings, your ideas or your personality
d) a short, clever phrase that an organisation uses, e.g. Nike's 'Just do it.'
e) not heavy; good in hot weather
f) a symbol for a group or an organisation, e.g. the Apple Computer Company's apple.

8.3

VOCABULARY types of film

1A Add the vowels.
1 act _i_ _o_ n f _i_ lm
2 h_o_rr_o_r f_i_lm
3 sc_i_-f_i_ f_i_lm
4 m_u_s_i_c_a_l
5 r_o_m_a_nt_i_c f_i_lm
6 c_o_m_e_dy
7 dr_a_m_a_

B Match the film reviews with the types of film above.

A
Ninety minutes in the scary world of vampires and blood ... 2

B
Childhood friends Jessica and Tim meet after ten years, and they want to be more than just good friends ...

C
Gene Walker is a modern-day Fred Astaire, dancing and singing his way through the streets of Cordoba ...

D
New York police officer Jack Hare takes a holiday in Miami, but finds himself working to save the country from a terrorist attack ...

E
A farmer in France wakes up and finds that all his animals can speak ... Chinese. Lots of laughs as the farmer teaches himself Chinese to talk to the animals.

F
A small Indian village has a visit from space tourists – aliens from another galaxy. A surprise as the aliens have more to learn from the locals than they think ...

G
Sally Bonner loses her parents in a train accident. She is blind and grows up alone with no friends ... but then Edmund, her teacher, helps Sally learn to play the piano.

FUNCTION recommending

2 Put the words in the box in the correct places in the conversation. You do not need two of the words.

| ~~recommend~~ | about | borrow | I | name | in |
| called | you | kind | | | |

A: Do you want to watch a film?
B: Sorry, I'm busy.
A: Oh. Well then, ¹can you / a good film? *recommend*
B: Hmmm ... ²What of films do you like?
A: Horror films, action films ...
B: Do you like sci-fi?
A: I don't know many sci-fi films.
B: ³There's a good film *The Matrix*.
A: ⁴What's it?
B: It's about the future and the way machines control us ...
A: ⁵Who's it?
B: Keanu Reeves, Laurence Fishburne ... Carrie-Ann Moss.
A: Oh, she's good. ⁶Do you think 'd like it?
B: Yeah, I think so. It's very exciting. I really enjoyed it.
A: ⁷Can I it?
B: Oh, I haven't got it, but you can rent it from the DVD shop.
A: OK, thanks.

LEARN TO link words

3A ▶ 8.2 Listen and write the consonant-vowel links in the sentences below.
1 Are you looking for‿a film?
2 Is it an action film?
3 Is anyone famous in it?
4 Do you want to borrow a DVD?
5 I haven't got a DVD player.
6 I've got it on video.

B Listen again and repeat.

C ▶ 8.3 Listen and circle the sentence you hear.
1 a) Are you looking for a film?
   b) Are you looking for a friend?
2 a) Is it an action film?
   b) Is it an interesting film?
3 a) Is Anna Faris in it?
   b) Is anyone famous in it?
4 a) Do you want to borrow a DVD?
   b) Do you want to buy a DVD?
5 a) I haven't got a DVD player.
   b) I haven't got a CD player.
6 a) I've got it on video.
   b) I've got an old video.

9.1 TRANSPORT

VOCABULARY transport collocations

A bus
B _____
C _____
D _____
E _____
F _____
G _____
H _____
I _____

1A Label pictures A–I.

B Match sentences 1–9 with pictures A–I.
1 It's got two wheels, you get on and off it and it doesn't use petrol. C
2 It's usually got two pilots and can carry a lot of people.
3 It's got four wheels and you pay the driver at the end of the journey.
4 It's got four legs and you ride it.
5 It's got two wheels and it uses petrol.
6 It's got a lot of wheels and you need a ticket.
7 It hasn't got any wheels and it can't carry a lot of people.
8 It hasn't got any wheels, it uses no petrol, and it's free.
9 It's got four or more wheels and you pay at the start of the journey.

2 Complete the conversations with the correct form of the verbs below.

| ~~get off~~   go by (×2)   go on   take   ride   come by   get on |

1 A: Can you tell me the way to the Sports Centre?
   B: Yes, you take the number 195 bus and you _get off_ at the third stop.
2 A: How did you travel to Paris?
   B: I _____ train.
3 A: Is this Kenji's first bike?
   B: Yes, and he _____ it everywhere.
4 A: What's the best way to get to the airport?
   B: You can go by bus or you can _____ a taxi.
5 A: How do you go to school?
   B: I usually _____ foot.
6 A: How does Stefanie go to work?
   B: She _____ car.
7 A: Where are you?
   B: I'm at Berlin airport and I _____ a plane to South Africa, so I can't talk.
8 A: Did you drive here?
   B: No, I _____ bus.

9.1

READING

3A Read the article and circle the correct answers.

1 A *commute* is …
   a) a type of transport
   b) the journey from home to work and back
   c) a part of a car.

2 Jim Kendrick won $10,000 because …
   a) he was the safest driver in Texas
   b) he drove the most kilometres in one year
   c) he travelled the furthest to work.

DO YOU THINK YOUR COMMUTE IS BAD? TRY 640 KILOMETRES A DAY!

Do you think gas* prices are too high? Well, be happy that you aren't Jim Kendrick of Texas in the USA.

5 Every weekday, Kendrick drives 320 kilometres from his home in San Antonio, Texas, to his job at AbleCargo in the port of Houston … and then 320
10 kilometres back again! He leaves work at 5a.m. and gets home and has dinner with his wife at 9p.m.

For his daily journey, Kendrick
15 won the competition 'America's Longest Commute'. His three-and-a-half-hour commute was longer than all the other people in the competition, and
20 is a lot more than the average American commute of twenty-five minutes.

'I was surprised to win,' said Kendrick, who won $10,000.
25 'I was sure that someone else had a longer commute. But it's great – $10,000 is just enough to buy gas for another year.'

Why does he do it? 'Well, my
30 wife and I have a beautiful house in San Antonio and our lifestyle is important to us.'

'The drive gives me a lot of energy. Sometimes, when I
35 drive my Ford Mustang down the highway, I feel like a professional racing car driver.'

How much longer does he want to do this commute? 'Another
40 five or ten years,' Kendrick said. 'I don't see any reason to stop. But gas prices are high, so maybe I need to look for a job nearer home.'

*gas (American English) = petrol (British English)

B Match sentence halves 1–6 with a)–f). Write the line number from the article where you found the information.

1 Jim won the contest because
   f – line 16

2 He was surprised to win because
   _____

3 He was happy about the money because
   _____

4 He does the commute because
   _____

5 He feels good when he drives because
   _____

6 He's thinking about changing jobs because _____

a) he doesn't want to change his lifestyle.
b) he spends about $10,000 a year on gas.
c) he thought someone else drove further.
d) gas prices are so high.
e) he feels like a racing car driver.
f) his commute was the longest.

GRAMMAR articles

4 Complete the text with *a/an*, *the* or no article (-).

Jim lives in ^{1} _a_ house near ^{2} _____ San Antonio, Texas. He's got ^{3} _____ job at AbleCargo in ^{4} _____ Houston, Texas, in ^{5} _____ USA. AbleCargo is ^{6} _____ shipping company, and Jim's ^{7} _____ engineer there. He drives seven hours every day, and gets ^{8} _____ home at 8.30 and has ^{9} _____ dinner at 9p.m. He likes ^{10} _____ fast cars, and he drives ^{11} _____ Ford Mustang. Jim doesn't commute at ^{12} _____ weekend.

5 Add *the* (×6) and *a/an* (×4) to these sentences. One sentence does not need any extra words.

1 Yes, /̬ bus station is down this street on left. *(the)*

2 Rajiv is actor in Mumbai.

3 I haven't got car, but I've got motorbike.

4 Town Hall opens at 9.30 in morning.

5 I love planes and flying. I always ask for window seat.

6 Keith often works at home in evening.

7 Is Manchester in UK?

8 I often go home by taxi at night.

9.2

VOCABULARY adjectives (1)

1A Complete the adjectives in this article about transport.

HOW DO YOU TRAVEL AROUND THE CITY?

I go to work by rollerblades. It's a ¹fast_____ way to travel and it's very ²hea_____ because I get lots of exercise.

Sometimes it feels quite ³dan_____ with so many cars around me, and it's a little ⁴inc_____ because I need to change into shoes when I go into my office. But roller blades are a lot of fun.

Tony Jones, film producer

rollerblades

I go everywhere by skateboard. True, it takes a long time to learn because it's ⁵dif_____ to ride one, but it's very ⁶con_____ – when I go into a shop I just pick up the skateboard and carry it like a book!

Joel Williams, musician

skateboard

I use my scooter all around the city. It's ⁷saf_____, it's ⁸eas_____ to ride and it's more ⁹com_____ than roller blades or a skateboard, because balancing isn't a problem. Sometimes you see scooters with motors on them, but those are really ¹⁰pol_____. 'Go green,' I say!

Nanci Levine, student

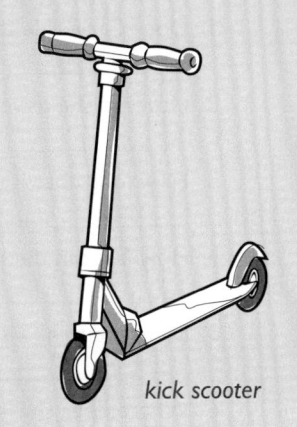

kick scooter

B ▶ 9.1 Listen and check.

C Listen again and repeat. Write the adjectives in the correct place according to the stress.

1 O	2 Oo
fast	
3 Ooo	4 oOo
5 oOoo	6 ooOoo

READING

2A Read the article. How does the writer feel?

| happy relaxed angry hungry funny |

No more wheels!
A shopkeeper speaks out

'I have a small food shop in the city centre, and I really don't like customers coming into the shop on wheels. A businessman comes in on a kick scooter, and he thinks it's funny to do his shopping on the scooter. I don't think it's funny, I think it's dangerous. And the skateboarders, they're even worse. They say they ride skateboards because it's fast and convenient, you know, it's easy to pick up the skateboard when they walk into a shop, but they don't pick up the skateboard, they ride it up and down my shop. But the worst of all are the rollerbladers. They fly into the shop, of course they don't take off the rollerblades because it's inconvenient, and they crash into customers and knock things down. It's terrible! So now I have a new rule: No more wheels. Shoes only!'

B Read the article again. Are sentences 1–6 true (T) or false (F)?

1 The writer has a restaurant. F
2 He thinks the businessman is a funny person.
3 To the writer, kick scooters are not safe.
4 He thinks kick scooters are are better than skateboards.
5 Skateboarders usually pick up their skateboards when they're in his shop.
6 Rollerbladers are the most dangerous, he thinks.

9.2

GRAMMAR can/can't, have to/don't have to

3A Complete the conversations with the correct form of *can*.

1 A: _Can I park_ my car here? (I / park)
  B: No, _____. (you / not)

2 A: _____ your bike on the pavement because it's too dangerous. (You / not / ride)
  B: Oh, OK.

3 A: _____ on the train? (people / smoke)
  B: No, _____. (they / not)

4 A: _____ to the theatre? (we / walk)
  B: Yes, _____, but it's a long way. (we)

5 A: _____ into the city centre, but not cars. (Taxis / drive)
  B: OK, thanks.

B Complete the conversations with *can't* or *don't have to*.

Conversation 1
A: What clothes do you have to wear for the new job?
B: I _don't have to_ wear a suit and tie, but I have to wear a white shirt and I _____ wear jeans.

Conversation 2
A: It's late ... after midnight.
B: Yes, but we _____ get up early tomorrow. It's Saturday.

Conversation 3
A: You _____ drive down this road. It's for buses only.
B: Oh, sorry.

Conversation 4
A: I haven't got any money with me.
B: It's OK. You _____ pay me now. Give me the money tomorrow.

4 Underline the correct alternatives.

A: Hey, do you want to do something tonight? I ¹*can't / don't have to* work.
B: Let's see ... No, I ²*can't / don't have to* meet you tonight – I ³*can / have to* work late.
A: Well, ⁴*can we / do we have to* meet tomorrow?
B: Sorry, I ⁵*can't / don't have to*, I'm busy. But I ⁶*can / have to* do something on Saturday.
A: Great. We ⁷*can / have to* go to that new Italian restaurant, La Spezia.
B: Hmm ... Saturday night is usually crowded. ⁸*Can we / Do we have to* book a table or ⁹*can we / do we have to* just go there?
A: It isn't so popular now, so we ¹⁰*can't / don't have to* book. And if we ¹¹*can't / don't have to* get a table, we ¹²*can / have to* go somewhere else.
B: Great! See you on Saturday, then.

LISTENING

5A Look at the picture of Carin Van Buren on her balancing scooter. Do you think the statements are true (T) or false (F)?

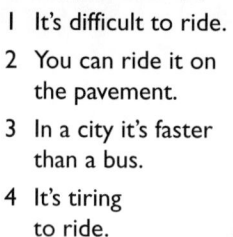

1 It's difficult to ride.
2 You can ride it on the pavement.
3 In a city it's faster than a bus.
4 It's tiring to ride.

B ▶ 9.2 Listen and check.

C Listen again and answer the questions.
1 Does Carin ride the scooter to work?
  Yes, she does.
2 How did she travel to work before?
  _____
3 How long does it take to learn?
  _____
4 How fast can the scooter go?
  _____
5 Does she think a scooter is better than a bike?
  _____
6 Where does she leave her scooter at work?
  _____
7 How does she feel when people laugh at her on her scooter?
  _____
8 Does she like it when people stop her and ask her questions?
  _____

9.3

VOCABULARY | excuses

1 Complete the excuses.
1. I didn't h_e_ _a_ _r_ my al_ _ _ cl_ _ _ _.
2. We slept late and mi_ _ _ _ _ our plane.
3. I lo_ _ _ my ke_ _ _.
4. My car br_ _ _ _ d_ _ _ _.
5. The traf_ _ _ _ was b_ _ _.

FUNCTION | apologising

2A Put the words in the correct order to complete the conversation.

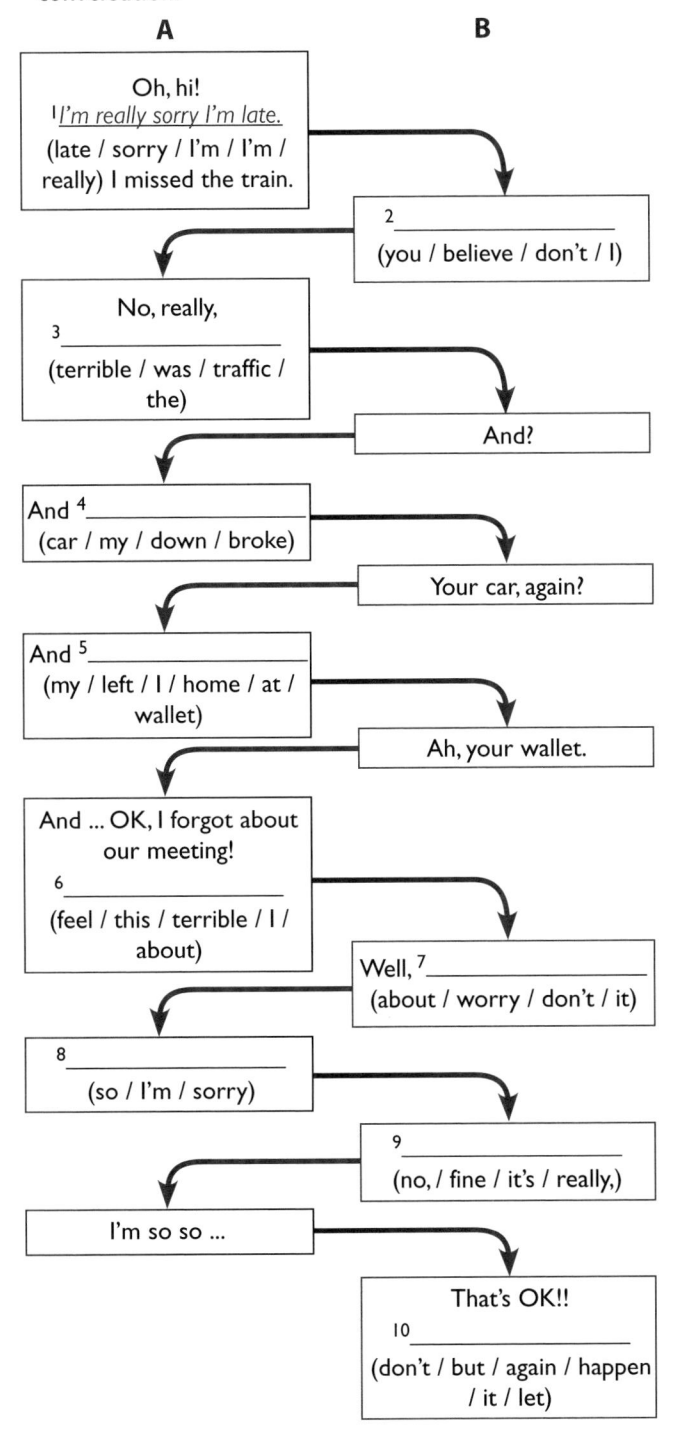

A

Oh, hi!
¹ *I'm really sorry I'm late.*
(late / sorry / I'm / I'm / really) I missed the train.

No, really,
³ _____
(terrible / was / traffic / the)

And ⁴ _____
(car / my / down / broke)

And ⁵ _____
(my / left / I / home / at / wallet)

And ... OK, I forgot about our meeting!
⁶ _____
(feel / this / terrible / I / about)

⁸ _____
(so / I'm / sorry)

I'm so so ...

B

² _____
(you / believe / don't / I)

And?

Your car, again?

Ah, your wallet.

Well, ⁷ _____
(about / worry / don't / it)

⁹ _____
(no, / fine / it's / really,)

That's OK!!
¹⁰ _____
(don't / but / again / happen / it / let)

B ▶ 9.3 Listen and repeat.

LEARN TO | tell a long story

3 Write Bruce's email from the notes.

Dear Alexis,
I'm really sorry about last night. I know it was your birthday. But I had an unlucky evening ...
First of all, I / leave / the house late because I / lose / my keys.
Then I / miss / the bus, so I / phone / a taxi, but the taxi / break down / and I / wait / thirty minutes for another taxi.
After that, I / get / to the restaurant an hour late, but I / leave / your present in the taxi.
I / phone / the taxi company, but they / not answer, so I / go / into the restaurant, but you / not be there.
Finally, I / go / home and / try / to phone you, but you / not answer.
Now I don't know what to do. I'm really sorry.
Love,
Bruce

First of all, I left the house late because ...
_____
_____
_____
_____
_____
_____
_____
_____
_____

VOCABULARY | airport

4 Put the letters of the words in brackets in the correct order to complete the story.

We had a terrible time at the airport. We missed our train and arrived forty minutes before the plane ¹ *took off* (okto fof). We ran to the desk,² _____ (deckche ni) and got our boarding passes. Then we went through ³ _____ (irucytes) and ⁴ _____ (protsaps nolcrot) – no problems. In the ⁵ _____ (pratedeur gunole) we didn't do any ⁶ _____ (xat-refe pishpong) because we only had ten minutes. We ran to the ⁷ _____ (teag), but we were too late so we didn't ⁸ _____ (teg no) the plane. What a disaster!

REVIEW AND CHECK 3: UNITS 7–9

GRAMMAR verb forms

1A Underline the correct alternatives.

Jesse's festival blog

Jesse McCormack is a member of the rock group the Stringers. He ¹*writes* / *is writing* most of the band's songs and ²*plays* / *is playing* lead guitar. This is his summer festival blog.

Saturday 4th August

I ³*write* / *'m writing* my blog today at our fourth festival this summer ... but it's the biggest with more than 25,000 people and we ⁴*have* / *'re having* a great time. The atmosphere here is amazing and people are very friendly. We usually ⁵*arrive* / *are arriving* the day before we play, but this time we ⁶*come* / *came* here two days ago.

Most people have tents, but in fact you ⁷*don't have to* / *can't* sleep in a tent. You ⁸*can* / *can't* sleep in your car. And there are the usual festival rules, for example you ⁹*can* / *can't* use glasses for drinks – you ¹⁰*have to* / *don't have to* use plastic cups. This is a good idea because sometimes people, often children, ¹¹*walk* / *are walking* around with no shoes on.

There's only one hour before we start our show. Danny ¹²*talks* / *'s talking* to a woman from Radio One. Saul ¹³*practises* / *is practising* our first song. Our manager, Dave, ¹⁴*calls* / *is calling* us so I ¹⁵*have to* / *can* stop now. More tomorrow!

B Complete the interview with the correct form of the present simple or present continuous.

Janna: This is Janna Towli from Radio One and I ¹*'m talking* (talk) to Danny Wright from the Stringers. Hi, Danny.

Danny: Hi, everyone.

Janna: So Danny, ²_____ (you / enjoy) yourself at the festival?

Danny: Yeah, it's cool.

Janna: We've got some questions. First, from Luka. He asks: '³_____ (Jesse / write) all the songs or ⁴_____ (you / write) any of them?'

Danny: Oh, Jesse is the songwriter. I just ⁵_____ (sing) the songs.

Janna: And from Viktoria: 'What's your favourite Stringers song?'

Danny: Erm ... You never ⁶_____ (say) 'I love you.'

Janna: OK, right. And the last question, from Abby. She asks: 'What ⁷_____ (Danny / wear) today?'

Danny: Me? Well, today I ⁸_____ (wear) a Stringers T-shirt and jeans. My usual! Oh, there's Dave, our manager. I have to go.

Janna: Thanks for talking to us. Good luck with the show!

Danny: Thanks!

VOCABULARY alphabet puzzle

2 Complete the sentences with words beginning with the letters A–Z.

A I'm sorry I'm late. I didn't hear my *alarm* clock.

B My grandfather had a moustache and a big black *beard*.

C The tram stop is close to my flat, so it's very _____ for me.

D Riding a bike is quite _____, so you have to wear a helmet.

E The opposite of a *crowded* beach is an _____ beach.

F The White House is one of the most _____ buildings in the world.

G I want to see the Eiffel Tower. Where do I _____ off the bus?

H *Frankenstein* was one of the first _____ films. It was quite scary.

I The opposite of *boring* is _____.

J The Amazon _____ is 7 million square kilometres.

K Do you _____ the way to the bus station?

L François is _____ on his bed. He doesn't feel very well.

M I got up late and I _____ my train.

N The children in the next room are too _____ – I can't work.

O Do you go by car or _____ foot?

P Cars are more _____ than bikes. Bikes are greener.

Q Be _____! The baby's sleeping.

R Can you _____ a good DVD?

S Tourists always visit Red _____ in Moscow.

T I was late because the _____ was bad.

U Alan's shoes are too small, so they're very _____.

V She was born in a small _____ in Belgium.

W The traffic is _____ at five o'clock than at three o'clock.

X How do you spell the opposite of *cheap*? e_____.

Y Hi, Liz. It's Jon. I waited for _____ for two hours! What happened?

Z My holiday was great. We saw the Great Wall. It was ama_____!

56

REVIEW AND CHECK 3: UNITS 7–9

GRAMMAR comparatives and superlatives

3 Complete the information with the correct comparative or superlative form of the words in the box.

| tall | cheap | hot | quiet | interesting | ~~good~~ | slow | convenient | cold | fast |

SHANGHAI

When is the best time to go?

The ¹ _best_ months to visit are May and October, when it's 19–24°C. July and August are ² _____ months, when it can be 28°C. November to April are ³ _____ months, when it's 3–14°C.

How can I get around?

You can travel by bus or by metro. Buses are ⁴ _____ than the metro, especially in the morning and evening when the traffic is bad. The metro is ⁵ _____ than buses, but there are only two metro lines. The ⁶ _____ way to travel around the city is by taxi because there are lots – they go everywhere and they aren't very expensive.

I only have one day! What can I see?

Visit ⁷ _____ building in China, the 492-metre Shanghai World Financial Centre. The floor is glass and it feels like walking in the sky. Walk along the Bund, next to the river – it's very central, but it's a lot ⁸ _____ than the noisy city centre. And visit the Shanghai Museum – most visitors to the city say this is ⁹ _____ thing to see in Shanghai.

Where can I stay?

Shanghai has hundreds of hotels, and there are many two-star and three-star hotels for travellers on a budget – of course, these are ¹⁰ _____ than the 4-star luxury hotels. Check the internet for recommendations from other travellers.

FUNCTION recommending; giving directions

4A ▶ RC 3.1 Listen to the conversations and choose the correct ending to the sentence.

Jurgen recommends a restaurant to Greg but …

a) Greg doesn't understand and takes the wrong street.
b) he gives bad directions and Greg and doesn't find the restaurant.
c) Greg decides to stay home and eat pizza.

B Listen again. Are the sentences true (T) or false (F)?

1 It's Jurgen's wife's birthday.   F
2 Greg and his wife like Chinese food.
3 Jurgen recommends a Chinese restaurant.
4 The restaurant is near the pharmacy.
5 Greg and his wife find the restaurant.
6 They have pizza at the restaurant.

C Listen again and complete the sentences.

1 What kind of food _do you like_ ?
2 Do you think my wife _____ ?
3 Can you tell _____ ?
4 Go down Hillside Road past the pharmacy _____.
5 Then go straight _____ 200 metres.
6 Oh, no – I'm so _____.
7 I feel terrible _____.
8 Don't worry _____.

GRAMMAR articles

5 Complete the text with a/an, the or no article (-).

POLAND – DAY 7

The best way to see ¹ _the_ city of ² _____ Krakow is in ³ _____ Trabant – the classic eastern-European car. The tour starts at 9.00a.m. in ⁴ _____ city centre, where you meet your tour guides Irek and Kasia. Irek is ⁵ _____ university student and Kasia is ⁶ _____ history teacher, and together they know Krakow better than most professional guides. You start the tour on ⁷ _____ foot and visit Cloth Hall in ⁸ _____ centre of Grand Square. You then go by ⁹ _____ car and visit Nowa Huta and the Jewish quarter. Lunch is at ¹⁰ _____ restaurant near the castle. ¹¹ _____ Polish food is quite rich, so try not to eat too much! In ¹² _____ afternoon, Irek and Kasia can show you Wawel Castle or take you back to your hotel.

TEST 3: UNITS 7–9

TEST

Circle the correct option to complete the sentences.

1. Sitting on the beach is _____ working.
   a) relaxing than   b) better than   c) more nice than

2. There was a bridge over the _____.
   a) desert   b) river   c) mountain

3. I _____ my MP3 player.
   a) listening to   b) 'm listening to   c) 'm listening to

4. What _____ like?
   a) does Jon look   b) Jon does look   c) Jon looks

5. A: Do I _____ the bus here for the museum?
   B: No, at the next stop.
   a) go by   b) ride   c) get off

6. I didn't get a seat because the train was _____.
   a) comfortable   b) uncomfortable   c) crowded

7. Sorry I'm late. I _____ my train.
   a) lost   b) missed   c) left

8. A: What _____?
   B: I'm working on the computer.
   a) you are doing   b) are you doing   c) do you doing

9. I don't think _____ this DVD. It's too scary.
   a) you'd like   b) you like   c) you recommend

10. My wife works _____. She's a writer.
    a) at home   b) at the home   c) home

11. _____ to the airport by bus?
    a) You can go   b) Do you can go   c) Can you go

12. Go _____ until the end of the street.
    a) straight   b) straight on   c) strait on

13. It was difficult to walk in the _____ because of all the trees.
    a) mountain   b) jungle   c) village

14. The children _____ very well at the moment.
    a) aren't feeling   b) don't feeling   c) aren't feel

15. He _____ slim with short black hair.
    a) 's got   b) 's   c) has

16. Spanish is _____ than English.
    a) easyer   b) easier   c) more easy

17. Children _____ pay. It's free for them.
    a) don't have to   b) can't   c) haven't to

18. A: I laughed a lot at this DVD. It's very funny.
    B: Oh, so it's a _____.
    a) drama   b) musical   c) comedy

19. A: Is there a post office near here?
    B: Yes, go down here and it's _____.
    a) on the left   b) on left   c) left

20. I always go by underground because it's fast and _____.
    a) convenient   b) polluting   c) dangerous

21. It's _____ hotel in Saudi Arabia.
    a) the bigger   b) the bigest   c) the biggest

22. The sign says 'No Smoking' so you _____ smoke here.
    a) have to   b) don't have to   c) can't

23. My grandmother is _____.
    a) in sixties   b) in her sixties   c) in the sixties

24. A: Do you often phone your parents?
    B: Yes, I talked to _____ last night.
    a) them   b) him and her   c) they

25. _____ are good for you.
    a) Vegetables   b) The vegetables   c) Vegetable

26. Who is _____ player in the football team?
    a) most bad   b) the worst   c) the baddest

27. _____, the train arrived. It was four hours late.
    a) First of all   b) After   c) Finally

28. Leonie _____ black.
    a) always is wearing
    b) is wearing always
    c) always wears

29. A: Where's the tourist information centre?
    B: You _____ left and walk for about five minutes.
    a) take   b) turn to   c) turn

30. A: Have you got _____?
    B: No, I haven't, but I've got two brothers.
    a) a sister   b) the sister   c) sister

TEST RESULT /30

10.1 THE FUTURE

GRAMMAR *be going to; would like to*

1A Look at the table and complete sentences 1–10 with the correct form of *be going to* or *would like to*.

	Plans next week	Plans next year	Wishes for the future
Jim, USA	start new job at the bank – Monday	look for a new flat not stay at parents' house	be very rich
Soo Min, South Korea	have haircut – Tuesday	go to university	work in TV
Bill and Jane, Ireland	visit daughter Lynn and family – Sat/Sun	not have a holiday	move nearer Lynn

1 Jim *'s going to start* his new job at the bank on Monday.
2 He _____ for a new flat next year.
3 He _____ at his parents' house.
4 He _____ very rich.
5 Soo Min _____ a haircut on Tuesday.
6 She _____ to university next year.
7 She _____ in TV.
8 Bill and Jane _____ their daughter at the weekend.
9 They _____ a holiday next year.
10 They _____ nearer their daughter.

B Write questions for the people with *be going to* or *would like to*.
1 Which bank / you / work at, Jim?
  Which bank are you going to work at, Jim?
2 Where / you / look for / a new flat, Jim?
  _____
3 When / you / go / to university, Soo Min?
  _____
4 Why / like / work / in TV, Soo Min?
  _____
5 How / you / travel, Bill and Jane?
  _____
6 Why / like / move / nearer your daughter, Bill and Jane?
  _____

C Match answers a)–f) with questions 1–6 in Exercise 1B.
a) Because I want to be famous. 4
b) We're going by train.
c) In the city centre.
d) We'd like to see our grandchildren more.
e) In September next year.
f) At HSBC bank.

2 Put the words in order to make questions. Then write short answers about you.
1 TV / you / to / evening / watch / are / this / going?
  Are you going to watch TV this evening?
  Yes, I am. / No, I'm not.
2 like / work / would / TV / to / you / in?
  _____
3 weekend / you / family / see / next / are / to / going / your?
  _____
4 for / English / to / useful / be / you / is / going?
  _____
5 like / new / would / phone / a / you / buy / to / mobile?
  _____
6 your / study / classmates / year / you / going / English / next / to / are / and?
  _____
7 in / like / live / country / you / to / would / another?
  _____
8 home / your / like / now / to / go / would / classmates?
  _____

59

10.1

READING

3A Read the article and circle the best title.
1 Lottery winners around the world
2 Sisters win lottery
3 Another teenage lottery winner

First there was Tracey Makin in 1998, then Michael Carroll in 2002, and then Callie Rogers in 2003 – all of them were teenagers when they won the lottery. Tracey was sixteen at the time and won £1,055,171. Callie was the same age when she won £1,800,000 and Michael was nineteen when he won £9,700,000.

Now eighteen-year-old Ianthe Fullagar is the newest in this group of teenage lottery winners. She won £7,000,000 and we asked her about her future.

'I'm not going to change my plans very much. I'm still going to go to university. I'm going to live like a normal student and not a millionaire. I love my baked beans on toast.'

It was only the second time that she played the EuroMillions Lottery. She bought her ticket from a newsagent's and watched the lottery result on television.

First on her shopping list is a holiday in Egypt and a replacement for her ten-year-old Ford Ka. 'I'm going to fly to Cairo and spend about a month travelling around the country. When I come back, I'm going to sell my old car and buy a new one. I'd like to get a bigger one.'

B Read the article again and answer the questions.
1 Who won the largest amount of money?
   Michael Carroll
2 Who won the smallest amount of money?
   _____
3 Who are the youngest teenage winners?
   _____
4 Does Ianthe want to change her life?
   _____
5 Does she often buy lottery tickets?
   _____
6 What is she going to do with the money?
   _____
7 Why does she want to buy a new car?
   _____

VOCABULARY plans

4A Complete the puzzle with the words from the box and find the message.

| ~~nothing~~ stay at buy clubbing learn a holiday start move a new suit go for |

1. do **nothing**
2. ... a walk
3. get ...
4. have ...
5. go ...
6. ... house
7. ...
8. ... a hotel / a new job
9. ... to swim
10. ... a boat

Message: _____.

B Complete the conversations.

Conversation 1
A: What are you going to do this weekend?
B: I'm going jo**gging** on Saturday morning and then in the evening I'm going to meet Bob and we're going for a dr_____ in the pub.

Conversation 2
A: So, what are your plans?
B: Well, we're going to get ma_____ next year and we'd like to mo_____ to another country, maybe Spain. We'd like to bu_____ a house there, and start a fa_____, maybe have three or four children.

Conversation 3
A: What's your son going to do?
B: He's going to stay with some fr_____ in São Paulo. He wants to do a co_____ and le_____ Portuguese and then he'd like to get a jo_____ with a computer company in Brazil.

Conversation 4
A: What are you going to do with your lottery money?
B: First, I'm going to st_____ work! I'm going to ha_____ a big party, too. Then I want to bu_____ a big boat and tr_____ round the world!

Conversation 5
A: Are you going to buy pr_____ for all your friends?
B: Of course! And then I'm going to go sh_____ in Paris to buy some fantastic designer clothes.

10.2

VOCABULARY Phrases with *get*

1A Add the vowels to the adjectives.
1. Marco got _sunburnt_ (snbnt), so he ...
2. I got _____ (thrsty), so I ...
3. Adrian got _____ (brd) at school, so he ...
4. They got _____ (wt), so they...
5. Ed and Leo got _____ (hngry), so they ...
6. I got very _____ (ht), so I ...
7. Helena got _____ (lst), so she ...
8. We got _____ (cld), so we ...

B Match sentence halves 1–8 above with a)–h).
a) was an hour late for the meeting. 7
b) put on our coats.
c) had a second breakfast.
d) texted some of the other students in the class.
e) changed into dry clothes.
f) took off my sweater.
g) went for a drink with Carson.
h) stayed indoors for the next two days.

C ▶ 10.1 Listen and write the adjectives in the correct place according to the vowel sound.

1 /ʌ/ e.g. c<u>u</u>p	2 /ɒ/ e.g. j<u>o</u>b	3 /e/ e.g. r<u>e</u>d
s<u>u</u>nburnt		
4 /ɜː/ e.g. h<u>er</u>	**5 /ɔː/ e.g. f<u>our</u>**	**6 /əʊ/ e.g. g<u>o</u>**

2 Look at the table and the meanings 1–4 of *get*. Write the words and phrases below in the correct column.

1 become	2 arrive	3 buy	4 obtain
get ...	get ...	get ...	get ...
hungry			

a hamburger, to school, a new computer, ~~hungry~~, lost, some help, to work, a new car, home, a glass of water, a job, tired

LISTENING

3A ▶ 10.2 Listen to four people who survived in difficult situations. Match speakers 1–4 with places a)–d).

Speaker 1   a) jungle
Speaker 2   b) mountain
Speaker 3   c) desert
Speaker 4   d) sea

B Listen again and circle the best answers.
1 Speaker 1 _____.
   a) ate fish ✓
   b) drank seawater
   c) was cold
2 Speaker 1 _____.
   a) got sunburnt
   b) got tired
   b) saw a lot of sharks
3 Speaker 2 _____.
   a) got cold
   b) walked all day
   c) got very thirsty
4 Speaker 2 _____.
   a) saw lots of insects
   b) had food with her
   c) sometimes took her shoes off
5 Speaker 3 _____.
   a) was on the mountain for three nights
   b) got lost because of the snow
   c) made a fire
6 Speaker 3 _____.
   a) slept on the ground
   b) got hungry
   c) stayed warm
7 Speaker 4 _____.
   a) got very hungry
   b) got thirsty
   c) didn't get bored
8 Speaker 4 _____.
   a) had some food with her
   b) ate plants
   c) ate insects

10.2

GRAMMAR will, might, won't for prediction

4 Complete sentences 1–8 with *'ll*, *will* or *won't* and a verb from the box.

~~get~~ be (×2) miss win come know love

1 Wear your coat or you'*ll get* cold.
2 Do you think Brazil _____ the World Cup?
3 It's very late. I'm sure the shop _____ open.
4 I don't want to go to the party! I _____ any people there.
5 Come on! We _____ the train.
6 Read this book. I'm sure you _____ it.
7 Oh no! I'm late again. The boss _____ happy.
8 You can invite Alain, but he _____. He doesn't like jazz music.

5 Underline the correct alternatives in the text.

SURVIVE IN THE CITY

People always talk about survival in the jungle, at sea, etc., but I'll tell you a really dangerous place: the city! Here are my tips for survival.

- Don't drive. Traffic is usually terrible and you ¹*might not* / *'ll* / *won't* spend more time in your car than seeing the city.

- Ask people for help – most people ²*will* / *might* / *won't* be happy to stop and help you.

- Don't stand in the street with a map in your hand and a camera around your neck. People ³*will* / *might not* / *won't* know you're a tourist. That's not a problem, but someone ⁴*will* / *might* / *might not* come and take your money.

- Wear normal clothes, not expensive ones. With expensive clothes, people ⁵*will* / *might not* / *won't* think you've got lots of money and yes – they ⁶*'ll* / *might* / *won't* take it away from you!

- Carry an umbrella. It often rains and with an umbrella you ⁷*'ll* / *might* / *won't* get wet.

- Don't stay out too late or it ⁸*'ll* / *might* / *might not* be easy to find a bus or a taxi.

- Give waiters a good tip, maybe 10%. You ⁹*'ll* / *might* / *might not* go back to the same restaurant and the waiter ¹⁰*will* / *might not* / *won't* forget you!

6 ▶ 10.3 Listen and number the sentences in the order you hear them.

1 a) You'll get cold. 2
   b) You get cold. 1
2 a) We'll miss the train.
   b) We miss the train.
3 a) I'm sure you'll hate it.
   b) I'm sure you hate it.
4 a) They'll know you're a tourist.
   b) They know you're a tourist.
5 a) I'll stay at home.
   b) I stay at home.
6 a) I'll never go out.
   b) I never go out.

WRITING too, also, as well

7 Are *too*, *also* and *as well* in the correct place? Tick three correct sentences. Correct the wrong sentences.

1 The bus is a good way to travel, and the underground is ~~too good~~.
2 If you buy a travel card for the underground, you can also use it on the bus.
3 You can ask shopkeepers for help – they're very friendly, and they'll know the city as well.
4 It's generally a safe city, but it can be dangerous also to walk alone late at night in some areas.
5 It isn't a good idea to carry a lot of money, and leave your expensive watch too at home.
6 You can get delicious food in cafés and as well in street markets.
7 Don't walk too far, and also wear comfortable shoes – then you won't get tired.
8 At night, taxis are as well convenient, but they're expensive.

8 Write a short text giving advice for a visitor to your town or city. Use *too*, *also*, *as well* and the phrases below to help you. Write 80–100 words.

The _____ is a good way to travel …
It's a good idea to carry …
You can ask _____ for help, and you can ask …
It can be dangerous to …

10.3

VOCABULARY adjectives

1 Put the letters in order to make adjectives. Start with the underlined letter.

1 zi<u>a</u>mang — _amazing_
2 cl<u>e</u>enextl — _____
3 o<u>c</u>lo — _____
4 rel<u>o</u>wfund — _____
5 <u>f</u>nittfasac — _____
6 ta<u>r</u>eg — _____
7 ow<u>e</u>meas — _____
8 tri<u>b</u>lilan — _____

FUNCTION making suggestions

2A Complete the conversation with the words in the box.

| <s>would</s> | How | don't | about | idea | feel | let's | Why |
| Have | Sounds | stay | Brilliant | | | | |

Tim: So, Gordon, what ¹ _would_ you like do today?
Gordon: I don't know. ² _____ you got any ideas?
Tim: What ³ _____ going to a concert?
Gordon: Hmmm ... That might be difficult. We ⁴ _____ like the same music. You like rock, I like hip-hop.
Tim: Oh. That's true. ⁵ _____ about inviting some friends?
Gordon: I don't really ⁶ _____ like doing that.
Tim: OK then. ⁷ _____ don't we ⁸ _____ home and watch TV?
Gordon: That's a good ⁹ _____. What's on?
Tim: Let me see ... Uh, *Castaway* with Tom Hanks.
Gordon: ¹⁰ _____!
Tim: And ¹¹ _____ have popcorn, too.
Gordon: ¹² _____ good!

B ▶ 10.4 Listen and check.

LEARN TO respond to suggestions

3A Correct the mistakes in sentences 1–5 and a)–e).

1 Let go shopping.   (corrected: Let's)   e
2 How about go for a bike ride?
3 Why don't we going to an art gallery?
4 What about staying at home and cook something?
5 Who about making spaghetti and meatballs?

a) That don't sound very interesting. Looking at paintings is boring!
b) I don't really feel like do that. I'm too tired.
c) Sound good. You make the meatballs, I can make the pasta.
d) Brilliant! What would you like eat?
e) That isn't very good idea. I haven't got much money.

B Look at the sentences in Exercise 3A again. Match suggestions 1–5 with responses a)–e).

VOCABULARY weather

4 Add the vowels to the weather words and write them in the correct place in the crossword.

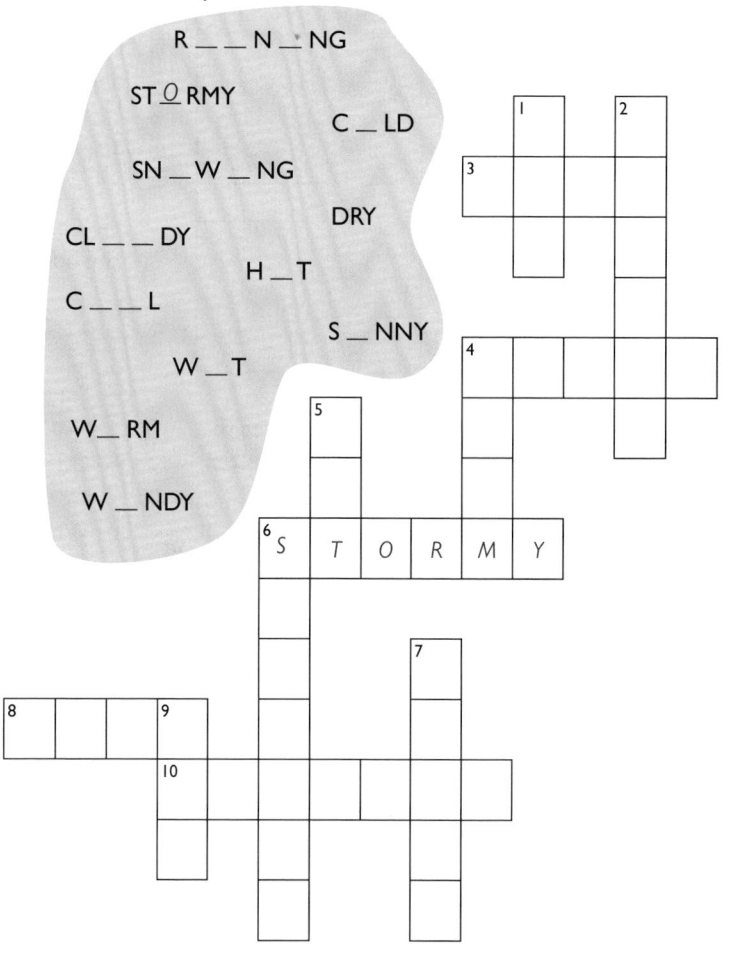

R _ _ N _ NG
ST _O_ RMY
C _ LD
SN _ W _ NG
CL _ _ DY
DRY
H _ T
C _ _ L
S _ NNY
W _ T
W _ RM
W _ NDY

Crossword answer at 6: S T O R M Y

11.1 HEALTH

VOCABULARY the body

1A Find twelve words for parts of the body.

S	T	O	M	A	C	H
M	K	T	H	U	M	B
O	N	O	S	E	N	T
U	E	H	F	E	E	T
T	E	E	T	H	C	O
H	H	A	N	D	K	E
F	O	D	B	A	C	K

B ▶ 11.1 Listen and repeat.

C Listen again and write the words in the correct place according to the vowel sound.

1 /e/ red	2 /æ/ happy
h<u>ea</u>d	
3 /iː/ meat	4 /əʊ/ no
5 /ʌ/ fun	6 /aʊ/ now

2 Put the letters in order to make health problems. Start with the underlined letter.

1 I feel _sick_ . (ki<u>s</u>c)
2 My leg _____. (<u>sh</u>utr)
3 I've got a bad _____. (<u>ch</u>adeeha)
4 I've got a _____ _____. (ro<u>s</u>e <u>t</u>rahot)
5 My _____ hurts. (delho<u>s</u>ur)
6 I've got awful _____. (ca<u>h</u>ottohe)
7 I've got a _____ _____. (<u>s</u>ero y<u>e</u>e)
8 I feel _____. (b<u>r</u>eritel)
9 I've got a _____. (metteru<u>p</u>are)
10 I've got a _____. (gu<u>c</u>oh)

GRAMMAR should/shouldn't

3A Read the leaflet about travel health. Check any new words in your dictionary.

B Complete the information with should/shouldn't and the words in brackets.

TRAVEL HEALTH: BEFORE YOU GO

We answer your FAQs (frequently asked questions) about health on holiday:

¹ _Should I see_ (I / see) my doctor before I go on holiday?

Yes, ² _____ (you / speak) to your doctor or your local travel centre about six weeks before you leave.

³ _____ (I / get) any vaccinations?

Your doctor or nurse can give you information or you can check on the internet. ⁴ _____ (You / not have) a lot of vaccinations together, so start early.

What else ⁵ _____ (I / do)?

⁶ _____ (You / visit) your dentist as well, because dentists can be very expensive in other countries. ⁷ _____ (You / take) a Traveller's First Aid Kit with suncream, plasters and painkillers, but ⁸ _____ (you / not open) these before you travel. Officials at the airport might ask to check them.

Any other advice?

Well, ⁹ _____ (you / not travel) when you have a bad earache or a cold. And it's important to relax, but ¹⁰ _____ (you / not drink) alcohol or coffee in the airport or on the plane, because they'll make you feel worse.

4 Complete the conversation with should/shouldn't and a verb from the box. Add the correct pronouns (I or you).

| go (×2)   watch   sleep   do (×2)   change   eat |

A: I'm going to fly to Japan soon and I'm worried about the time difference, you know, getting tired after the journey.
B: Oh yes, jet lag can be difficult. ¹ _You should go_ to bed early for two or three nights before you travel.
A: What else ² _____?
B: When you're on the plane, ³ _____ all the food they bring, it's too much. And ⁴ _____ your watch to Japanese local time.
A: And ⁵ _____ on the plane?
B: Yes, you need to rest, so ⁶ _____ all the movies or stay awake the whole time. It's a long journey! What time do you arrive?
A: At two in the afternoon.
B: You'll be very tired, but ⁷ _____ to bed. ⁸ _____ some exercise. It's a good idea to go for a walk and then wait and sleep when it's dark.
A: Thanks. That's good advice.

64

11.1

READING

WALKING – THE PERFECT SPORT?

Forget about tennis, swimming, skiing and jogging. Walking is the easiest and cheapest way to stay fit. It's free, you don't need special clothes or equipment, you don't need a trainer or a special place. Anybody can do it anytime: young people, older people, alone or in groups.

OK – perhaps it's not really a sport, but it IS the most popular physical activity and one of the best ways to stay healthy. What are the benefits? Walking is good for your heart and your legs; regular walkers say they sleep better and feel happier; and smokers say they don't smoke so much.

Maybe you don't have very much time, so here are some ideas to help you start walking:

- Walk, don't drive, to the local shop. If you have a lot to carry, take a small backpack.
- If you have children, walk with them to and from school.
- Get off the bus or train a stop or two early. This will give you some extra daily exercise – and it's cheaper, too!
- Take a walk in your lunch hour at school or work.
- Once a week take a longer walk, and go on a completely new route; this helps to keep things interesting.

There are walkers' clubs all over the world. Join one – walking is a great way to meet people and make new friends!

5A Read the article above and number topics a)–d) in the correct order.

a) Why is walking better than other sports?   1
b) How can you find time for walking?
c) Who can you walk with?
d) Why is walking good for your health?

B Read the article again and tick the ideas the article talks about.

1 Walking isn't expensive.   ✓
2 You have to wear good walking shoes.
3 Age isn't important.
4 Walking is good for headaches.
5 You should go shopping on foot.
6 Get up earlier in the morning, and do some extra exercise every day.
7 Take a different walk every week so you don't get bored.
8 You can meet people more easily when walking.

C Find words 1–7 in the text. Then match the words with their definitions a)–g).

1 equipment   a) with no other people
2 a trainer   b) a bag that you carry on your back
3 alone   c) connected to your body, e.g. _____ exercise
4 physical   d) the things you use for an activity, e.g. a machine in the gym
5 benefits   e) a way from one place to another
6 a backpack   f) good things
7 a route   g) a teacher

D Cover the article and try to complete the sentences. Then check your answers with the text.

Maybe you don't have very much time, so here are some ideas to help you start walking:

- Walk, don't drive, [1]_____ the local shop. If you [2]_____ a lot to carry, take a small backpack.
- If you [3]_____ children, walk [4]_____ them to and [5]_____ school.
- Get off the bus or train a stop or two early. This will give you some extra daily exercise – and it's cheaper, [6]_____!
- Take a walk [7]_____ your lunch hour [8]_____ school or work.
- Once a week [9]_____ a longer walk, and go on a completely new route; this helps to keep things interesting.

There are walkers' clubs [10]_____ over the world. Join one – walking is a great way to [11]_____ people and [12]_____ new friends!

65

11.2

VOCABULARY common verbs

1A Complete the diagrams with a verb from the box.

| hear | understand | ~~forget~~ | read | run |
| climb | swim | concentrate | remember | |

1 _forget_ — a name / my PIN number / my ticket

2 _____ — fast / 800 metres / down a road

3 _____ — your password / your mother's birthday / your first teacher

4 _____ — English / my teacher / the problem

5 _____ — a magazine / a newspaper / music

6 _____ — a tree / a mountain / a tower

7 _____ — a noise / something outside / the door close

8 _____ — in a river / in a lake / 100 metres

9 _____ — on your homework / on your work / on a computer game

B Complete the sentences with verbs from Exercise 1A.
1 I'm too tired and I can't _concentrate_.
2 Sorry, I don't _____. I don't speak Chinese.
3 I can't _____ that! It's too high.
4 Help! Help! I can't _____!
5 I can't _____ this article. Where are my glasses?
6 Don't _____ your keys.
7 Speak up! I can't _____ you.
8 Slow down. We have time and we don't have to _____.
9 I can never _____ my mobile number. I have to write it down.

LISTENING

2A ▶ 11.2 Listen to the radio programme about finding your 'real' age. Number the pictures in the order you hear about them.

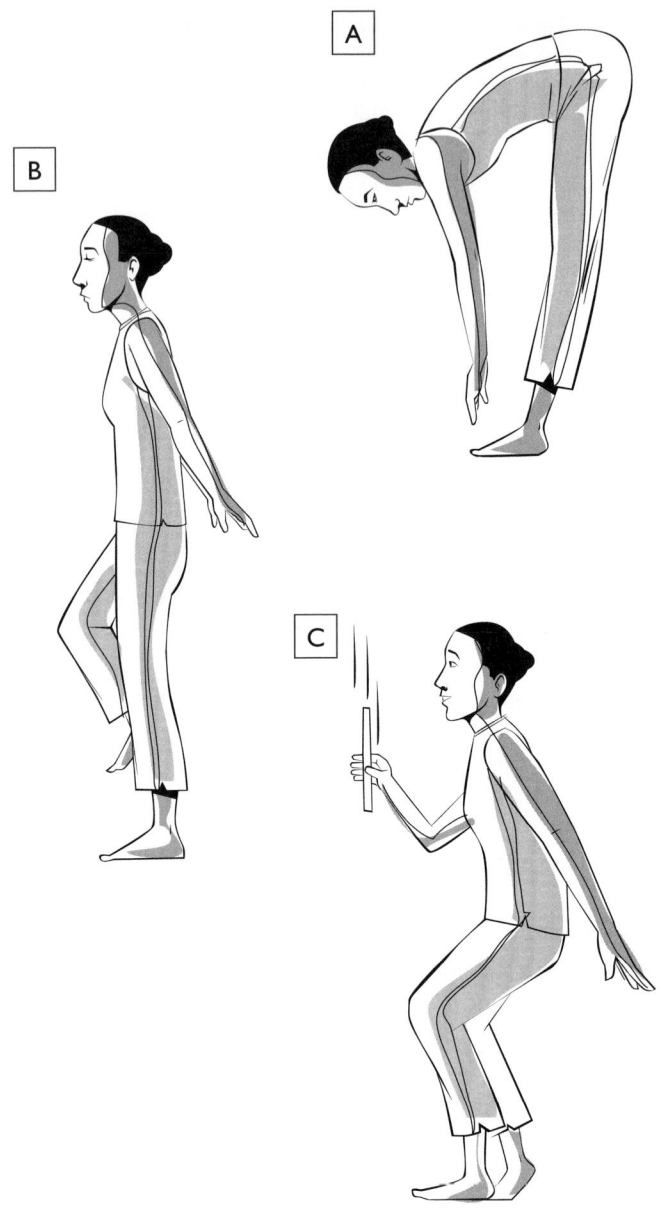

A
B
C

B Listen again and circle the correct information about the interviewer.
1 Her 'birthday' age is _____.
   a) under 20   b) 20–29   c) 30–39 (circled)
2 Her time (in seconds) for the balance test is _____.
   a) 11–15   b) 16–20   c) 21–25
3 She catches the ruler _____.
   a) near the beginning   b) in the middle   c) at the end
4 She can touch her _____.
   a) toes   b) ankles   c) knees
5 Her real age is _____ her 'birthday' age.
   a) younger than   b) the same as   c) older than

11.2

GRAMMAR adverbs of manner

3 Underline the correct alternative.
1. A: Your mum drives really *slow / slowly*.
   B: Yes, well you know that *slow / slowly* drivers don't have many accidents.
2. A: Jeff is quite *lazy / lazily* about doing tasks around the house.
   B: That's true, he does them *lazy / lazily*, but he does them in the end!
3. A: The teacher talks very *quiet / quietly*.
   B: Yes, and the students aren't *quiet / quietly*, so it's difficult to hear.
4. A: I found the shop *easy / easily*, thanks to your clear directions.
   B: Well, in fact, it's rather *easy / easily* to find.
5. A: Our team played *bad / badly* and we lost the match.
   B: That's surprising, I thought the other team was *bad / badly*.
6. A: You're so *energetic / energetically* when you get up in the morning. How do you do it?
   B: I read somewhere that if you get up *energetic / energetically*, you'll feel good all day.
7. A: You came in rather *noisy / noisily* last night.
   B: Sorry, I didn't mean to be so *noisy / noisily*.
8. A: This exercise isn't very *hard / hardly*.
   B: No? Well, work *hard / hardly* to the end because the second part is difficult.

4A Complete the sentences with the adverb form of the words in brackets.
1. You have to drive _carefully_ (careful) and _____ (safe). You can't drive _____ (dangerous) or _____ (fast).
2. You have to work very _____ (hard) and often very _____ (late) at night but you get long summer holidays. You don't have to speak _____ (loud), but it helps.
3. You should eat _____ (healthy) and go to bed _____ (early). You don't have to walk or run _____ (fast), but you have to see _____ (clear).
4. You don't have to read music _____ (perfect), but it helps. You have to sing _____ (good), but you don't have to sing _____ (loud).

B Look at the sentences in Exercise 4A again. What are the jobs for each one? Underline the correct alternative.
1. <u>a bus driver</u> / a racing driver
2. a teacher / a politician
3. a footballer / a golfer
4. a jazz singer / an opera singer

5 Complete the sentences with an adjective or adverb.
Conversation 1
A: Are you OK?
B: No, I don't feel very we_ll_____. Can I lie down somewhere?
A: Yes, over here.
B: I'm really tir_____. I slept terri_____ last night.

Conversation 2
A: This room's very comf_____.
B: Yes, but it's quite noi_____. I can hear the people downstairs.
A: Well, we don't have to stay here all evening. I'm hun_____.
B: Yes, we can eat che_____ in the café tonight and then we can go to that exp_____ Italian restaurant tomorrow.

Conversation 3
A: I sing very ba_____.
B: No, you don't. You sing beau_____.
A: Thank you. That's ki_____ of you.

WRITING adverbs in stories

6A Write the adverbs.
1. slow   _slowly_
2. quick   _____
3. angry   _____
4. nervous   _____
5. careful   _____

B Complete the joke with the adverbs from Exercise 6A.
A man walked ¹ _nervously_ into the dentist's office. The dentist looked ² _____ at the man's teeth and then said, 'I have to take one tooth out. I can do it ³ _____ – it'll only take five minutes and it'll cost $100.'

'A hundred dollars for five minutes' work!' the man said ⁴ _____. 'That's too expensive!'

'Well,' answered the dentist, 'I can do it ⁵ _____ if you want!'

11.3

VOCABULARY problems

1 Complete the conversations with the verbs in the box.

| ~~cut~~ drop lift stand fall push |

1. A: Be careful with that knife!
   B: Why?
   A: You might _cut_ your finger.
2. A: What's the matter?
   B: This box is too heavy. I can't _____ it.
3. A: I can't ride my bike uphill.
   B: So what do you do?
   A: I usually get off and _____ it.
4. A: I can carry these dishes.
   B: Don't carry all of them. You'll _____ them!
   A: I'll be OK. Oh, no!
5. A: It's very windy tonight.
   B: Yes, I think that tree might _____ down.
6. A: Hi, Jenny. It's me.
   B: Hi, Frank. Where are you?
   A: I'm on the train. It's really crowded so I have to _____.

FUNCTION offering to help

2A Put the words in 1–4 and a)–d) in the correct order.

1. my / problem / MP3 / there's / a / player / with
   There's a problem with my MP3 player.
2. favourite / was / that / my / vase
   _____
3. tired / really / I'm
   _____
4. in / cold / here / it's
   _____

a) coffee / let / you / a / make / me
   _____
b) look / me / let
   _____
c) you / I'll / buy / one / another
   _____
d) I / window / shall / close / the?
   _____

B Look at the sentences in Exercise 2A again. Match 1–4 with offers a)–d).

3A Read Jim's 'To do' list. Then use offers of help to complete the conversation.

TO DO
Phone Noriko in Tokyo
Email Moscow office
Get flowers for Ellie – send them to hospital
Meet Anne at airport (5.30)

Ruth: Are you OK, Jim?
Jim: No. I have to meet Anne at 5.30 and look at this list!
Ruth: ¹_Let_ me _help_. I'm not busy at the moment.
Jim: Oh, can you? Thanks!
Ruth: No problem. ² _____ I _____ Noriko?
Jim: Yes, please.
Ruth: And then I ³_____ _____ the Moscow office.
Jim: Can you tell them I'll phone tomorrow?
Ruth: OK. And I ⁴_____ _____ some flowers for Ellie. I'm going to the hospital to see her tonight anyway.
Jim: Fantastic! ⁵_____ me _____ you the money.
Ruth: It's OK. Give it to me tomorrow.
Jim: Thanks a lot. I ⁶_____ _____ the same for you any time!

B ▶ 11.3 Listen and check. Then listen and repeat.

LEARN TO thank someone

4 Circle the correct answer.
1. A: Are you OK? Let me carry that.
   B: a) Yes.   b) No problem.   **c) Thanks a lot.**
2. A: Shall I speak to Mr Chen for you?
   B: a) That's kind of you.   b) You're welcome.   c) It's a problem.
3. A: I'll drive you home.
   B: a) You're welcome.   b) Shall I do it?
   c) Thanks. I'm very grateful.
4. A: Thank you very much.
   B: a) Yes.   b) You're welcome.   c) Your welcome.
5. A: Is this seat free?
   B: Sure.
   A: a) Thanks a lot.   b) No problem.   c) You're welcome.
6. A: I'll buy lunch.
   B: a) Really? Please.   b) Really? Sure.   c) Really? Thanks.

12.1 EXPERIENCES

VOCABULARY outdoor activities

1A Put the letters in order to make activities. Start with the underlined letters.

1 og higfins   go fishing
2 ch<u>tw</u>a sri<u>db</u>   _____
3 bl<u>mic</u> a no<u>m</u>autni   _____
4 e<u>dr</u>i a sro<u>he</u>   _____
5 wi<u>sm</u> n<u>i</u> a vi<u>rr</u>e   _____
6 li<u>s</u>a a to<u>ba</u>   _____

B ▶ 12.1 Listen and check.

C Listen again and repeat. Write the activities in the correct place according to the stress.

1 oO	2 oOo	3 ooO
	go fishing	
4 ooOo	5 oooOo	

WRITING postcard phrases

2A Complete the postcard with phrases a)–h).

¹ Verbier ,
² _____
³ _____,
⁴ _____. There's lots of snow so the skiing is perfect. The hotel's beautiful – a little noisy because there's a big group staying here, but it's a lovely old building in the centre of the village. The food's great too – really tasty!

Speaking of food, it's dinner in five minutes so ⁵ _____!

⁶ _____ and ⁷ _____.

⁸ _____

a) I hope you're all OK
b) I'm having a great time
c) I must go now
d) I'll speak to you soon
e) 5th January
f) ~~Verbier~~
g) Love, Jim
h) Dear Mum and Dad

B Now cross out four unnecessary words in the phrases you wrote in the postcard.

GRAMMAR present perfect

3 Write the past participle of the verbs.

1 be   been
2 climb   _____
3 do   _____
4 travel   _____
5 have   _____
6 ride   _____
7 drink   _____
8 play   _____
9 meet   _____
10 fly   _____

4A Look at the table and complete the sentences.

	Ethan	Amy	Tom and Lily
go to South America	✓	✗	✓
see Red Square	✗	✓	✓
eat Mexican food	✗	✓	✗
visit the Louvre gallery in Paris	✗	✗	✓
swim in the Black Sea	✓	✗	✗

1 Ethan _has been_ to South America.
2 Amy _____ to South America.
3 Tom and Lily _____ Red Square.
4 Ethan _____ Red Square.
5 Amy _____ Mexican food.
6 Tom and Lily _____ Mexican food.
7 Tom and Lily _____ the Louvre gallery in Paris.
8 Amy _____ in the Black Sea.

B Complete the questions.

1 _Has_ Ethan _swum_ in the Black Sea?
2 _____ Ethan and Amy _____ the Louvre gallery in Paris?
3 _____ Lily _____ Mexican food?
4 _____ Amy _____ Red Square?
5 _____ Tom and Lily _____ to South America?
6 _____ Tom _____ in the Black Sea?

C Write short answers to questions 1–6 in Exercise 4B.

1 Yes, he has.
2 _____
3 _____
4 _____
5 _____
6 _____

12.1

READING

5A Read Jim's travel blog and write the correct day under each picture.

A — Day 1
B
C
D
E

| Destinations | Our Travellers | Forums | Flights | Hotels | Cars | Hostels | Tours | Travel Insurance |

Day 1
We arrived in Piraeus early this morning. Liz has never seen the Parthenon. I've been to Athens once before, so I'm going to be her tour guide. We're going there tonight!

In the afternoon, we went by train from Piraeus into the city of Athens, and walked up to the Parthenon – amazing!

Day 2
Back to Athens again and this time we found a restaurant in the Plaka area. We've eaten Greek food many times back in New Zealand, but this is real Greek food! This is the first time in my life that I've tried octopus and it was delicious!

Day 3
We stayed overnight in Athens and then took a bus down to Cape Sounion in the afternoon to visit the Temple of Poseidon. We've seen many sunsets in our lives, but this was the most beautiful – the sun going down into the Aegean Sea.

Day 4
We left Piraeus early this morning and sailed for twenty hours to the island of Santorini. We arrived in the old port late in the evening. Tomorrow morning we're going up to the village – by donkey! I've ridden horses, camels, and elephants but I've never ridden a donkey!

Day 5
Donkey disaster! I'm writing this from a hospital bed in Athens. We started our donkey ride this morning and I made a big mistake: I walked behind the donkey and it kicked me in the stomach! There was no hospital on the island, so they took me by helicopter to Athens. I've broken three bones ... and I still haven't ridden a donkey. But I *have* flown in a helicopter!

B Read the blog again. Are the sentences true (T) or false (F)?

1 Jim is a tour guide.   F
2 Jim hasn't eaten Greek food before.
3 Jim liked the octopus.
4 They watched the sunrise near the Temple of Poseidon.
5 Jim and Liz travelled to Santorini by boat.
6 Jim enjoyed riding the donkey.
7 Jim flew back to Athens.
8 Now he's back home in New Zealand.

C Correct the false sentences.

1 *Jim isn't a tour guide.*

6A Imagine it's before the holiday. Read the blog again and write short answers to the questions.

1 Has Liz ever seen the Parthenon?   *No, she hasn't.*
2 Has Jim ever been to Athens?   _____
3 Has Jim ever eaten octopus?   _____
4 Have Jim and Liz ever seen a sunset?   _____
5 Has Jim ever ridden a donkey?   _____

B Now imagine it's after the holiday. Read the questions again and write short answers.

1 *Yes, she has.*
2 _____
3 _____
4 _____
5 _____

LISTENING

1A Match activities 1–8 with pictures A–H.
1 go on a roller coaster   B
2 get lost
3 be on TV
4 sing in a karaoke club
5 go to the cinema alone
6 fly in a helicopter
7 swim in a lake
8 drive in bad weather

B Complete the quiz with the past participle of the verbs in brackets.

FEAR OR FUN?

Have you ever ...

1 _been_ on a roller coaster? (go)

2 _____ lost in a city? (get)

3 _____ on TV? (be)

4 _____ in a karaoke club? (sing)

5 _____ to the cinema alone to see a film? (go)

6 _____ in a helicopter? (fly)

7 _____ in a lake? (swim)

8 _____ in really bad weather? (drive)

C ▶ 12.2 Listen to four conversations. Which situations from Exercise 1B do the people talk about?

Conversation 1   _6_
Conversation 2   _____
Conversation 3   _____
Conversation 4   _____

D Listen again. Write when the person did the activity.

Conversation 1   _five years ago_
Conversation 2   _____
Conversation 3   _____
Conversation 4   _____

12.2

GRAMMAR present perfect and past simple

2 Underline the correct alternatives in conversations 1–3.

Conversation 1

A: ¹*Did you ever fly* / *Have you ever flown* in a helicopter?

B: No, I ²*didn't* / *haven't*. ³*Did* / *Have* you?

A: Yes, I ⁴*did* / *have*. Just once, when I ⁵*went* / *'ve been* helicopter skiing, five years ago.

Conversation 2

B: ⁶*Have you ever sung* / *Did you ever sing* in a karaoke bar?

A: No, but I ⁷*sang* / *'ve sung* at a party. It ⁸*was* / *'s been* last year sometime. No, two years ago. At a birthday party.

A: What ⁹*did you sing* / *have you sung*?

B: I can't remember ... Oh, yes – 'I Did it My Way'.

Conversation 3

B: ¹⁰*Did you ever drive* / *Have you ever driven* in really bad weather?

A: Yes. I ¹¹*drove* / *'ve driven* up to Scotland to visit my grandparents in 2007, and it just ¹²*snowed* / *has snowed* non-stop.

3 Complete the conversations with the correct form of the verbs in brackets.

Conversation 1

A: ¹ *Have you ever ridden* (you / ever / ride) a horse?

B: Yes, I have. I ²_____ (ride) one in Argentina last year.

A: ³_____ (you / like) it?

B: Yes, it ⁴_____ (be) fun, but the horse ⁵_____ (not go) very fast.

Conversation 2

A: Does Emilio go everywhere by motorbike?

B: Yes, he does.

A: ⁶_____ (he / ever / hurt) himself?

B: Yes, he ⁷_____ (break) his arm twice.

A: Really? How ⁸_____ (he / do) that?

B: Both times the weather ⁹_____ (be) bad and he ¹⁰_____ (fall) off the bike.

VOCABULARY prepositions

4 Look at the map and complete the directions with prepositions from the box.

| ~~through~~ | down | up | under | towards |
| away from | across | over | into | through |

Get off the train and walk ¹ *through* the station and ²_____ the steps. There's a big square in front of the station with a clock tower on the other side. Walk ³_____ the square ⁴_____ the clock tower. Walk past the clock tower and go straight on until you see a bridge going ⁵_____ the road. Walk ⁶_____ the bridge and soon you'll see a shopping centre on your left. It's called WhiteWays. Walk ⁷_____ the shopping centre and at the other side you'll come out in Kirkby Street. Walk along Kirkby Street ⁸_____ the shopping centre. Then turn right into Sedgefield Road. My flat is in number thirty-five. The door's usually open so just come ⁹_____ the hall. Walk ¹⁰_____ the stairs to the first floor. My door is the blue one.

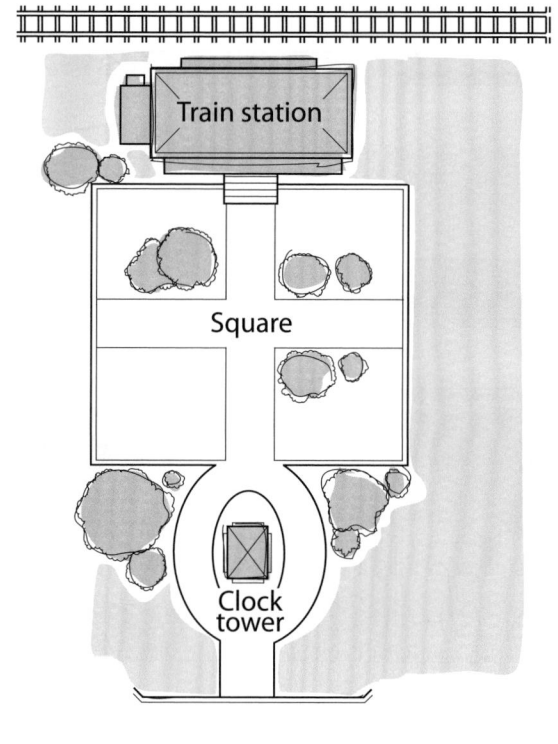

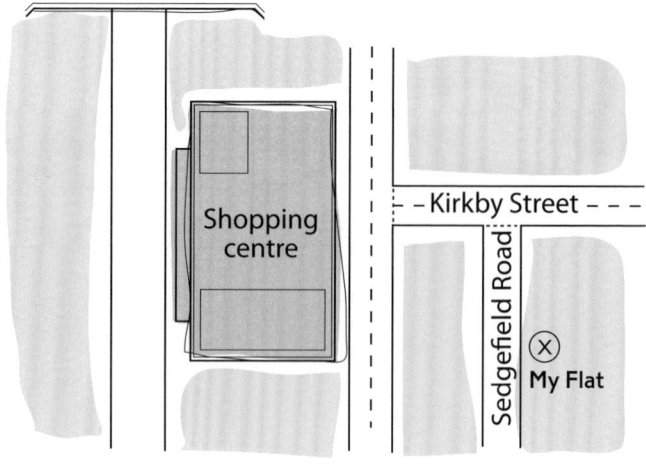

12.3

VOCABULARY telephoning expressions

1 Complete Susie's answerphone messages with verbs in the correct form.

1. This is Lisa from the health clinic. I l<u>eft</u> a message on your answerphone yesterday. Can you p_____ the clinic, please?
2. Hi, Susie. It's Meg. Can you c_____ me back? I'm at home this evening.
3. Hi. It's me, Bernie. Did you t_____ a message for me last night from Simon?
4. Hello. This is Sports Mad. Can you r_____ us, please? There's a problem with your trainers.
5. Hi, Susie. It's Fallon. I got your message and I'm ph_____ you back.
6. Hi, it's me again. I know you're there! A_____ the phone!

FUNCTION telephoning

2 Tick two correct sentences from telephone conversations. Correct the other six sentences.

1. Just ask ~~she~~ *her* to call me.
2. Could you say me the number?
3. OK, I call you back.
4. Could I leave a message to her?
5. Let me check that.
6. Hi, Frank. I'm Sally.
7. Good morning. Could I chat with Mr Suriano, please?
8. Just a moment.

3 Write the telephone conversations.

Conversation 1

A: Hi, Xavier. This / Bea.
   Hi, Xavier. This is Bea.

B: Hi, Bea. How / you?
   _____

A: I / OK. Michelle / there?
   _____

B: Yes, but she / sleep.
   _____

A: leave / message / her?
   _____

B: Of course.

A: Just ask / to call / me.
   _____

B: OK. Bye.

Conversation 2

A: Hello. / speak / the manager, please?
   Hello. Can I speak to the manager, please?

B: Just / moment. I / sorry, he / busy / moment. / call / back later?
   _____

A: It / very important.
   _____

B: I / take / message?
   _____

A: No thanks. I / phone back later.
   _____

LEARN TO say telephone numbers

4A Write the telephone numbers in words. Put a comma between number groups.

1. 3234996   *three two three, four double nine six*
2. 6882975   _____
3. 0757281   _____
4. 6232889   _____
5. 9897766   _____
6. 0870 5338992   _____

B ▶ 12.3 Listen and check. Then listen and repeat.

VOCABULARY feelings

5 Complete the adjectives.

1. Don't be a<u>frai</u>d. I'll go first.
2. Don't be e_____d. Everybody forgets my name.
3. Don't be n_____s. The exam will be easy, I'm sure.
4. Don't be f_____d. It's only a small snake!
5. Well done. I'm very p_____d of you.
6. Don't get e_____d. It isn't a very expensive watch!

73

REVIEW AND CHECK 4: UNITS 10–12

GRAMMAR verb forms

1A Complete the article with the correct form of the verbs in brackets. Use the past simple, the present perfect, *would like to* or *be going to*.

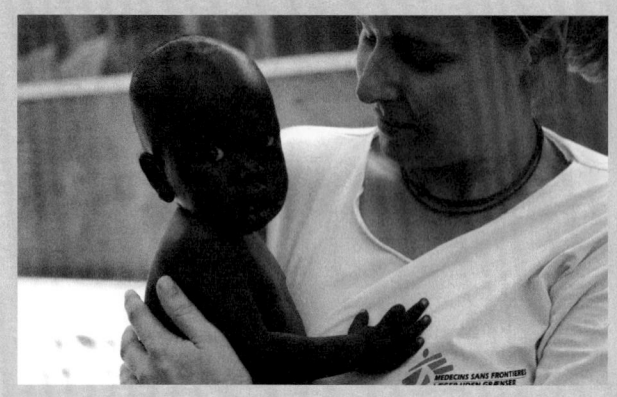

Irish nurse Liz Johnson works with the international aid agency, Médecins Sans Frontières (MSF). She talked to us about her experiences.

'About seven years ago I ¹ *saw* (see) a TV programme about MSF and I ² _____ (decide) to work for them. I ³ _____ (join) MSF three months later.'

'I love my work. I ⁴ _____ (go) to a lot of different places in the world and I ⁵ _____ (meet) some amazing people: doctors, nurses, helpers and patients. In fact, four years ago in Sudan I ⁶ _____ (meet) my husband, Jacques, a French doctor. We now travel and work together. I'm very proud of him.'

Last week Liz and Jacques ⁷ _____ (return) to France after six months work in Haiti. What are their plans for the future? 'We've got some definite plans: Jacques ⁸ _____ (speak) at a big MSF meeting next week and then we ⁹ _____ (have) a one-week holiday in Spain. After that we aren't sure. Next, we ¹⁰ _____ (open) a hospital, but we don't know in which country.'

B Put the words in order to make questions for Liz.

1 did / decide / you / for / when / to / MSF / work?
   When did you decide to work for MSF?

2 you / to / a / have / been / lot / different / of / countries?
   _____

3 meet / you / husband / did / when / your?
   _____

4 to / Jacques / going / week / where / speak / 's / next?
   _____

5 do / you / like / to / next / would / what?
   _____

C Now imagine you are Liz. Answer the questions.

1 *About seven years ago.*
2 _____
3 _____
4 _____
5 _____

VOCABULARY revision

2A Add vowels to the words in each group.

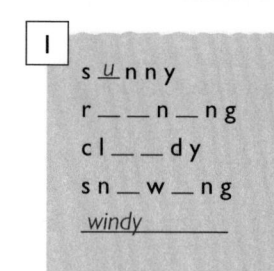

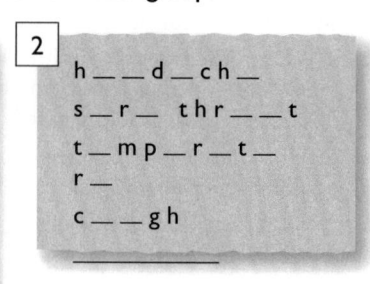

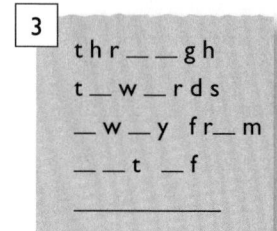

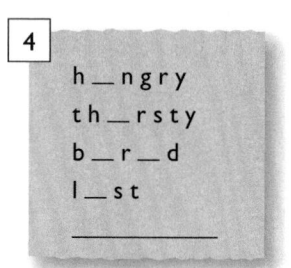

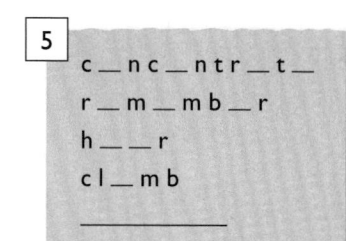

1
s u n n y
r _ _ n _ n g
c l _ _ d y
s n _ w _ n g
windy

2
h _ _ d _ c h _
s _ r _   t h r _ _ t
t _ m p _ r _ t _ r _
c _ _ g h
_____

3
t h r _ _ g h
t _ w _ r d s
_ w _ y   f r _ m
_ _ t   _ f
_____

4
h _ n g r y
t h _ r s t y
b _ r _ d
l _ s t
_____

5
c _ n c _ n t r _ t _
r _ m _ m b _ r
h _ _ r
c l _ m b
_____

6
_ x c _ l l _ n t
w _ n d _ r f _ l
c _ _ l
b r _ l l _ _ n t
_____

7
s h _ _ l d _ r
k n _ _
f _ n g _ r
_ l b _ w
_____

B Match phrases a)–g) with the correct group 1–7 in Exercise 2A.

a) It's ...   /
b) The party was ...
c) We got ...
d) Turn left and then walk _____ the car park.
e) I've hurt my ...
f) I've got a ...
g) I can't ...

C Add the words in the box to the correct group in Exercise 2A.

| ~~windy~~   amazing   runny nose   into   understand   sunburnt   thumb |

REVIEW AND CHECK 4: UNITS 10–12

GRAMMAR should/will/might

3A Read the text and write D (Daniel), R (Rebecca) or DR (both) next to problems 1–6.

1 wants to change jobs   R
2 works too much
3 lives unhealthily
4 doesn't have any friends
5 is bored with work
6 has money problems

life coaching*

Improve your life and reach your dreams …

Read about two of our customers and how life coaching has helped them:

Daniel is a successful businessman, but he finds it difficult to make friends so at weekends he stays at home and spends a lot of time alone on his computer. On weekdays, he often stays in the office late. He's also overweight and says he's never done much exercise. He'd like to become healthier and go out and meet people, maybe find a girlfriend, but he doesn't know where to start.

Rebecca loves dancing and she teaches a dance class once a week. She works for an electronics company, but she doesn't like her job. She thinks it's boring and works long hours, but she needs the money because her rent is very high. She'd like to teach dance all the time, but she doesn't know how to start.

*coaching = training, teaching

B Read the life-coaching advice and underline the correct alternatives.

> Daniel ¹<u>should</u> / 'll look for activities he can do with other people. He ²should / shouldn't join a club or group, for example a walking club or a cooking group because then he ³'ll / might meet people who enjoy the same things. When he's with other people he ⁴should / shouldn't ask them lots of questions and he ⁵should / shouldn't show interest in their answers. People love talking about themselves and they ⁶'ll / won't think he's a great guy! Who knows? He ⁷'ll / might find a girlfriend one day!

> Rebecca ⁸shouldn't / might not wait any more. She's in the wrong job. She ⁹should / 'll contact the Association of Dance Teachers – she can find them on the internet and they ¹⁰might / 'll give her advice about starting a new business. At the moment she ¹¹won't / shouldn't leave her job. The best thing is to work part-time, but her company ¹²might / might not agree. She ¹³should / shouldn't start teaching more classes – lots of people want to learn to dance and I'm sure she ¹⁴won't / might not find it difficult to reach her dream.

VOCABULARY Plans

4 Find 12 verb phrases for future plans.

W	T	R	G	R	W	Y	H	I	H
H	A	V	E	A	C	H	I	L	D
A	I	S	T	A	Y	I	N	M	O
V	U	G	M	V	F	D	N	G	S
E	G	O	A	B	R	O	A	D	S
A	O	S	R	G	O	A	S	Z	M
B	F	H	R	G	G	C	T	C	E
A	O	O	I	G	S	O	A	S	S
R	R	P	E	R	P	U	Y	E	P
B	A	P	D	C	E	R	A	S	O
E	W	I	L	R	X	S	T	V	R
C	A	N	A	Z	G	E	H	B	T
U	L	G	E	T	A	J	O	B	B
E	K	Q	S	C	K	X	M	L	X
G	O	F	O	R	A	M	E	A	L

FUNCTION telephoning, offering and suggesting

5A Complete the poem.

'Could I ¹<u>speak</u> to Susie Dee?'
'She's not at ²h_____. She's back at three.'
Could you ³p_____ her back tonight?'
'I'll ⁴l_____ a message. Is that all right?'
'Just a ⁵m_____, I need a pen.'
'She's got my ⁶n_____. My name's Ben.'
'⁷L_____ me check, your name is Jack?'
'Oh, never mind – I'll ⁸c_____ her back.'

• • •

'Well, hello Susie! How are you?'
'I'm fine. What ⁹w_____ you like to do?'
'Why ¹⁰d_____ we meet and have a chat?'
'I don't really ¹¹f_____ like doing that.'
'Then how ¹²a_____ a walk together?'
'¹³S_____ good. Let me check the weather.'
'It's going to ¹⁴r_____ – that's not ideal.'
'So ¹⁵l_____ stay in and cook a meal!'

B ▶ RC4.1 Listen to the poem. Then say it with the recording.

TEST 4: UNITS 10–12

TEST

Circle the correct option to complete the sentences.

1. You dance _____.
   a) beautiful   b) good   c) well

2. A: It's Estelle's birthday on Saturday.
   B: Yes, _____ her a camera. I ordered it last week.
   a) I'm going to give
   b) I'd like to give   c) I give

3. A: Should I tell Felipe?
   B: _____.
   a) Yes, you should tell.
   b) No, you shouldn't.
   c) Yes, you shouldn't.

4. Mack ran quickly _____ Anya and said, 'I'm so happy to see you!'
   a) away from   b) towards   c) across

5. Jan _____ to Germany.
   a) never has been   b) was never   c) has never been

6. I've got _____.
   a) headache   b) a cough   c) sore throat

7. Have you ever _____ in a thermal spa?
   a) swim   b) swam   c) swum

8. A: Oh, no. A snake!
   B: Don't be afraid. I'm sure it _____ you.
   a) won't hurt   b) 'll hurt   c) might not

9. Hi, _____ Fabio. Is Luigi there?
   a) I'm   b) it's   c) is this

10. A: I feel worse today.
    B: You _____.
    a) should to go home
    b) shouldn't go to bed
    c) should go to bed

11. A: Where _____ in Malta?
    B: At the Carlton Hotel.
    a) you're going to stay
    b) are you going to stay
    c) you would like to stay

12. They _____ yesterday.
    a) 've been fishing   b) 've gone fishing
    c) went fishing

13. Peter's very _____ today.
    a) seriously   b) quiet   c) noisily

14. We _____ a great barbecue – about twenty people came.
    a) went   b) had   c) got

15. A: Tom Grady has got a temperature and he _____ says his arms and legs hurt.
    B: I'll phone his mother. I think he's got flu.
    a) also   b) too   c) as well

16. He jumped out of _____.
    a) a helicopter   b) a bridge   c) an elephant

17. I can't _____ on this test. It's too noisy here.
    a) understand   b) concentrate   c) remember

18. I always carry lots of water with me so I don't get _____.
    a) dry   b) thirsty   c) hungry

19. Sorry, I can't talk at the moment. Can I _____ in half an hour?
    a) leave a message   b) take a message
    c) phone you back

20. I love Gladiator. I _____ it about ten times.
    a) saw   b) see   c) 've seen

21. My _____ hurts.
    a) shoulder   b) flu   c) temperature

22. You have to go _____ passport control and security.
    a) out of   b) through   c) into

23. He drove _____ through the city.
    a) fastly   b) slow   c) fast

24. A: What shall we do tonight?
    B: _____ stay in and watch a DVD.
    a) Let's   b) Why we don't
    c) How about

25. A: Did Jake ask you to his wedding?
    B: Yes, but I _____ go because it's in Canada and it's very expensive to fly there.
    a) might   b) might not   c) 'll

26. _____ that for you?
    a) Let me carry   b) Shall I carry   c) I'll carry

27. Have you ever been to China?
    a) No, I haven't.   b) Yes, I have been to.
    c) Yes, I have gone.

28. We _____ get married!
    a) going to   b) 're going to   c) 're going

29. I hurt my _____ yesterday and I can't walk.
    a) thumb   b) finger   c) toe

30. I _____ around the world.
    a) 'd like to travel   b) 'm like to travel
    c) like travel

TEST RESULT   /30

AUDIOSCRIPT

UNIT 7 Recording 1

1. empty
2. noisy
3. cheap
4. boring
5. uncomfortable
6. slow
7. expensive
8. quiet
9. fast
10. comfortable
11. crowded
12. interesting

UNIT 7 Recording 2

Hello, it's 9.48a.m. on Monday the second of December. I'm Nick Young and I'm on the Trans-Siberian train. Welcome to my audio diary. First of all, some facts: the Trans-Siberian is the longest train journey in the world. It's 9,300 kilometres and takes seven days …

…

So, this is day one – we left the city an hour ago and I'm here in my compartment. It's quite comfortable with two beds, one for me and one for Anton. Anton's from Sweden and he's very friendly. He doesn't speak much English but that's not a problem.

…

Hi, Nick here. It's day three and we're in Siberia. Out of the window you can see snow and forests and small villages for kilometre after kilometre. It's beautiful. About every two hours the train stops at a small station and there are women selling bread, fish, fruit or vegetables. We often buy food for lunch or dinner. When we get back on the train, we chat and read and have more cups of tea. Then we have lunch and then dinner and then we go to bed. It's all very relaxing.

…

Hi there. This is my last audio diary on this journey. In one hour we get into Vladivostok station! Last night the Russian lady in the carriage next door had her fiftieth birthday party. It was crowded but we had a good time!
So what do I think about the Trans-Siberian train? Fantastic! And my best memories? Great dark forests, small Russian villages, and some good new friends. I really think this is the best journey of my life!

…

UNIT 7 Recording 3

Conversation 1
A: So, the park's between the cinema and the pharmacy.
B: No, it's behind the cinema and the pharmacy.

Conversation 2
A: So the supermarket's between the cinema and the pharmacy.
B: No, it's between the cinema and the post office.

Conversation 3
A: So, the cinema is the fourth building on the left.
B: No, it's the third building on the left.

Conversation 4
A: So, the café is the fourth building on the left.
B: No, it's the fourth building on the right.

Conversation 5
A: So, the post office is opposite the bank.
B: No, it's opposite the museum.

Conversation 6
A: So, the town hall is opposite the bank.
B: No, it's next to the bank.

UNIT 8 Recording 1

1. Hello … Oh, hi Rob … No, we're at the new exhibition at the National Gallery and we're looking at the Klimt paintings … Yeah, they're fantastic … OK, see you later.
2. Nellie, it's me, Russ … Hi, yeah, we're queuing to buy tickets for the concert. Do you want to come? I can get you a ticket … Two…? Oh, who's your new friend … ? Right. See you soon.
3. Hi … Oh, look, I can't talk now – we're just going in to a concert … It's the Mozart … Yeah, the Requiem … Sorry, I've got to go.
4. Hi, Felicity … Fine, thanks … Listen, do you want to have a coffee later … ? After the match – maybe around four o'clock … Yeah, it's Nadal again – he's amazing … Oh, you're watching the match on TV … ? Right, see you at four.
5. Zsuzsa, I just had to call you. The new designs, they're fantastic – everything's black and white, you know. Kate's wearing white and Fabio's in all-black – black jeans, a black sweater and black jacket … OK, yeah, I'll take some pictures … Talk to you later.

UNIT 8 Recording 2

1. Are you looking for a film?
2. Is it an action film?
3. Is anyone famous in it?
4. Do you want to borrow a DVD?
5. I haven't got a DVD player
6. I've got it on video.

UNIT 8 Recording 3

1. Are you looking for a friend?
2. Is it an action film?
3. Is anyone famous in it?
4. Do you want to buy a DVD?
5. I haven't got a CD player.
6. I've got it on video.

UNIT 9 Recording 1

1. fast
2. healthy
3. dangerous
4. inconvenient
5. difficult
6. convenient
7. safe
8. easy
9. comfortable
10. polluting

UNIT 9 Recording 2

R = Reporter   C = Carin
R: We're in Amsterdam, the Netherlands, and we're talking to Carin van Buren. Carin's riding a kind of scooter with a motor. Carin, what is this … er … machine called?
C: It's a balancing scooter.
R: And do you ride it around the city?
C: Yes, I use it to go to work. Before this year I went to work by bike or sometimes by bus. Then I saw a balancing scooter on the internet and thought, that looks good, and I bought one!
R: Is it difficult to ride?
C: No, it's actually very easy.
R: And how long does it take to learn to ride?
C: It takes about two hours. Yes, it took me two hours.
R: Can you ride it on the pavement here?
C: No, you can't. You have to ride it on the road or you can use the bike paths.
R: And how fast does it go?
C: The maximum speed is twenty-five kilometres an hour but I usually go slower than that.
R: Do you feel safe on it?
C: Yeah – yes, I do. I always wear a helmet. The scooter doesn't go very fast and it's easy to stop.
R: And is it better than travelling by bus or bike?
C: I think so. By bus it took about forty-five minutes to go to work and now it takes me twenty minutes by scooter. And it's better than a bike because I'm not hot when I arrive at work.
R: Where do you leave your scooter at work?
C: I take it into my office and I leave it near my desk.

R: Really?
C: Yeah, it isn't a problem.
R: Is it tiring to ride?
C: Yes, it *is* quite tiring. You can't really relax.
R: Is there anything else you don't like about the scooter?
C: Sometimes people laugh at me and I feel quite stupid. Oh yes, and people often stop me and ask questions about it! I don't like that.

UNIT 9 Recording 3

A: Oh, hi. I'm really sorry I'm late. I missed the train.
B: I don't believe you.
A: No, really, the traffic was terrible.
B: And?
A: And my car broke down.
B: Your car, again?
A: And I left my wallet at home.
B: Ah, your wallet.
A: And … OK, I forgot about our meeting! I feel terrible about this.
B: Well, don't worry about it.
A: I'm so sorry …
B: No, really, it's fine.
A: I'm so so …
B: That's OK!! But don't let it happen again.

RC3 Recording 1

G = Greg   J = Jurgen
G: Hey, Jurgen. It's my wife's birthday tomorrow. Can you recommend a good restaurant?
J: Well, what kind of food do you like?
G: We both like Chinese food and … er … French food.
J: There's a good restaurant called *Bouchon* in town. It serves French food.
G: Do you think my wife would like it?
J: Yes, I think so. It's quite romantic.
G: Where is it?
J: It's in a small street near the cinema.
G: Can you tell me the way?
J: From the cinema, you go down Hillside Road past the pharmacy and turn left.
G: Left at the pharmacy. OK …
J: Then go straight on for about two hundred metres. Take the second right and *Bouchon* is on the right. It isn't far.
G: Great – thanks!
…
J: Hi, Greg. Did you find the restaurant?
G: No!
J: Oh? Why?
G: Your directions were all wrong! You said to turn *left* at the pharmacy.
J: Oh, no …

G: And we did, but it took us completely the wrong way!
J: Oh, no – I'm so sorry. I always mix up left and right.
G: Hm. My wife was really angry.
J: I feel terrible about this.
G: In the end we went home and ordered pizza!
J: Oh, no …
G: Ah, well. Maybe next year! Don't worry about it, really.

UNIT 10 Recording 1

sunburnt, thirsty, bored, wet, hungry, hot, lost, cold

UNIT 10 Recording 2

Speaker 1
Well, the most difficult thing was that there was so much water, but I was so thirsty. Food wasn't a big problem because I caught fish and ate them. Of course I got sunburnt after the first day because I had nothing to put on my head. And I was afraid of sharks – once I saw one, but it just swam around the raft for a few minutes and then it went away.

Speaker 2
I felt very small and very tired. I walked all night, very slowly because of the sand, and I tried to stay cool in the daytime, but it was so hot. On the second day I found some water – that was very lucky – but then I wanted to walk more, not just stay by the water. I wanted to try to find my way back to the town. I had food with me, so I didn't get hungry – just very thirsty. Once I saw a snake, and I was afraid that one might go into my shoe, so I never took my shoes off.

Speaker 3
There was snow everywhere, everything was white, and that's why I got lost – I didn't see the path. I was up there only one night, but it was the longest night of my life. The most important thing was staying warm. I didn't have enough clothes with me, so I got terribly cold. I wanted to make a fire, but everything was wet. I slept on the ground and got colder. I didn't think about food, I wasn't really hungry, but just so thirsty … it was difficult, very difficult.

Speaker 4
There was water, so I didn't get thirsty. And I didn't get too hungry because I knew what kind of plants to eat. Of course I got very lost, I walked day and night … but you know you can never, ever get bored there. There are so many different types of plants and animals and insects, it was beautiful … so yes, I felt tired and lost, but not bored.

UNIT 10 Recording 3

1 You get cold.
   You'll get cold.
2 We'll miss the train.
   We miss the train.
3 I'm sure you'll hate it.
   I'm sure you hate it.
4 They know you're a tourist.
   They'll know you're a tourist.
5 I stay at home.
   I'll stay at home.
6 I'll never go out.
   I never go out.

UNIT 10 Recording 4

T = Tim   G = Gordon
T: So, Gordon, what would you like to do today?
G: I don't know. Have you got any ideas?
T: What about going to a concert?
G: Hmmm … That might be difficult.
T: Why?
G: We don't like the same music. You like rock, I like hip-hop.
T: Oh. That's true. How about inviting some friends?
G: I don't really feel like doing that.
T: OK then. Why don't we stay home and watch TV?
G: That's a good idea. What's on?
T: Let me see … Uh, *Castaway* with Tom Hanks.
G: Brilliant!
T: And let's have popcorn, too.
G: Sounds good!

UNIT 11 Recording 1

head, toe, neck, teeth, hand, knee, feet, mouth, back, nose, thumb, stomach

UNIT 11 Recording 2

I = Interviewer   A = Adrian
I: In today's programme I'm at the Real Age Clinic with Doctor Adrian Clark. Adrian, how can I find out my 'real' age?
A: OK, how old are you?
I: I'm thirty-one.
A: OK. We call that your 'birthday' age. Right. I'm going to ask you to do some tests and then I can tell you if your real age is younger or older than thirty-one.
I: OK.
A: We'll start with three simple tests. First of all is the Balance Test. Come over here, please. OK, you have to close your eyes and stand on one leg.
I: Stand on one leg. Right.
A: And I'm going to time you.

I: Whoa … this is quite difficult. I feel a bit stupid. I wasn't very good at that. How long was it?
A: You did fourteen seconds.
I: That isn't very good, is it?
A: Well, most people under twenty find this test easy but not many people over thirty can stand on one leg for more than twenty-five seconds. The average for your age is about fifteen to twenty seconds … so fourteen seconds is OK.
I: Right. What's the next test?
A: The second test is the Ruler Test. Which hand do you write with?
I: My right hand.
A: OK, hold out your right hand and open your thumb and first finger. I'm going to hold this ruler above your hand. I'll say 'now' and you have to catch it.
I: OK.
A: Are you ready?
I: Yes.
A: Now … Oh, well done. You caught it … in the middle.
I: Is that good?
A: Yes, at twenty you should catch the ruler half way down – in the middle. People over forty-five don't usually catch it!
I: Oh, good … that's better.
A: And the next test. Can you touch your toes?
I: Yes, that's easy.
A: Ah, yes – but you have to keep your legs straight.
I: Ah. I can touch my knees … and …
A: No, be careful. Go slowly. That's enough. You can touch your ankles. That's quite good for your age.
I: So … how did I do?
A: Not bad. Your 'real' age from these three tests is … twenty-nine. Now I'm going to ask you some questions about your lifestyle and general health.

UNIT 11 Recording 3

A: Are you OK, Jim?
B: No. I have to meet Anne at 5.30 and look at this list!
A: Let me help. I'm not busy at the moment.
B: Oh, can you? Thanks!
A: No problem. Shall I phone Noriko?
B: Yes, please.
A: And then I'll email the Moscow office.
B: Can you tell them I'll phone tomorrow?
A: OK. And I'll get some flowers for Ellie. I'm going to the hospital to see her tonight anyway.
B: Fantastic! Let me give you the money.

A: It's OK. Give it to me tomorrow.
B: Thanks a lot. I'll do the same for you any time!

UNIT 12 Recording 1

1 go <u>fi</u>shing
2 watch <u>birds</u>
3 climb a <u>moun</u>tain
4 ride a <u>horse</u>
5 swim in a <u>ri</u>ver
6 sail a <u>boat</u>

UNIT 12 Recording 2

Conversation 1
A: Have you ever flown in a helicopter?
B: No, I haven't. Have you?
A: Yes, I have. Just once, when I went helicopter skiing – five years ago.
B: That sounds interesting. What's helicopter skiing?
A: A helicopter takes you up the mountain and you ski from there.
B: And how was it?
A: It was fun. I enjoyed it.

Conversation 2
A: Matt, have you ever sung in a karaoke club?
B: No, but I've sung at a party. It was last year sometime. No, two years ago. At a birthday party.
A: What did you sing?
B: I can't remember … Oh, yes – *I Did It My Way*. It was fun. I can't sing, but it was a good laugh. Why are you asking?
A: I'm going to a karaoke club tonight and I'm feeling quite nervous about it.
B: You'll be all right. Just relax and enjoy it!

Conversation 3
A: What's the matter?
B: I have to drive to Dublin tomorrow and look at the rain! Have you ever driven in really bad weather?
A: Yes. I drove up to Scotland to visit my grandparents in 2007 and it just snowed non-stop – it was impossible to see the road ahead.
B: Sounds dangerous.
A: Yes, so I stopped and stayed overnight in a hotel. After that I always visit them by train!
B: Yeah, that's a good idea. Maybe I'll go by train.

Conversation 4
A: Look at this picture. It looks scary! Have you ever been on a roller coaster like that?
B: Yes, when I was about nineteen in Munich. A friend of mine took me on a really big roller coaster.
A: Were you afraid?

B: No. After ten seconds I closed my eyes and didn't open them until it stopped!

UNIT 12 Recording 3

1 three two three, four double nine six
2 six double eight, two nine seven five
3 oh seven five, seven two eight one
4 six two three, two double eight nine
5 nine eight nine, double seven double six
6 oh eight seven oh, five double three, eight double nine two

RC4 Recording 1

A: Could I speak to Susie Dee?
B: She's not at home. She's back at three. Could you phone her back tonight?
A: I'll leave a message. Is that all right?
B: Just a moment, I need a pen.
A: She's got my number. My name's Ben.
B: Let me check, your name is Jack?
A: Oh, never mind – I'll call her back.
A: Well, hello Susie! How are you?
C: I'm fine. What would you like to do?
A: Why don't we meet and have a chat?
C: I don't really feel like doing that.
A: Then how about a walk together?
C: Sounds good. Let me check the weather.
   It's going to rain – that's not ideal.
A: So let's stay in and cook a meal!

ANSWER KEY

UNIT 7

7.1

1A

2 uncomfortable 3 fast 4 crowded
5 interesting 6 quiet 7 expensive
8 boring 9 cheap 10 noisy

B

1 slow, fast 2 noisy, boring, quiet, crowded 3 comfortable, interesting
4 expensive 5 uncomfortable

2

2 South Africa's **hotter** than Italy.
3 I'm **older** than my brother.
4 Indian food is **spicier** than English food.
5 Lena's **more intelligent** than me.
6 Cola is **sweeter** than lemonade.
7 Chinese is more difficult **than** English.
8 Crisps are **worse** for you than chips.

3

2 better 3 more interesting 4 more romantic 5 closer 6 colder 7 bigger
8 friendlier

4A

No, they aren't good travel partners.

B

2 T 3 T 4 TM 5 T 6 M 7 M 8 TM

C

2 the apartment 3 the apartment 4 the hotel 5 Mike 6 Tim 7 Tim 8 Mike

7.2

1

1 lake 2 bridge 3 river 4 jungle
5 market 6 mountain 7 city 8 village
9 famous building 10 desert
You have 'a great time'!

2A

1 C 2 A 3 B

B

2 The cheapest is *Family fun*.
3 The most comfortable is *Luxury weekend*.
4 The noisiest is *Family fun*.
5 The longest is *Mountain adventure*.
6 The easiest is *Luxury weekend*.
7 The most difficult is *Mountain adventure*.
8 The shortest is *Luxury weekend*.
9 The most uncomfortable is *Mountain adventure*.
10 The coldest is *Mountain adventure*.

3A

2 What's the shortest word on this page?
3 Which is the most interesting text in units 1–6 of this book?
4 Which is the best exercise on this page?
5 What's the most difficult grammar point in English?
6 Who's the happiest person in your family?
7 Who's the friendliest person in your English class?
8 Which is the worst restaurant in town?

B

1 sentence
2 a / 1
3–8 student's own answers

4A

His train goes from Moscow.

C

2 T 3 T 4 F 5 F 6 F 7 T 8 T

D

4 Nick can't see any lakes.
5 They buy food from women at stations.
6 They drink a lot of tea.

5A

Hi, it's Nick again. We started the day with a surprise – but not a good one. Anton and **I went** to the dining car for **breakfast** and there wasn't any food. That wasn't a big problem because I had some **biscuits** and we **drank** some tea, but then we went back for lunch and it was the same situation. The waiter **told** us that there's a station where they usually get food, but the food truck wasn't there.

Nobody on the train was worried about this **because** almost everybody **brought** their own food. A guy called Egor **gave** us half of his roast chicken, and a Chinese couple gave us some bread. **People** were so kind. Anton and I talked about how to thank them ... so **I taught** them some English songs, and it **was** really just a big party. My best day on the train!

7.3

1

2 car park 3 swimming pool 4 theatre
5 library 6 bus station 7 art gallery
8 tourist information 9 park 10 museum

2

2 turn 3 straight 4 past 5 Dawson 6 into
7 on / ahead 8 left

3

2 2c 3 3a 4 4b

4A

2 the cinema and the post office. 3 the third building on the left. 4 the fourth building on the right 5 the museum
6 next to

B

2 No, it's between the cinema and the (post office.)
3 No, it's the (third) building on the left.
4 No, it's the fourth building on the (right.)
5 No, it's opposite the (museum.)
6 No, it's (next to) the bank.

UNIT 8

8.1

1

2 having 3 running 4 staying 5 swimming
6 sleeping 7 writing 8 trying 9 beginning
10 giving

2A

2 's / is taking
3 are standing, listening
4 's / is walking, isn't listening
5 's / is sitting, drinking
6 are chatting, aren't watching
7 's / is looking
8 's / is selling

B

B Roger C Megan D Paolo E Philip
F Wesley G Zoe H Lisa I Kalila J Jo and Sam

C

2 Who's / Who is Zoe talking to?
3 Where are Zoe and Paolo sitting?
4 How many bags are Jo and Sam carrying?
5 Who's / Who is Wesley taking a photo of?
6 What's / What is Roger doing?
7 Who's / Who is laughing?
8 What's / What is Zoe drinking?

D

2 She's talking to Paolo.
3 They're sitting at a café/at a table.
4 They're carrying four bags.

Answer key

5 He's taking a photo of Jake.
6 He's talking/speaking on his mobile (phone).
7 Paolo's laughing.
8 She's drinking a coffee.

3
2 Is your phone ringing?
   Yes, it is. / No, it isn't.
3 Are you doing this exercise with a pen?
   Yes, I am. / No, I'm not.
4 Are any other people sitting in the room?
   Yes, they are. / No, they aren't.
5 Is music playing in the room?
   Yes, it is. / No, it isn't.
6 Are you enjoying this exercise?
   Yes, I am. / No, I'm not.
7 Is your teacher writing on the board?
   Yes, he/she is. / No, he/she isn't.
8 Are your classmates drinking coffee?
   Yes, they are. / No, they aren't.

4
2 for 3 of 4 to 5 about 6 on 7 on 8 at

5A
2 e 3 d 4 a 5 b

B
1 really likes 2 wants 3 going into
4 wants 5 Some of

6A
David took Julia's phone.

B
2 them 3 we 4 she 5 it 6 her 7 we
8 her 9 he 10 his 11 it 12 her 13 him
14 his 15 it 16 they

8.2

1A
A Tom B Bruce C Robert D Sam
E Mike F William

B
2 Belinda's got short dark hair. She isn't very slim.
3 Jay's got short curly blonde hair. She isn't very slim.
4 Keira's got long dark hair. She's very slim.

2A
2 'm having
3 'm sitting
4 aren't working
5 don't usually start
6 doesn't like
7 works
8 Is she looking
9 looks
10 'm phoning

3
2 's cooking / is cooking
3 's helping / is helping
4 are (you) doing
5 'm watching / am watching
6 are you wearing
7 don't usually wear
8 wear
9 'm standing / am standing
10 don't (usually) stand
11 get
12 'm waiting / am waiting

4
Across: 1 skirt 3 shoes 5 dress 6 jeans
          8 tie 9 socks 10 shirt
Down: 2 trousers 3 sweater 4 coat
          6 jacket 7 suit 8 top

5A
1 Wool / cotton 2 more comfortable
3 comfortable and cheap

B
2 F 3 T 4 F 5 F 6 T

C
2 e 3 a 4 f 5 c 6 d

8.3

1A
2 horror film 3 sci-fi film 4 musical
5 romantic film 6 comedy 7 drama

B
B 5 C 4 D 1 E 6 F 3 G 7

2
2 What **kind** of films do you like?
3 There's a good film **called** The Matrix.
4 What's it **about**?
5 Who's **in** it?
6 Do you think **I'd** like it?
7 Can I **borrow** it?

3A
2 Is‿it‿an‿action film?
3 Is‿anyone famous‿in‿it?
4 Do you want to borrow‿a DVD?
5 I haven't got‿a DVD player.
6 I've got‿it‿on video.

C
1b) Are you looking for a friend?
2a) Is it an action film?
3b) Is anyone famous in it?
4b) Do you want to buy a DVD?
5b) I haven't got a CD player.
6a) I've got it on video.

UNIT 9

9.1

1A
B helicopter C bike D horse E taxi
F plane G train H motorbike I foot

B
2 F 3 E 4 D 5 H 6 G 7 B 8 I 9 A

2A
2 went by 3 rides 4 take 5 go on 6 goes by 7 'm getting on 8 came by

3A
1 b 2 c
2 c line 25 3 b line 27 4 a line 29
5 e line 36 6 d line 42

4
2 – 3 a 4 – 5 the 6 a 7 an 8 – 9 –
10 – 11 a 12 the

5
1 Yes, **the** bus station is down this street on **the** left.
2 Rajiv is **an** actor in Mumbai.
3 I haven't got **a** car, but I've got **a** motorbike.
4 **The** Town Hall opens at 9.30 in **the** morning.
5 I love planes and flying. I always ask for **a** window seat.
6 Keith often works at home in **the** evening.
7 Is Manchester in **the** UK?
8 ✓

9.2

1A
2 healthy 3 dangerous 4 inconvenient
5 difficult 6 convenient 7 safe 8 easy
9 comfortable 10 polluting

C
1 safe 2 healthy, easy 3 dangerous, difficult, comfortable 4 polluting
5 convenient 6 inconvenient

2A
angry

B
2 F 3 T 4 T 5 F 6 T

3A
1 you can't 2 You can't ride
3 Can people smoke / they can't
4 Can we walk / we can 5 Taxis can drive

B
1 can't 2 don't have to 3 can't
4 don't have to

Answer key

4

2 can't 3 have to 4 can we 5 can't
6 can 7 can 8 Do we have to 9 can we
10 don't have to 11 can't 10 can

5A

1 F 2 F 3 T 4 T

C

2 By bus or bike. 3 About two hours.
4 25 kilometres an hour. 5 Yes, she does.
6 Near her desk. 7 Stupid. 8 No, she doesn't.

9.3

1

1 alarm clock 2 missed 3 lost, keys
4 broke down 5 traffic, bad

2A

2 I don't believe you.
3 the traffic was terrible.
4 my car broke down.
5 I left my wallet at home.
6 I feel terrible about this.
7 don't worry about it.
8 I'm so sorry.
9 No, really, it's fine.
10 But don't let it happen again.

3

First of all, I left the house late because I lost my keys. Then I missed the bus, so I phoned a taxi but the taxi broke down and I waited thirty minutes for another taxi. After that, I got to the restaurant an hour late, but I left your present in the taxi. I phoned the taxi company, but they didn't answer, so I went into the restaurant, but you weren't there. Finally, I went home and tried to phone you, but you didn't answer.

4

2 checked in
3 security
4 passport control
5 departure lounge
6 tax-free shopping
7 gate
8 get on

REVIEW AND CHECK 3

1A

2 plays 3 'm writing 4 're having 5 arrive
6 came 7 don't have to 8 can 9 can't
10 have to 11 walk 12 's talking 13 is
practising 14 is calling 15 have to

B

2 are you enjoying 3 Does Jesse write
4 do you write 5 sing 6 say
7 's Danny wearing 8 'm wearing

2

C convenient D dangerous E empty
F famous G get H horror I interesting
J jungle K know L lying M missed
N noisy O on P polluting Q quiet
R recommend S Square T traffic
U uncomfortable V village W worse
X (e)xpensive Y you Z (ama)zing

3

2 the hottest 3 the coldest 4 slower
5 faster 6 most convenient
7 the tallest 8 quieter
9 the most interesting 10 cheaper

4A

sentence b

B

2 T 3 F 4 T 5 F 6 F

C

2 would like it 3 me the way 4 and turn
left 5 on for about 6 sorry 7 about this
8 about it, really

5

2 – 3 a 4 the 5 a 6 a 7 – 8 the 9 –
10 a 11 – 12 the

TEST

1 b 2 b 3 c 4 a 5 c 6 c 7 b 8 b 9 a
10 a 11 c 12 b 13 b 14 a 15 b 16 b
17 a 18 c 19 a 20 a 21 c 22 c 23 b
24 a 25 a 26 b 27 c 28 c 29 c 30 a

UNIT 10

10.1

1A

2 's / is going to look for
3 isn't / is not going to stay
4 'd / would like to be
5 's / is going to have
6 's / is going (to go)
7 'd / would like to work
8 are going to visit
9 aren't / are not going to have
10 'd / would like to move

B

2 Where are you going to look for a new flat, Jim?
3 When are you going / are you going to (go to) university, Soo Min?
4 Why would you like to work in TV, Soo Min?
5 How are you going to travel, Bill and Jane?
6 Why would you like to move nearer your daughter, Bill and Jane?

C

b) 5 c) 2 d) 6 e) 3 f) 1

2

2 Would you like to work in TV?
   Yes, I would. / No, I wouldn't.
3 Are you going to see your family next weekend?
   Yes, I am. / No, I'm not.
4 Is English going to be useful for you?
   Yes, it is. / No, it isn't.
5 Would you like to buy a new mobile phone?
   Yes, I would. / No, I wouldn't.
6 Are you and your classmates going to study English next year?
   Yes, we are. / No, we aren't.
7 Would you like to live in another country?
   Yes, I would. / No, I wouldn't.
8 Would your classmates like to go home now?
   Yes, they would. / No, they wouldn't.

3A

3 Another teenage lottery winner

B

2 Tracey Makin 3 Tracey and Callie
4 No, she doesn't. 5 No, it was only the second time she played the lottery.
6 She's going to have a holiday and buy a new car. 7 Because her car is too small.

4A

1 nothing 2 go for 3 a new suit
4 a holiday 5 clubbing 6 move 7 stay at
8 start 9 learn 10 buy

Message: Life's a lottery

B

1 drink
2 married, move, buy, family
3 friends, course, learn, job
4 stop, have, buy, travel
5 presents, shopping

10.2

1A

2 thirsty 3 bored 4 wet 5 hungry 6 hot
7 lost 8 cold

B

b) 8 c) 5 d) 3 e) 4 f) 6 g) 2 h) 1

C

1 hungry 2 hot, lost 3 wet 4 thirsty
5 bored 6 cold

2

1 lost, tired
2 to work, home, to school
3 a new car, a hamburger, a new computer
4 some help, a job, a glass of water

3A

Speaker 1: d
Speaker 2: c
Speaker 3: b
Speaker 4: a

B

 4 b 5 b 6 a 7 c 8 b

4 won't know 5 'll
won't come

7 won   't

6

2 a) 1, b) 2
3 a) 1, b) 2
4 a) 2, b) 1
5 a) 2, b) 1
6 a) 1, b) 2

7

2 ✓
3 ✓
4 It's generally a safe city, but it can **also** be dangerous to walk alone late at night in some areas.
5 It isn't a good idea to carry a lot of money, and leave your expensive watch at home, **too**.
6 You can get delicious food in cafés and in street markets **as well**.
7 ✓
8 At night taxis are convenient, but they're expensive **as well**.

10.3

1

2 excellent 3 cool 4 wonderful
5 fantastic 6 great 7 awesome 8 brilliant

2A

2 Have 3 about 4 don't 5 How 6 feel
7 Why 8 stay 9 idea 10 Brilliant 11 let's
12 Sounds

3A

2 How about go**ing** for a bike ride?
3 Why don't we **go** to an art gallery?
4 What about stay**ing** at home and cook**ing** something?
5 **What/How** about making spaghetti and meatballs?
a) That **doesn't** sound very interesting. Looking at paintings is boring!
b) I don't really feel like do**ing** that. I'm too tired.
c) Sound**s** good. You make the meatballs, I can make the pasta.
d) Brilliant! What would you like **to** eat?

e) That isn't **a** very good idea. I haven't got much money.

B

2 b 3 a 4 d 5 c

4

Across: 3 cool 4 windy 6 stormy
         8 cold 10 raining
Down: 1 hot 2 cloudy 4 warm 5 wet
         6 snowing 7 sunny 9 dry

UNIT 11

11.1

1A

S	T	O	M	A	C	H
M	K	T	H	U	M	B
O	N	O	S	E	N	T
U	E	H	F	E	E	T
T	E	E	T	H	C	O
H	H	A	N	D	K	E
F	O	D	B	A	C	K

C

1 neck
2 hand, back
3 teeth, knee, feet
4 toe, nose
5 thumb, stomach
6 mouth

2

2 hurts 3 headache 4 sore throat
5 shoulder 6 toothache 7 sore eye
8 terrible 9 temperature 10 cough

3B

2 you should speak 3 Should I get
4 You shouldn't have 5 should I do
6 You should visit 7 You should take
8 you shouldn't open 9 you shouldn't travel 10 you shouldn't drink

4

2 should I do 3 you shouldn't eat 4 you should change 5 should I sleep 6 you shouldn't watch 7 you shouldn't go 8 you should do

5A

b) 3 c) 4 d) 2

B

3, 5, 7, 8

C

2 g 3 a 4 c 5 f 6 b 7 e

D

1 to 2 have 3 have 4 with 5 from 6 too
7 in 8 at 9 take 10 all 11 meet 12 make

11.2

1A

2 run 3 remember 4 understand 5 read
6 climb 7 hear 8 swim 9 concentrate

B

2 understand 3 climb 4 swim 5 read
6 forget 7 hear 8 run 9 remember

2A

1 B 2 C 3 A

B

2 a 3 b 4 b 5 a

3

1 A: slowly B: slow 2 A: lazy B: lazily
3 A: quietly B: quiet 4 A: easily B: easy
5 A: badly B: bad 6 A: energetic
B: energetically 7 A: noisily B: noisy
8 A: hard B: hard

4A

1 safely, dangerously, fast
2 hard, late, loudly
3 healthily, early, fast, clearly
4 perfectly, well, loudly

B

2 a teacher 3 a golfer 4 a jazz singer

5

1 tired, terribly
2 comfortable, noisy, hungry, cheaply, expensive
3 badly, beautifully, kind

6A

2 quickly 3 angrily 4 nervously
5 carefully

B

2 carefully 3 quickly 4 angrily 5 slowly

11.3

1

2 lift 3 push 4 drop 5 fall 6 stand

2A

2 That was my favourite vase.
3 I'm really tired.
4 It's cold in here.
a) Let me make you a coffee.
b) Let me look.
c) I'll buy you another one.
d) Shall I close the window?

B

1 b 2 c 3 a 4 d

3A

2 Shall I phone
3 'll / will email
4 'll / will get
5 Let me give
6 'll / will do

Answer key

4
2 a 3 c 4 b 5 a 6 c

UNIT 12

12.1

1A
2 watch birds 3 climb a mountain 4 ride a horse 5 swim in a river 6 sail a boat

C
1 watch birds 3 ride a horse, sail a boat 4 climb a mountain 5 swim in a river

2A
2 e 3 h 4 b 5 c 6 a 7 d 8 g

B
I'm having a great time
I must go now
I hope you're all OK
I'll speak to you soon

3
2 climbed 3 done 4 travelled 5 had 6 ridden 7 drunk 8 played 9 met 10 flown

4A
2 hasn't been 3 have seen 4 hasn't seen 5 has eaten 6 haven't eaten 7 have visited 8 hasn't swum

B
2 Have / visited 3 Has / eaten 4 Has / seen 5 Have / been 6 Has / swum

C
2 No, they haven't. 3 No, she hasn't. 4 Yes, she has. 5 Yes, they have. 6 No, he hasn't.

5A
B Day 3 C Day 2 D Day 5 E Day 4

B
2 F 3 T 4 F 5 T 6 F 7 T 8 F

C
2 Jim has eaten Greek food many times back in New Zealand.
4 They watched the sunset near the Temple of Poseidon.
6 Jim didn't ride the donkey – he walked behind it and it kicked him.
8 He isn't back home, he's in hospital in Athens.

6A
2 Yes, he has. 3 No, he hasn't. 4 Yes, they have. 5 No, he hasn't.

B
2 Yes, he has. 3 Yes, he has. 4 Yes, they have. 5 No, he hasn't.

12.2

1A
2 F 3 C 4 E 5 A 6 D 7 H 8 G

B
2 got 3 been 4 sung 5 been 6 flown 7 swum 8 driven

C
Conversation 2 4
Conversation 3 8
Conversation 4 1

D
Conversation 2 2 years ago
Conversation 3 2007
Conversation 4 when he was about 19

2
2 haven't 3 Have 4 have 5 went 6 Have you ever sung 7 've sung 8 was 9 did you sing 10 Have you ever driven 11 drove 12 snowed

3
2 rode 3 Did you like 4 was 5 didn't go 6 Has he ever hurt 7 's broken 8 did he do 9 was 10 fell

4
2 down 3 across 4 towards 5 over 6 under 7 through 8 away from 9 into 10 up

12.3

1
1 phone 2 call 3 take 4 ring 5 phoning 6 Answer

2
2 Could you **tell** me the number?
3 OK, I'**ll** call you back.
4 Could I leave a message **for** her?
5 ✓
6 Hi, Frank. **It's** Sally.
7 Good morning. Could I **talk/speak to** Mr Suriano, please?
8 ✓

3
1
A: Hi, Xavier. This is Bea.
B: Hi, Bea. How are you?
A: I'm OK. Is Michelle there?
B: Yes, but she's sleeping.
A: Could I leave a message for her?
B: Of course.
A: Just ask her to call me.
B: OK. Bye.

2
A: Hello. Can I speak to the manager, please?
B: Just a moment. I'm sorry, he's busy at the moment. Could you call back later?
A: It's very important.
B: Can I take a message?
A: No thanks. I'll phone back later.

4
2 six double eight, two nine seven five
3 oh seven five, seven two eight one
4 six two three, two double eight nine
5 nine eight nine, double seven double six
6 oh eight seven oh, five double three, eight double nine two

5
2 embarrassed 3 nervous 4 frightened 5 proud 6 excited

REVIEW AND CHECK 4

1A
2 decided 3 joined 4 've / have been 5 've / have met 6 met 7 returned 8 's / is going to speak 9 're / are going to have 10 'd / would like to open

B
2 Have you been to a lot of different countries?
3 When did you meet your husband?
4 Where's Jacques going to speak next week?
5 What would you like to do next?

C
2 Yes, I have. 3 Four years ago. 4 At a big MSF meeting. 5 (We'd like) to open a hospital.

2A
1 raining, cloudy, snowing
2 headache, sore throat, temperature, cough
3 through, towards, away from, out of
4 hungry, thirsty, bored, lost
5 concentrate, remember, hear, climb
6 excellent, wonderful, cool, brilliant
7 shoulder, knee, finger, elbow

B
b 6 c 4 d 3 e 7 f 2 g 5

C
2 runny nose 3 into 4 sunburnt 5 understand 6 amazing 7 thumb

3A
2 DR 3 D 4 D 5 R 6 R

B
2 should 3 'll 4 should 5 should 6 'll 7 might 8 shouldn't 9 should 10 'll 11 shouldn't 12 might not 13 should 14 won't

84

4

(word search grid with circled answers including HAVE A CHAT, STAY IN, GO FOR A MEAL, GET A JOB, etc.)

5A

2 home 3 phone 4 leave 5 moment
6 number 7 Let 8 call 9 would 10 don't
11 feel 12 about 13 Sounds 14 rain
15 let's

TEST

1c 2a 3b 4b 5c 6b 7c 8a 9b 10c 11b
12c 13b 14b 15a 16a 17b 18b 19c
20c 21a 22b 23c 24a 25b 26b 27a
28b 29c 30a

Pearson Education Limited
Edinburgh Gate
Harlow
Essex CM20 2JE
England
and Associated Companies throughout the world.

www.pearsonELT.com

© Pearson Education Limited 2011

The right of Frances Eales and Steve Oakes has been asserted by them in accordance with the Copyright, Designs and Patents Act 1988.

All rights reserved; no part of this publication may be reproduced, stored in a retrieval system, or transmitted in any form or by any means, electronic, mechanical, photocopying, recording, or otherwise without the prior written permission of the Publishers.

First published 2011

Third impression 2014

ISBN: 978-1-4082-9198-6

Set in Gill Sans Book 9.75/11.5
Printed in Slovakia by Neografia

Acknowledgements

Text permissions

We are grateful to the following for permission to reproduce copyright material:

Text
Extract Chapter 5 adapted from "Do you eat to live or do you live to eat?" Anita Nagy blog 7 September 2006, http://www.bbc.co.uk/worldservice/learningenglish/communicate/blog/student/0000007386.shtml, reproduced with permission from Anita Nagy; Extract Chapter 8 adapted from "History of the T-shirt", www.t-shirt-buyers-guide.org, copyright © T-Shirt-Buyers-Guide.org; Extract Chapter 10 adapted from "Teenage lottery winner: 'So which bank should I trust with my £7m jackpot?'", Daily Mail, 1 October 2008 (Hull, L.), copyright © Solo Syndication 2008.

In some instances we have been unable to trace the owners of copyright material, and we would appreciate any information that would enable us to do so.

The publisher would like to thank the following for their kind permission to reproduce their photographs:

(Key: b-bottom, c-centre, l-left, r-right, t-top)

6 Photolibrary.com: Corbis (bl), 10 Photolibrary.com: Purestock (tl), 12 Getty Images: Stephen Mallon (br). 17 Jupiter Unlimited: Stockxpert (br). 18 Photolibrary.com: White (tr). 20 Jupiter Unlimited: Stockxpert (tr). 24 Photolibrary.com: Niall McDiarmid/Red Cover (t). 25 Courtesy of Pueblo Inglés: courtesy of Pueblo Ingles (tr). 31 Getty Images: Paul Visconti/StockFood Creative (tl). 32 Photolibrary.com: Yvette Cardozo/Index Stock Imagery (cl). 34 Rex Features: Chris Weeks/BEI (tl). 35 Getty Images: Ian Cook/Time & Life Pictures (cl). 36 Getty Images: Photodisc/SD Productions (tc). 41 Getty Images: Michelle Pedone (br). 42 iStockphoto: (br). 44 Jupiter Unlimited: Goodshoot (tr). 49 Alamy Images: Photos 12 (cr). Getty Images: Tom Schierlitz (tr/Suit). Jupiter Unlimited: Stockxpert (tl/Jeans) (tl/Socks) (tr/Coat) (tr/Jacket) (tl/Shirt) (tr/Trousers) (tl/Shoes) (tr/Jumper) (tl/Dress) (tr/Skirt) (tr/Top). shutterstock: Elnur (tl). 52 Getty Images: Ghislain & Marie David de Lossy (c). 54 Photolibrary.com: Huntstock (tr). 56 Alamy Images: Natalie Jezzard (tc). 60 Press Association Images: Dave Thompson (cl). 62 Corbis: Radius Images (br). 65 Jupiter Unlimited: Photos.com (tr). 74 Medecins Sans Frontieres: Mikkel Dalum (tl) (the picture shown is not 'Liz Johnson' but a generic MSF worker)

All other images © Pearson Education

Every effort has been made to trace the copyright holders and we apologise in advance for any unintentional omissions. We would be pleased to insert the appropriate acknowledgement in any subsequent edition of this publication.